THE ART OF
M&A
Strategy

THE ART OF M&A Strategy

A Guide to Building Your Company's Future Through Mergers, Acquisitions, and Divestitures

Kenneth Smith

Alexandra Reed Lajoux

McGraw Hill

New York Chicago San Francisco Lisbon London
Madrid Mexico City Milan New Delhi
San Juan Seoul Singapore
Sydney Toronto

The McGraw-Hill Companies

1 2 3 4 5 6 7 8 9 0 QFR/QFR 1 6 5 4 3 2 1

ISBN 978-0-07-175621-1
MHID 0-07-175621-3

e-ISBN 978-0-07-176016-4
e-MHID 0-07-176016-4

This book is printed on acid-free paper.

To my father, Norman Alfred Smith, and to the memory of my mother, Charlotte Elizabeth Smith.

Ken Smith

To the memory of my father, Stanley Foster Reed, and my mother, Stella Swingle Reed.

Alexandra R. Lajoux

CONTENTS

PREFACE

A major merger or acquisition can be a company-defining moment. On the one hand, the right business combination at the right price, with good execution, can reposition the company, accelerate profitable growth and shareholder return, and even change the game for the industry as a whole. On the other hand, a bad deal—whether the failure is in the concept, the price, or the execution—can quickly destroy shareholder value in an otherwise healthy company.

Yet, despite the risks, strategic M&A is here to stay because the business environment is changing, and companies must change to compete. New technology, re-regulation, and continued globalization are driving restructuring in almost every sector. Technology advancements are resulting in new business models, such as e-commerce and social marketing, calling for new skills and partnerships. The changing regulatory landscape for broad industry sectors such as health care and financial services will alter the economics of many businesses and drive mergers and divestitures as companies reposition to compete. Globalization is presenting new opportunities for international value chains and international markets, and in so doing it is changing the requirements for competitive scale and scope from the domestic to the global context.

POTENTIAL VALUE OF MERGERS

In such an environment, mergers, acquisitions, and divestitures are powerful and increasingly important weapons of strategy. The term *weapons* is apt: the word *strategy* derives from the Greek word *strategein*, to lead an army in battle. If an industry is restructuring, mergers may be a requirement to maintain competitive scale or may be the only means to achieve leadership. If a company's strategy calls for growth, new market entry, or repositioning in the value chain, acquisitions can be the fastest means of achievement. If a portfolio of businesses or products (whether acquired or homegrown) requires pruning, divestitures can enhance shareholder value for the seller and buyer alike.

When acquisitions are pursued for strategic reasons, they are much more likely to succeed for shareholders. Indeed, many strategic acquisitions have created substantial shareholder value, not only in deal implementation but also by catalyzing transformation. IBM's acquisition of Lotus earned many times the premium paid for Lotus and in addition was a key step in IBM's transformation from a hardware company to a software and services company. The merger of Canadian National Railways with Illinois Central created the first North American railway from sea to sea to sea and created a growth stock in an old industry. Thomson-Reuters is the product of successive divestures and acquisitions that converted a newspaper chain in a declining industry into a global leader in information services.

Make or Break

However, while the execution of a well-planned strategic deal can make a company, it can also break a company. Some of the worst deals of the last decade across a range of industry sectors serve to illustrate the risks: in telecommunications, BCE's investment in Teleglobe, which then spiraled into bankruptcy; in life sciences, Upjohn's initial attempt to integrate Pharmacia, failing to recognize that the two companies were an ocean apart in corporate culture as well as geography; in professional services, Paris-based Cap Gemini's retention of only a fraction of the assets it acquired from Ernst & Young Consulting because the best assets had legs and walked away from the stock-based retention incentives; in consumer products, the Quaker Oats acquisition of Snapple and its subsequent sale at a fraction of the value—earning this deal a place among the 10 transactions dubbed by Robert Bruner as "Deals from Hell."[1]

Note that these were all otherwise reasonably successful, well-run companies.

THE DOWNSIDE: VALUE DESTRUCTION

Acquisition failures do not have to make the headlines to be disasters for shareholders. An international study of more than two thousand large transactions (billion dollar plus) in North America and Europe in the last decade found that over half have destroyed shareholder value.[2] Among these, many have been doomed from the outset by an ill-conceived strategy or, more often, unrealistically optimistic expectations of the "synergies"—the ways in which two companies would complement, supplement, or leverage each other to make "1 plus 1 equal 3." In the worst cases, strategies have been hastily developed when the market presents an irresistible opportunity. In many other cases, the deal had the potential to create value, but the means of value creation were considered only superficially. As a result, the synergies were overestimated or the means to achievement were underestimated; so the price paid for the company was in excess of the value created after the deal. Well in excess of $1 trillion in shareholder value has dissipated in the last decade—not in deals that fell apart but in deals that simply failed to deliver.

WHY THIS BOOK?

Therefore, given the ongoing importance of M&A in strategy as our industries restructure, and given the mixed results of M&A in the past, this book's ambition is to guide and motivate better use of mergers, acquisitions, and divestitures in business strategy and better performance for shareholders.

- Part I outlines how M&A can create value in strategy. For each of a range of corporate strategy situations, the role and rationale for M&A as a tool are outlined and examples provided. The strategic contexts considered include building and managing a business portfolio (e.g., diversification, optimizing a business portfolio, role of buy and sell side); participating in industry consolidation; growth (e.g., developing the product or market, capturing value chain opportunities, achieving vertical integration, etc.); and using acquisitions to create "real options" (i.e., strategic options for future development). Well-known historical examples illustrate successful strategies of each type that have been achieved through M&A.
- Part II is a guide to the development and execution of a successful M&A strategy. M&A is high risk and may not be the only means to achieve strategic outcomes, so this part of the

book begins with a review of strategic planning and outlines how to determine the role of M&A, if any, considering the industry context, the competitive imperatives, and strategy options. Assuming M&A is selected as one of the strategic weapons, subsequent chapters outline how to search and screen partner candidates, how to choose between buying and selling, and how the board of directors should be engaged in M&A decisions. The chapters highlight strategic considerations in deal structuring, negotiations, due diligence, and post-deal implementation. (However, detailed guides for these latter subjects are beyond the scope of this book.)

- Part III moves from M&A as an event to sustained strategic M&A programs. In particular, the chapters examine globalization and the global restructuring of industries. This analysis suggests that M&A will be a requirement for most companies and that superior M&A capabilities will be needed to compete. When M&A is central to strategy, effective postmerger integration is critical, so the text examines the most strategic aspects of postmerger integration. Advisors can play a role throughout the M&A process, and an outline of how to choose the right advisor at each stage is provided. Finally, noting that M&A skills may have little to do with the skills of the underlying businesses, the text examines the core competencies required for successful M&A programs. The superior skills needed for M&A as a basis of competitive advantage are defined and examples are provided. It should be noted that, although Part III focuses on companies for whom M&A is central to strategy, the more occasional acquirer may also find its guidance useful.

PLATFORM FOR GROWTH

This book is addressed to professionals, business leaders, directors, and students of business who need to know about M&A strategy in order to compete in restructuring industries. Practitioners of M&A make up the primary audience for the book, including leaders and staff of corporate development departments, consultants, investment bankers, accountants, and lawyers that support M&A. Given the high profile of strategy and M&A decisions, we hope that CEOs and corporate directors will also derive value from reading the book and having it on hand for reference.

We hope that all readers of this book will consider it a platform for sustainable corporate growth—and for future dialogue. We welcome your comments.

Kenneth Smith kensmith@uoguelph.ca
Alexandra R. Lajoux arlajoux@nacdonline.org

Endnotes

1. Robert F. Bruner, *Deals From Hell: Lessons That Rise Above the Ashes* (New York: John Wiley, 2005). The 10 hellish transactions are the 1968 merger of Pennsylvania Railroad with New York Central Railroad, the 1986 leveraged buyout of Revco Drugstore, the 1989 acquisition of Columbia by Sony, the 1991 acquisition of NCR by AT&T, the 1998 proposed merger between Renault and Volvo, the 1994 acquisition of Snapple by Quaker Oats, the 1999 acquisition of The Learning Company by Mattell, the 2001 merger of AOL and Time Warner, the near-merger between Dynegy and Enron that same year, and the Tyco acquisition program that launched in 2002.
2. Analysis based on SECOR database of over 2,000 large deals over 10 years; a discussion of the shareholder value metric and key findings from various analyses over the past 15 years can be found in the Appendix to Part I.

ACKNOWLEDGMENTS

The main ideas of this book came from the authors' experience working on issues of strategy, mergers, acquisitions, and divestitures over many years. We are grateful to have had the opportunity to work and contribute on such important issues. In particular, Ken Smith extends his gratitude to the clients he has served in his decades as a management consultant.

We would also like to thank our colleagues in professional services for the many opportunities to work together and to exchange and develop ideas. In particular, we acknowledge colleagues at the Mergers and Acquisitions Leadership Council, the Institute of Corporate Directors, and the National Association of Corporate Directors. This book benefits from the authors' quantitative research on merger success and failure. Ken is grateful for the support in this research of many colleagues and, in particular, for the work of Susan Hershman, Yang Liu, Eliza O'Neil, Paula Stavro-Leanoff, Sari Katz, Frank Daufenbach, and Lisa Woznica, who contributed to new insights; and also for the support of SECOR Consulting—which has permitted our use of the database, analysis, and selected reports—work led by Ken while at the firm. Earlier joint work with Alexander Triantis and Jean-Rene Halde also contributed to important ideas presented in this book. For her part, Alexandra would like to acknowledge her collaborations with Robert A. G. Monks, Peter Nesvold, Jeff Anapolsky, Charles M. Elson, the late J. Fred Weston; and Stanley Reed, her late father, who receives a dedication in this book.

The writing of the book also benefited from the diligent research and fact checking of Eric Wilson and Sadhana Sridharan, and the support of the College of Management and Economics at the University of Guelph.

Finally, the book could not have been completed without the great patience, tolerance, and encouragement of those around us; for Ken they include his family, most notably Cathy, George, and Emma. Alexandra also thanks family and friends.

THE ART OF
M&A
Strategy

PART I

How M&A Creates Value in Strategy

Today it is common to refer to a "strategic acquisition" or to develop an "M&A strategy," but M&A was not always considered as part of strategy, and for good reason. Although M&A is now recognized as an important component of strategic growth, M&A in decades past was dominated by financially based transactions of empire builders and corporate raiders. M&A strategy was missing from the corporate tool kit of most other corporations.

EXTREMES DOMINATED

On one extreme were the deals carried out by holding companies in the 1970s, amassing conglomerates of unrelated companies. These were the days of J. B. Fuqua of Fuqua Industries, Harold Geneen of ITT, Jimmy Ling of LTV, Henry Singleton of Teledyne, and Tex Thornton of Litton. These were visionaries capable of planning, but the strict antitrust regulations of the day discouraged the purchase of a competitor, customer, or supplier; made vertical and horizontal mergers difficult; and forced diagonal moves. As a result, these buyers often lacked any strategy to create value through these acquisitions. This led to depressed market valuations as market analysts assigned the so-called conglomerate discount.

On the other extreme, a decade later, the 1980s saw the rise of the "corporate raiders" and others aimed at creating value—quickly—out of companies with undervalued stock, including the conglomerates built up in the previous decade. For example, the highly diversified ITT divested its core telecommunications assets in the mid-1980s. The tone for deals of that decade was set by buyers such as Carl Icahn, T. Boone Pickens, and Jay Pritzker—names more famous than the companies they bought and sold. Companies had typically become targets by their lack of a value creating strategy—underperforming for shareholders and thus failing to "keep the raiders at bay." However, the interests of the new owners were often short term, seeking a quick return through the sale of assets and implementation of unsustainable cost reductions. So, while value was created, it was sometimes at the expense of the long-term interests of the target company.

In between these extremes and spanning two decades, a range of company-to-company deals suffered from the same general lack of strategy. Even when the principals could articulate the strategic intent they rarely found concrete means to turn those strategies into greater financial value. Like the diversification of the 1970s and the raids of the 1980s, these various M&A programs could hardly be called strategic, and they largely failed the shareholder.

The cumulative result of the deals of the 1970s and 1980s was a gradual erosion of long-term shareholder value in the acquiring companies—a result that became clear in the 1990s. The first of several shareholder value based assessments of acquisitions (led by one of the authors) appeared in *BusinessWeek* in 1995.[1] The study evaluated acquisitions from 1990 to 1995 based on the acquiring company's total return to shareholders during the three years following each deal, relative to industry peers.[2] While some deals performed better than others, the basic conclusion was a case against mergers from the shareholder perspective: simply put, acquiring companies had an inferior return relative to their industry's; their shareholders would have been better off selling the stock short as soon as they became aware of each deal.

By the turn of the twenty-first century, companies began to use M&A as a strategic tool. A number of acquisitive holding companies arose, funded by private equity. These entities have offered high returns to their investors overall, with the exception of the latter part of the decade when a global financial crisis hit. The stellar example is Berkshire Hathaway, which had a 76 percent total return from January 2000 to January 2010 despite a sharp decline in returns the latter part of the decade.[3] And Berkshire shares crossed into the January 2011 finishing line with a 21.4 percent return, outperforming the benchmark S&P's 12.8 percent.[4]

STRATEGIES FOCUSED ON VALUE CREATION

Today, as we start the second decade of the century, shareholder value has become the key metric of corporate performance and, in particular, of success and failure of acquisitions. Perhaps this focus on shareholder value has had an impact on M&A strategy and performance. Deal success rates for growth-oriented transactions and international deals improved in the last decade.[5]

This improving deal performance coincides with a more strategic role for M&A, as changes in the business environment are compelling most companies to consider M&A as integral to their strategies. Paradigm-shifting technology, spreading globalization, and extensive changes in public policy and regulation are altering value chains, industry boundaries, and the bases of competitive advantage. In such an environment, more adaptive strategies are required and, at every turn, the consideration or reconsideration of make, buy, or sell options.

In financial services, for example, the repeal of the Glass-Steagall Act in 1999 removed regulatory barriers in place since the Depression era. Companies were able to achieve cross-sector synergies not previously possible. Thus national banks acquired brokerages, investment banks, and trust companies and grew by acquisition across state and international borders as quickly as regulation and financial capacity allowed.

Acquirers gained enormous potential to create value in these deals—most importantly by developing North American or global scale in selected business lines to leverage technology, customer databases, and product-development capacity, which often meant more efficient marketing of a more complete and better targeted set of products and services. In addition, they had unprecedented opportunities to rationalize operations and to achieve the advantages of scale in sourcing, transaction processing, and technology development necessary to compete with larger international institutions.

The financial crisis and subsequent changes in regulation are again changing the value creation opportunities and therefore the strategies and the role of M&A. For example, the proposed rule from former Federal Reserve Chairman Paul Volcker (Volcker rule), would restore some of the walls that Glass-Steagall tore down by banning banks from buying securities in many circumstances. Will the brokerages be spun off? On a broader scale, will the consolidation of the U.S. banking industry lose momentum?

For example, will increased capital requirements and the death of the "too big to fail" philosophy slow the march to large national and international banks? Will fear of international contagion result in restrictions on cross-border deals?

In the energy industry, public policy is emerging that will shift demand from oil and gas to electric power for many purposes. And to generate that power, environmental policy is favoring nuclear and renewable energy over carbon fuels. The technological sophistication of the next generation of nuclear power offers advantages to large-scale players who can build and operate similar technology across several facilities. These capabilities are in short supply, so as coal gives way to nuclear as the source of base-load power, will major power generators need to merge to build and leverage nuclear capabilities?

Renewable sources provide an opposite pull in some respects. Run-of-river hydro, wind, and solar power are most likely to come from smaller operators who will sell their power to distributors. This is resulting in a fragmented network of suppliers. Will the network inefficiencies of these fragmented supply sources lead to repatriation by the utilities or consolidation of the suppliers?

In media and telecommunications, the long anticipated convergence is now driving industry restructuring. Whereas companies and industries had once been built according to the *form* of information (video, voice, and text defining the roles of cable companies, phone companies, and publishing houses, respectively), industries are now being organized around the *function* of the information. Witness the creation of Thomson-Reuters—an integrated business information company built by acquisition. Former newspaper chains have become multimedia news corporations either through acquisition of or sale to other media.

In addition, the Internet has accelerated the globalization of this industry. In many countries, regulatory protections for media are changing to allow foreign ownership and the formation of global communications companies such as Deutsche Telekom. In each segment of the industry, what will be the required scale and scope to compete?

Different and equally compelling forces are driving change in manufacturing, retailing, resources, transportation, and health care and pharmaceuticals. Virtually every sector is affected by the march of technology, the opportunities and threats of global markets, and the often-changing regulation and public policy at home and abroad. And in most cases the need or opportunity to reposition through acquisition, merger, sale, or spin-off must be considered.

THE ROLE OF M&A IN STRATEGY

Putting all this together you arrive at the thesis of Part I. Given the influence of technology, globalization, and regulatory change on the required scale, scope, and skills to compete, M&A will continue to shape our industries. For most companies, therefore, the consideration of M&A in strategy is fundamental. Furthermore, understanding the role of M&A in strategy and mounting a superior M&A program can be a source of significant competitive advantage.

M&A can play four broad roles in strategy. Chapter 1 looks at the role of M&A in the development of business portfolios. Holding companies and corporate raiders have been joined by more strategically motivated private equity companies, each seeking to build and maintain a portfolio of investments that will achieve specific risk-return outcomes. Among the largest of these are pension funds seeking to ensure a safe, sustainable future value. Many other private equity funds are owned by a few or many investors with a defined strategy to create value in the fund, and with a more specific strategic as well as financial rationale for each major investment.

Chapter 2 looks at the role of M&A in industries that are consolidating, domestically or internationally. The latter is particularly important to companies that now find themselves in globalizing industries. In the context of consolidation, merging may be necessary to maintain competitive scale and scope. The strategic question often comes down to whether to be a buyer or a seller.

Chapter 3 looks at the role of M&A in growth strategies. Profitable growth is a key driver of shareholder value; depending on the industry and company circumstances, competitive advantage may come from deeper penetration in current product or market segments or from new products or new markets. In each case there is a "make or buy" decision that defines the role of M&A.

Chapter 4 looks at acquisitions that create so-called real options. In such cases, the specific deal may not create value in and of itself. Rather, such deals can position the buyer for future steps that will create value, sometimes depending on circumstances that cannot be predicted with certainty. (However, these acquisitions should not be confused with those deals called "strategic" by their proponents simply because they cannot be justified in any other way.)

Of course, many deals play a combination of these four roles in strategy. It is nevertheless useful to examine them separately because each presents different challenges and commands different skills for success. In addition, there are important differences in the nature and transparency of the value creation opportunities and the difficulty in achieving them. It must be remembered that for deals to be successful, the new owner must create value in excess of the price paid. In a competitive market for control, therefore, there is opportunity to create this "excess" value only to the extent that the buyer can see or execute on greater opportunity than the market can.

These four roles for M&A, therefore, represent successively more complex and higher-potential M&A strategies, as illustrated in Exhibit I.1. A change in ownership alone has such excess value only if the new owner can foresee or extract improved performance from the business. In a change of ownership alone, such excess must all be found in the new owner's ability to foresee or extract better performance from the business.

In business combinations that offer cost synergies between the businesses, there is potentially much greater value at stake. However, in a consolidating industry such value is readily apparent to and readily achievable by other buyers as well. As a result, the market price will often reflect much of the potential for cost synergies, and the seller will, therefore, extract a large proportion of the value potential.

Exhibit I.1 Four deal strategies: buyer/seller perspectives of value.

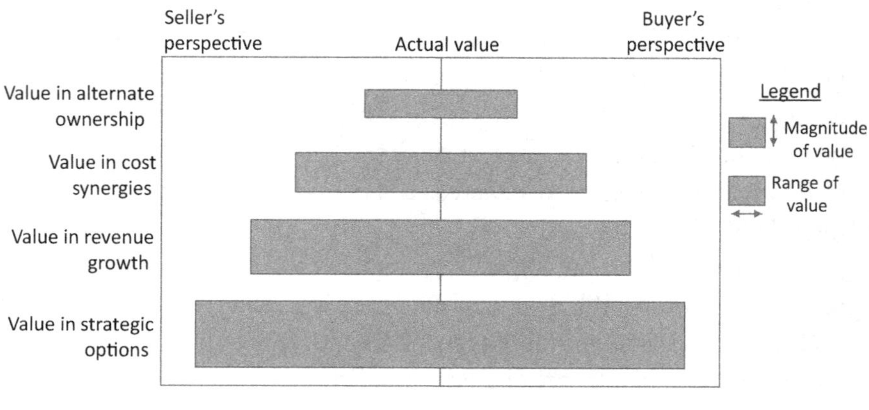

The value potential of revenue synergies tends to be more unique to the individual buyer and also more difficult to achieve. Therefore, less of the value in revenue synergies is negotiated away in the price—other bidders do not see the same revenue synergies and are reluctant to incorporate a large proportion of potential revenue synergies in the financial case for the deal. We shall also see that, while cost synergies are one-time events, revenue synergies are gifts that keep on giving. As a result, growth-oriented M&A strategies tend to create more value for shareholders in the long run.

Finally, the least transparent value potential and the most difficult strategies to execute are those that take many steps to implement and require placing bets on future circumstances. However, we shall see how such farsighted M&A strategies have built great companies.

Endnotes

1. "The Case Against Mergers," *BusinessWeek*, October 30, 1995, featuring research led by Ken Smith.
2. Total shareholder return is measured as the total capital value of the stock of a company (closing shareprice on a particular date) at the end of an investment period, plus any dividends paid during the period, expressed as a percentage of the total value of the company at the start of the investment period.
3. Jacob Wolkinsky, "Warren Buffett's Berkshire Hathaway Delivers Strong Results for the Decade," *Seeking Alpha* (blog), January 2, 2010, accessed May 30, 2011, http://seekingalpha.com/article/180560-warren-buffett-s-berkshire-hathaway-delivers-strong-results-for-the-decade.
4. Prieur du Plessy, "Berkshire Hathaway Stomps the S&P in 2010," *Seeking Alpha* (blog), January 9, 2011, accessed May 30, 2011, http://seekingalpha.com/article/245524-berkshire-hathaway-stomps-the-s-p-in-2010.
5. Ongoing research by Ken Smith at the University of Guelph, Canada, 2011, in collaboration with SECOR Consulting.

CHAPTER 1

Building and Managing a Portfolio of Businesses

Even then, we will make plenty of mistakes.[1]

—*Warren Buffet*

For most companies, M&A activity is optional. For a multibusiness portfolio company, however, it is quintessential. Acquisitions drive portfolio companies as their path to value and sometimes their reason for existence.

A portfolio company is an enterprise composed of multiple corporate entities and investments. These "holdings" have usually been acquired, but some may have resulted from the division of a prior business. This chapter focuses on those portfolio companies that maintain these entities as separate businesses—these portfolio companies look to add businesses to the portfolio and occasionally sell businesses from the portfolio. Some single business companies comprise multiple legal entities but are managed as one overall company—these are not the subject of this chapter.

We also distinguish portfolio companies from passive investment funds. Portfolio companies for our purposes hold all or a majority interest in many of the companies in their portfolios, either alone or with partners. As such they (perhaps with partners) effectively control the businesses in the portfolio. We exclude for our purposes funds that make equity investments but not controlling investments (not even with partners). Such companies buy and sell stock and play a passive role in the companies in which they have invested, whereas the portfolio companies buy and sell companies and are often in a position, either alone or with partners, to control the companies they hold. (Portfolio companies may have such passive investments as well as corporate holdings, but this chapter is concerned with only the latter.)

As noted in the introduction, it is the portfolio companies that dominated M&A in earlier decades and that have drawn much criticism. In particular, some such companies earned a so-called conglomerate discount from the capital markets. This dubious distinction meant that the market assessed the whole (the portfolio company) as being worth less than the sum of the parts (the sum of the market's valuations of the holdings). In other words, such portfolio companies were adding negative value.

This raises important questions about the role of corporate centers in these portfolios, how they can add value, and the role of M&A. In fact, many portfolio companies are highly successful and remain a major force in the M&A markets. We will use a characterization of management approaches for portfolio companies to look at how M&A can add value.

ROLE OF THE CORPORATE CENTER

How can portfolio companies add value?

A portfolio company can create value in excess of the value of the individual companies in many ways, including the following:

- Reducing risks to the shareholders by diversifying assets
- Improving returns on investments through superior selection of acquisition candidates
- Optimizing across holdings the use of tax credits, loss carry forwards, debt management, and other forms of "financial engineering"
- Exploiting skills and synergies available between businesses
- Consolidating assets as in an industry "roll up."

However, how the portfolio company adds value depends on the role and corresponding skills of the corporate center or parent company. In a portfolio of businesses, the corporate center can add value either by improving the performance of the units or by making changes to the portfolio. The latter is clearly the role of M&A—that is, the portfolio can be changed by selling units or buying new units.

However, the former also has a bearing on M&A strategy. Unit performance can be improved by changes in strategy, management disciplines, staff, or access to skills or resources—all of which can be influenced by what else is in the portfolio and/or how the portfolio is managed.

A typology of business portfolio companies can be defined by the differing roles of their corporate centers.

What roles can the parent company play in a portfolio of businesses?

The roles of portfolio parents—or corporate centers as they are increasingly called—can vary widely. Michael Goold of the Ashridge Strategic Management Centre and Nathaniel Foote of McKinsey & Company defined five scenarios for the corporate center based on the degree of business integration and the type of parent company intervention.2 Each scenario suggests the strategy to create value.

The *controller* role applies to a diversified portfolio in which the parent company does not intervene in the individual business, other than exercising its fiduciary duties on any boards of its holdings, including setting goals and budgets. The parent company's role is essentially to grow and allocate shareholder capital, usually within defined risk-return parameters. This is done through buying and selling of companies or shares of companies and through monitoring performance. Berkshire Hathaway Inc. and some of the large pension funds are examples.

The *coach* role may also apply to a diversified portfolio, but there is a greater direct role of the parent in the businesses of the portfolio. The coach aims to help the companies in the portfolio perform better through better management tools and processes. The application of Six Sigma across the holdings of General Electric Corporation is a good example. The role of coach also applies to a portfolio of businesses for which similar skills are required to manage, for example, businesses in a single industry, such as the newspaper chains.

The role of *orchestrator* applies to a portfolio of businesses that share some aspects of their business systems. The evolution of media serves to illustrate the nature of this role over that of the coach: with the prevalence of digital media, many of the former print media chains, such as Time Inc., are now managing content centrally and are bundling print and digital product for sale to consumers and advertisers. Thus each magazine remains a separate product, but elements of its business system may be shared or intertwined with others.

The first three roles are variants of holding companies with a defined basis for the corporate center to add value. The last two roles, the *surgeon* and the *architect*, apply to transformational interventions, such as turnarounds. The surgeon role applies to diversified holdings, but unlike the controller, the surgeon will be directly involved in the transformation. Some private equity firms, hedge funds, or "corporate raiders" are in the surgeon role.

The architect is also implementing transformational change, but in a portfolio of businesses with common skills or potentially shared business systems. The transformation of Thomson Corporation from essentially a newspaper chain into the Thomson-Reuters information services company illustrates an architect at work in the selection and disposal of assets and the integration of the new portfolio of businesses, clearly distinct from the work of the surgeon on unrelated companies in a portfolio.

There is, of course, some gray area between these five roles. Some parent companies may also change roles due to a change in strategy. Nonetheless, most portfolio companies fit into one of these types at a given time. The corresponding role defines, in part at least, their M&A strategies.

ROLE OF M&A FOR HOLDING COMPANY CENTERS

What is the role of M&A if the parent is in the "controller" role?

The parent as controller uses M&A to *buy*, *hold*, or *sell*. This type of portfolio is best illustrated by some large investment funds, such as Berkshire Hathaway Inc., and many of the large pension funds, such as the Canada Pension Plan Investment Board (CPPIB). These companies have developed superior skills for the selection and sale of assets. They are active investors only to the extent that they sit on the boards of the companies in which they invest and exert influence as directors, but they rarely determine the strategies or get involved in the operations of acquired companies.

Berkshire Hathaway Inc. is a holding company owning subsidiaries that engage in a number of diverse business activities, including property and casualty insurance and reinsurance, utilities and energy, freight rail transportation, finance, manufacturing, services, and retailing. Some well-known holdings include GEICO, the third-largest private passenger auto insurer; General Re, one of the largest reinsurers in the world; MidAmerican, an international energy holding company owning a wide variety of operating companies engaged in the generation, transmission, and distribution of energy; Burlington Northern Santa Fe Corporation (BNSF), one of the largest railroad systems in North America; Benjamin Moore, a formulator, manufacturer, and retailer of architectural and industrial coatings; Johns Manville, a leading manufacturer of insulation and building products; and Business Wire, the leading global distributor of corporate news, multimedia, and regulatory filings. Berkshire Hathaway holds investments in companies as well as whole companies.

The founder and chairman Warren Buffet (known as the Oracle of Omaha) and the company Berkshire Hathaway are legendary. Berkshire Hathaway has posted a 20.2 percent compound annual return since 1965, outperforming the S&P 500 by 10.8 percent over the same period.[3]

The approach to M&A is buy and hold; sell only if necessary:

> Regardless of price, we have no interest at all in selling any good businesses that Berkshire owns. We are also very reluctant to sell sub-par businesses as long as we expect them to generate at least some cash and as long as we feel good about their managers and labor relations.[4]

The corporate center's role as controller is reflected in its acquisition criteria, as stated in the 2009 annual report[5]:

> We are eager to hear *from principals or their representatives* about businesses that meet all of the following criteria:
>
> 1. Large purchases (at least $75 million of pre-tax earnings unless the business will fit into one of our existing units)
> 2. Demonstrated consistent earning power (future projections are of no interest to us, nor are "turnaround" situations)
> 3. Businesses earning good returns on equity while employing little or no debt
> 4. Management in place (we can't supply it)
> 5. Simple businesses (if there's lots of technology, we won't understand it)
> 6. An offering price (we don't want to waste our time or that of the seller by talking, even preliminarily, about a transaction when price is unknown)

While the foregoing criteria filter out some industries, Berkshire Hathaway's holdings nevertheless cover a wide breadth—financial services, railroads, manufacturing, media, and so forth.

The development of CPPIB, founded in 1997, makes for a good illustration of a public sector portfolio for which the parent is in a controller role. On its corporate website,[6] the CPPIB sets out its role and risk tolerance:

> The CPP Investment Board is a professional investment management organization based in Toronto. Our purpose is to invest the assets of the Canada Pension Plan in a way that maximizes returns without undue risk of loss. The CPP Fund was $127.6 billion at the end of 2010. Canada's Chief Actuary estimates that CPP contributions will exceed annual benefits paid through to the end of 2021. Thereafter a portion of the CPP Fund's investment income would be needed to help pay CPP benefits.

The latter point clearly identifies obligations that imply a lower risk tolerance than typical private sector funds.

The mandate is set out in legislation:

- To invest in the best interests of CPP contributors and beneficiaries
- To maximize long-term investment returns without undue risk, taking into account the factors that may affect the funding of the Canada Pension Plan and its ability to meet its financial obligations
- To provide cash management services to the Canada Pension Plan so that they can pay benefits.

The CPP Investment Board cannot conduct any business or activity that is inconsistent with these objectives.

Initially managed entirely through external fund managers, CPPIB has gradually developed deep asset selection skills in house, sector by sector. For each of the industry sectors in which CPPIB chooses to hold assets, finance expertise specific to the sector has been hired from industry or from the investment community. The sector team then seeks asset classes, regions, and eventually specific targets that are either undervalued or show significant potential for growth.

Although CPPIB has participated in many major acquisitions, it has usually syndicated large acquisitions so that the assessment, accountability, and exposure are shared by other capable investment managers. For example, their bid for BCE, a legacy Bell company, in 2008 was as the leader of a consortium that also included Caisse de dépôt et placement du Québec, the Public Sector Pension Investment Board, and seasoned buyout firm Kohlberg Kravis Roberts & Co. (The consortium was ultimately outbid by a $35.2 billion offer from another pension fund, this one led by the Ontario Teachers' Pension Plan. Following a series of legal rulings the deal was abandoned.)

However, CPPIB does own majority interest in numerous real estate holdings[7] and in 2010 made its first large-scale investment as the sole investor with the acquisition of Macquarie Communications Infrastructure Group.[8]

The large pension funds are a major force in the acquisition market. Companies like CPPIB and CALPERS (California Public Employees' Retirement System) have an endless supply of funds and are in a relentless search for safe and attractive investments. The sheer size of these funds makes them formidable competitors domestically and internationally.

There are, of course, many smaller public and private holding companies that fall into this category. There are differences in the risk-return profile of these companies and the focus of their investments by size, industry, and geography, for example. However, in each case they aim to deliver a return to their shareholders through superior selection of assets, as opposed to superior management. The role of the parent company is to buy, hold, and sell assets, so the strategy of the company is de facto its M&A strategy, and the role of acquisitions and divestitures is fundamental to value creation. The strategy in each case involves the selection of the sectors, the markets, and ultimately the companies that will deliver superior returns at a defined level of risk.

Note that virtually all of these companies list among their acquisition criteria the quality of the management of the target company. In other words, they are choosing good management because they choose not to manage. This is the primary distinction of the strategies of portfolio companies in the controller role.

What is the role of M&A if the parent is in the "coach" role?

The parent in the coach role uses M&A to *buy, develop,* or *sell.* This second type of holding company is also diversified and holds each asset separate. However, the coach seeks to add value directly through its ownership.

General Electric best illustrates this type of portfolio company. Like the first group, coaches seek good management. However, GE fully intends to add value to acquired companies through its management.

Three examples serve to illustrate the coach role in the case of GE. First is the legendary management training. The GE Way, as it is called, is a system of management development that includes training in the company's own Management Development Institute,[9] rotating through many jobs, and teaching a range of productivity tools. GE's leaders are so valued that, after Jack Welch's retirement, the potential successors that didn't get the top job were flooded with offers to go elsewhere.

Second, the spread of productivity tools at GE, best illustrated by Six Sigma, shows the coach at work. GE began moving toward a focus on quality in the late 1980s with the GE Work-Out, a high-involvement review of work practices that cut through bureaucracy to find better ways of operating. This created an open environment in which Six Sigma could be highly effective. Six Sigma is focused on quality: to achieve Six Sigma quality, a process must produce no more than 3.4 defects per million opportunities, where an "opportunity" is defined as a chance for nonconformance, or not meeting the required specifications.

GE's company website describes the parent company's role with respect to Six Sigma:

> Six Sigma is a vision we strive toward and a philosophy that is part of our business culture. . . . Ensuring consistent, predictable processes to Six Sigma, in turn, is embedding quality thinking—process thinking—across every level and in every operation of our Company around the globe.[10]

Finally, under Jack Welch, GE adopted the portfolio development strategy of growing each holding to be first or second in its industry or GE would exit. This is based on a belief that industry leaders have market advantages through brand strength and cost advantages through scale. GE has acquired companies below this threshold but seeks to build an industry leader position over time. As current CEO Jeff Immelt said of the 2007 acquisition of Smiths Aerospace:

> Smiths Aerospace is a world-class business and a great extension of our Aviation business. GE and Smiths fit together well because our product offerings are complementary, and because we have similar customers and deep domain expertise in this industry. . . . With this buy, GE Aviation brings a number of associated monitoring and component systems in-house, strengthening its control over all aspects of their engines and also gaining a

premium position. . . . This is what GE Aviation President and CEO Scott Donnelly means when he talks about "greater product scope and value to our customers.[11]

Many smaller private equity companies fit the role of coach. They select industries they know well and through the board play an active role in the strategy and development of each holding. The executives at the corporate center of these firms typically have a significant stake in the business and are expected to play a "hands on" role in the holdings.

For example, Apax, which was originally started in 1990 as a venture capital pioneer, owns companies in media (e.g., Cengage Learning), health care (e.g., NHS UK), fashion (e.g., New Look), and foreign exchange (e.g., Travelex)—these are all large businesses, and Apax no longer invests in venture capital. It has a strong focus on sector knowledge, and, in contrast to the examples referenced in the controller role, its investment professionals have operational rather than financial backgrounds. Subcommittees of the Apax Executive Committee "oversee the investment process from initial idea through due diligence and throughout the life of the investment to its eventual exit. At every stage in the process, the investment is subject to a rigorous process of scrutiny by these committees."[12]

In all cases, the assets remain separate, and synergies between them are very limited. However, the parent in the coach role is driving improvements through the board or through corporate assets (such as training centers) or corporate processes (such as strategic planning or Six Sigma).

Media companies, especially print media companies, provide examples of horizontally related properties that have been assembled so that a corporate center "coach" can add value based on industry knowledge. For example, newspaper chains like Gannett, Knight-Ridder, or Southam Inc. historically largely comprised very similar but separate businesses—major daily newspapers. As these portfolios were assembled, there was little synergy between the newspapers of two different cities. A major daily's advertising revenue was mostly from local advertisers (such as grocery, automotive, and classified ads), and most of the news was either local (e.g., city and state politics and current events) or needed to be written for the local audience (e.g., sports and national politics). Overarching these practical considerations was a widely held principle of publisher autonomy.

The greater value in the collective was not derived from integration, therefore, but rather from skilled oversight. Each chain had a formula, explicit or implicit, for the desired market positioning and the economic model. The corporate center reviewed strategy and performance of the individual properties regularly and would "help" with the implementation of corporate programs and guidelines when necessary. Skill transfer was also achieved through executive transfers between the corporate center and individual properties and between properties. There also came to be some corporate advertising resources and, rarely, a shared news gathering team. As these chains were built through acquisition, the coach role indeed added economic value. Many of the acquired newspapers had been family enterprises with founders much more focused on the headlines than on the bottom lines. While the new owners were sometimes accused of going too far and damaging the product, they more often offered better business methods and disciplines that complemented good publishing principles.

In such cases, the relevant skills of the coach were specific to the industry. The parent company intended to add value based on its newspaper expertise or management models rather than on generic management skills and productivity tools as illustrated earlier in the GE case. The role of M&A is to add properties that could benefit from similar skills, best practices, and disciplines and that fit, or could be made to fit, the model. There were similar chains developed in magazine publishing and broadcasting.

Note that in the case of the media industry, this strategy has now evolved as the industry has evolved. With digital media, the pull to centralized functions is gaining ground over publisher autonomy and product independence. Magazine "titles" (formerly called "properties") share much more from the corporate center, including technology platforms, Web management, and so forth. Acquisition rationale includes substantial integration.

In all cases, the role of M&A is to find situations where better management processes, tools, or knowledge (but not necessarily different managers) could improve results. As the center and the collective are intended to add continuing value, the goal is seldom to sell unless the goals cannot be met. The coach will buy and develop, or sell if necessary.

What is the role of M&A for the "orchestrator?"

The parent as orchestrator uses M&A to *buy* and *integrate*. Carrying the previous newspaper example into today's media industry, we find examples of the orchestrator. The modern digital media company, such as Time Inc., acquires valued media properties as it did in the predigital era, but now it is with a view of adding these properties to a shared digital media technology platform, developing content for use across media, and selling packaged advertising.

Companies that have seen value in vertical integration have acted as orchestrators to acquire and integrate the pieces of a business system or value chain. For example, the French nuclear company AREVA, a crown corporation, was established to reduce France's dependence on foreign energy.

AREVA acquired a portfolio that included every stage of the civil nuclear industry: uranium mining, fuel fabrication, reactor development and operation, and power transmission, and is now a multinational industrial conglomerate headquartered in Paris, France. It was created on September 3, 2001, by the merger of Framatome (now AREVA NP), Cogema (now AREVA NC), and Technicatome (now AREVA TA). Its main shareholder is the French public-sector company, the CEA, which owns 78.9 percent. The CEA's brief is similar to that of the U.S. Department of Energy. However, the German company Siemens also retains 34 percent of the shares of AREVA's subsidiary, AREVA NP, in charge of building the EPR, an advanced nuclear reactor.

Three main subsidiaries form the core of AREVA:

- AREVA NP (nuclear power): develops and builds nuclear reactors; Siemens had a 34 percent stake in AREVA NP until April 2011.
- AREVA NC (nuclear cycle): covers the whole nuclear fuel cycle, from mining to waste disposal. AREVA NC also owns Eurodif.
- AREVA TA (atomic technology): develops and builds research reactors and reactors for naval propulsion.

A fourth major division, AREVA T&D (transmission and distribution), was sold in 2004 to ALSTOM and Schneider Electric. While AREVA is mainly known for nuclear power, it also has interests in some other energy projects.

The vertical portfolio is further complemented by a number of equity partnerships. It is with the express intent of integration—by controlling

Exhibit 1.1. Vertical integration – example of parent as orchestrator.

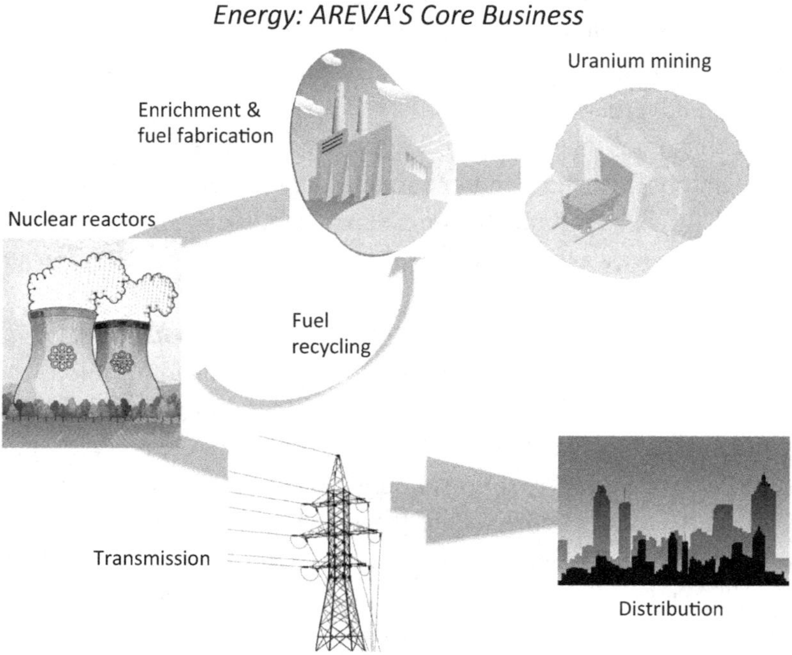

the value chain AREVA assures supply downstream and ultimately assures greater energy autonomy for the principal shareholder—France.

The development of the portfolio of consulting companies under Marsh & McLennan provides another example of the orchestrator adding value through M&A. Started in the United States in 1937 as the employee benefits department of Marsh & McLennan, Inc., the company took the name of William M. Mercer in 1959, when Marsh & McLennan acquired William M. Mercer Limited, a Canadian firm founded by William Manson Mercer in 1945. Marsh & McLennan now holds the Mercer Consulting Group, including actuarial services, HR consulting, and related outsourcing; and the Oliver Wyman Group, including Oliver Wyman (comprising the former strategy consultancy Mercer Management Consulting, the former financial services specialists Oliver Wyman, and change management specialists Delta), Lippincott (brand and identity consultants), and NERA Economic Consulting. These firms are among the international leaders in their respective fields.

While there is some synergy between these firms, there are more differences than similarities and they operate quite separately. Each recruits for quite different skill sets (e.g., actuaries at Mercer HR Services versus strategists at Oliver Wyman), and each sells to different parts of the corporation (e.g., the human resources department versus the line executives, respectively).

However, the parent company has orchestrated the development of each of these firms by integrating high-quality boutique consultancies into a recognized large-scale competitor in each case.

For example, when William M. Mercer was acquired by Marsh & McLennan in 1959 it was the largest pension and benefits firm in Canada, but it had only a small presence internationally. Over the course of 50 years under Marsh & McLennan's ownership, William M. Mercer acquired pension and benefit consulting firms around the world to become an international leader in the field. Of its 2010 acquisition of ORC Worldwide Mercer states the intention

> to become an unparalleled provider of global human resource intelligence and to further strengthen related international consulting, conference and educational services. Both firms have a significant global presence. ORC's strong market position and reputation in the United States, particularly in the area of international assignment expertise, complements Mercer's worldwide research capabilities and extensive global network of offices.[13]

The strategy consultancy known today as Oliver Wyman is the product of 20 years of acquisitions of high-quality boutique strategy consultancies, such as Temple, Barker & Sloan, Corporate Decisions, Strategic Planning Associates, and Delta in the United States; Johnson-Smith International in Canada; and Unternehmensberatung München and St. Gallen in Europe; and financial industry specialists Oliver Wyman in 2003, whose name is now used for the strategy consultancy and for the overall group.[14]

Professional services firms are notoriously poor acquirers—even McKinsey & Company has steered away from acquisitions after a failed attempt to enter IT strategy consulting through acquisition in the 1990s. Marsh & McLennan brought M&A skills to the consulting industry and built leading competitors in each chosen consulting sector.

Marsh & McLennan has also been reasonably effective at integration, a challenge in professional services firms so driven by their distinct histories, cultures, and egos. For example, after the acquisition of Strategic Planning Associates (SPA) there was little natural inclination for SPA partners to work with the former Temple, Barker, and Sloane (TBS) partners that had previously been brought into the group, at that point called the Mercer Consulting Group. SPA had offices in Washington, D.C., New York, and London, while TBS was in Boston, and they operated largely in different sectors. Management, however, recognized the complementary nature of the offerings and skills—SPA focused on corporate strategy and TBS on operations. The prize was to combine these skills in each other's clients to increase revenue per client. Mercer orchestrated the integration by implementing a compensation system for partners that double counted all revenue gained from joint sales. A partner from one firm was able to get help from the other at no cost to expand sales into areas previously inaccessible. Likewise, a partner invited to help would say "yes" because of the opportunity to earn sales credit in a new client.

The preceding examples show how the orchestrator uses M&A to fill in missing pieces or add businesses that will derive benefit from the shared resources. The orchestrator must facilitate the required integration without undermining the value of the entities acquired.

ROLE OF M&A FOR TRANSFORMATIONAL CENTERS

What is the role of M&A if the parent is in the role of "surgeon"?

The parent in the surgeon role uses M&A to *buy*, *turnaround*, and *sell*. This is what is known as the buyout firm. While this can happen in the other types of portfolio companies, it is the explicit strategy of the buyout firm, sometimes called "corporate raider" or "takeover artist." The role of M&A activity is to find problem companies that can be fixed and later to plan the exit.

Kohlberg Kravis Roberts & Co. (KKR) exemplifies the role of the surgeon. As a global leader in private equity investing, KKR executed the first leveraged buyout in excess of $1 billion, several of the largest buyouts in history, the first friendly tender offer in the buyout of a public company, and the largest completed or announced buyouts in the United States, the Netherlands, Denmark, India, Australia, Turkey, Singapore, and France.[15]

> Our approach is to work as partners with the management of our portfolio companies and remain deeply involved in the operations of our businesses. We work closely with our portfolio companies to drive operational improvements throughout all areas of their businesses. This includes sales

> and profit growth, market share leadership, innovation and prudent investments in R&D, geographic expansion, cost improvements, and other value-creating activities. Our portfolio companies span 14 industry segments, and are located throughout the U.S., Europe, and Asia.

This hands-on role is in distinct contrast with portfolio manager roles described earlier. In addition, KKR sends in executives from the KKR Capstone operations team to improve all aspects of portfolio company operations, including pricing, market strategies, sales force management, growth strategies, cost reduction, sourcing and purchasing, and capital efficiency issues.

KKR's acquisition of Toys "R" Us, Inc., illustrates the approach. KKR acquired Toys "R" Us, retailer of toys and baby products, for $6.6 billion in 2005 in a consortium with Bain Capital and Vornado Realty Trust. During the next several months, the new owners replaced more than half of the senior executives, while testing new store concepts and overhauling the company's marketing strategy. At time of writing, a long-anticipated initial public offering (IPO) is expected in late 2011or in 2012.[16]

Other corporate raiders have been less constructive, sometimes extracting value for the owners without regard for the future of the company. It is these acquirers that are mimicked by the character Gordon Gekko in the 1987 film *Wall Street* and the 2010 sequel *Wall Street: Money Never Sleeps*.

Ideally the surgeon's patient survives the operation, so the surgeon can buy, turnaround, and sell for profit.

What is the role of M&A for the "architect"?

The parent as architect uses M&A to *sell*, *buy*, and *restructure*. Thomson, now Thomson-Reuters, illustrates well the role of the parent as architect in a transformation. Beginning with Roy Thomson's own radio station in 1932, the Thomson Corporation was built first as a media company. Capitalizing on advertising revenue, Thomson bought additional radio stations and eventually newspapers. The newspaper franchise grew into a major chain across the United States, Canada, and the United Kingdom.

Such properties, well managed, generated a lot of cash, and Thomson made a variety of other investments in the 1960s and 1970s in retail, travel, and petroleum with acquisitions such as the Hudson Bay Company and a partnership with Getty Oil and Occidental Petroleum to develop North Sea oil.

The strategic restructuring of the portfolio began in the late 1990s as Thomson began a transformation into a subscriber-based information services company. Thomson recognized that it could add value in three ways:

1. Assemble information services products serving selected industries (e.g., law and finance) and become an essential source for those industries
2. Facilitate content synergies between the products in a sector to make each product better
3. Develop superior skills in database and information management that would benefit all sectors and all products.

To fund the acquisitions and development program, Thomson gradually divested most of its newspapers and diversified assets and issued an IPO for Thomson Travel. As the Internet emerged as the preferred interface, by virtue of the scale of information services Thomson was able to invest $600 million annually in digitization and development of Web platforms—well beyond what each product or even sector could have achieved individually. As Internet use grew from 1999 to 2009, Thomson more than doubled its revenues, completed the acquisition of Reuters, and became the largest information services company in the world.

The role of M&A for the architect of Thomson-Reuters was in the sale of assets that did not fit the new corporate design and the acquisition of the ones that did fit and that could drive or benefit from the restructuring.

There are some other examples of transformations using M&A. In several industries, manufacturers or resources companies have moved downstream to capture higher margins, selling off some or all of the original businesses. IBM's transformation from a computer hardware manufacturer to a predominantly software and services company is one example, with acquisitions such as Lotus and PWC Consulting and the spinoff of manufacturing operations like Celestica.

Some companies have moved downstream and remained vertically integrated, such as Centrica derived from British Gas and now an international company that has acquired assets from gas production to retailing.

Others have exited the upstream assets. Quebecor of Montreal, for example, was once integrated from pulp and paper production to printing and newspapers. It has long since shed the paper business and in 2010 sold its substantial graphics business, World Color Press, to Wisconsin's Quad/ Graphics for an estimated $1.3 billion plus.[17] Quebecor had developed World Color into the second-largest printer in the world through a series of acquisitions, but after it was in and out of bankruptcy, there was a clear preference for investments in cable, media, and entertainment, in which there were revenue synergies and growth.

Common elements of these examples are a change of industry or a superior positioning in the value chain, and the realization of synergy value in the selected industry. Acquisitions and divestitures usually play an integral role in these transformations.

DISTINCTIONS AND COMMON ELEMENTS

Is there a good, better, or best role for the corporate center of a portfolio of businesses?

The examples we have looked at so far provide positive illustrations of M&A in each type of portfolio company. However, there are also plenty of failures of each type. Each role is delivering characteristically different value from the corporate center, which in turn requires different skills and motivations. Many of the failures illustrate what can happen if the skills and motivations of the corporate center are misaligned with the role of M&A in value creation.

For example, many of the holding companies formed in the 1970s and 1980s fancied themselves as able to add value but did not. Attempts to diversify on the basis of financial insight (controller) or management skill (coach) often resulted in bad choices and/or lack of ability to compete in a different industry. For example, the Molson Companies Limited made acquisitions in hardware and chemicals that ultimately had to be reversed. Meanwhile, other brewers like Fosters and Interbrew (now Inbev) were creating global brewing giants.

Large companies like General Motors and Exxon Corporation got the idea that having a large department in something meant they could compete in that industry. They formed companies in areas like IT, office equipment, and consulting to add value as coach. These were generally uncompetitive under the weight of their respective corporations and were spun off or shut down.

Many of the telecoms invested in cell phones, media, and digital technologies to orchestrate the synergies promised by convergence. While some have made progress, the investments in acquisitions and R&D have been hugely expensive, and these companies have generally failed to compete effectively with the entrepreneurs of each successive technology wave.

The infamous AOL–Time Warner merger was to be transformational—in this case, the corporate vision was to architect media convergence. Although the concept was right, the corporate center had no apparent skills and no plan for implementing such a transformation.

Common to all these examples is that the role selected for the corporate parent, whether selected explicitly or implicitly, was incongruent with the history and skill sets of the particular corporation. Different skills are required for each role, so it must be clear what role the holding company will play, and there must be the capacity and skills at the corporate center to play that role successfully. This is discussed further in Parts II and III.

What do portfolio companies have in common with respect to the role of M&A?

All these companies are collections of companies. Although in some cases they realize synergies among the holdings, the holdings remain separate corporate entities. While there may be a range of value drivers for the individual companies in the portfolio, M&A is a core activity for the holding company. The holding company creates value for shareholders through acquisitions, divestitures, and, in some cases, through the role it plays in the management of the holdings.

Endnotes

1. Letter to Shareholders, Berkshire Hathaway Inc., Annual Report, 2009.
2. See "'Planned Parenthood': How and Why Headquarters Must Fine-Tune Its Role," *Business International* (newsletter), March 20, 1989.
3. Berkshire Hathaway Inc., Annual Report, 2010.
4. Berkshire Hathaway Inc., Annual Report, 2009.
5. Ibid.
6. CPPIB, "About Us," http://www.cppib.ca/About_Us/.

7. CPPIB, Annual Report, 2010.
8. CPPIB, Annual Report, 2010.
9. See "GE's Crotonville: A Staging Ground for Corporate Revolution," Noel M. Tichy, *Academy of Management Executive*, May 1989. http://www.jstor.org/pss/4164880.
10. *The Roadmap to Customer Impact*, http://www.ge.com/sixsigma/SixSigma.pdf.
11. *Defence Industry Daily*, May 1, 2007. http://www.defenseindustrydaily.com/ge-buys-smiths-aerospace-for-48b-02955/.
12. Apax Annual Reports, http://www.apax.com/inside-apax/annual-reports.aspx.
13. Mercer company website, www.mercer.com.
14. Oliver Wyman company website, www.oliverwyman.com.
15. Kohlberg Kravis Roberts & Co. website, www.kkr.com.
16. Thomas Lee, "Toys R Us Gains New Spirit," *Star Tribune*, September 12, 2011.
17. "U.S. Printer to Swallow Former Quebecor World," *CBC News*, January 26, 2010. http://www.cbc.ca/news/business/story/2010/01/26/quebecor-world-quad-graphics-takeover.html.

CHAPTER 2

Consolidation: Value in Cost Synergies

And then there were none.

—*Alfred Hitchcock*

Many industries undergo periods of consolidation in which some companies identify opportunity to achieve competitive advantage through increased scale or scope, and others must follow in order to remain competitive. The opportunities are often triggered by changes in the market related to technology, globalization, or regulation that make larger scale or scope possible or more important.

When companies in the same industry buy others to increase scale or scope, revenues are typically additive while costs are not. Simply put, it usually takes less than twice the costs to run a company twice the size in the same business. As mentioned in the Introduction to this book, the availability of such cost savings has been the principal motivation of many corporate combinations, including the acquisition of small players by larger ones as well as so-called mergers of equals. (We use the term *corporate combinations* to include mergers or acquisitions that result in a new, larger, *integrated* entity. This is distinct from the acquisitions made by holding companies discussed in the previous chapter, after which the target remains a separate company or "holding.")

Surprisingly, such acquisitions most often fail for shareholders. Over the last 20 years of study, large acquisitions of in-market, like companies have proven 40 percent more likely to fail than other deals. It seems the greater the opportunity for cost synergies, the greater the failure rates. However, this is not to say that these combinations have not created value. Rather, the value has been transferred overwhelmingly to the sellers.

This chapter explores this consolidation dilemma—a compelling economic justification to combine but a chronic failure of the buyers to capture value for shareholders. To understand M&A strategy in this arena, it is important to first understand why and how industries consolidate—the drivers, the benefits, and the limitations. Within this context, we then explore the alternate strategies of the players and what is critical to M&A strategy in a consolidating industry.

DRIVERS OF CONSOLIDATION

Why do so many industries consolidate?

Most industry consolidations are the result of the natural progression of an industry through its life cycle from differentiation in growth to similarity in a mature or declining market. When companies start up, their value usually lies in offering something new and different to the marketplace. At that time, their uniqueness in product or market access is their main advantage, and their small size or captive market works for them. However, innovations tend to attract imitations, and profitable markets attract competitors. Products and services that were once unique or unique within a defined market become standard or even commoditized.

Such product life cycles occur in every industry. For example, over the past 25 years the simple cell phone market has evolved from unique, high-cost products to inexpensive commodities. This market is now in turn giving way to smart phones, initially expensive and highly differentiated but rapidly copying each others' features. Initial innovators such as Palm could not maintain sufficient market share to benefit from scale economies and have yielded the market to the BlackBerry and iPhone.

Natural resource industries provide examples of companies that are derived from a local advantage versus a technology advantage. For example, the pulp and paper industry grew from local companies situated in or near a source of fiber and energy. The key ingredients were ownership or cutting rights for a rich and replenishing softwood forest, a river system to transport logs from distant reaches, and a waterfall or river that could be dammed to provide power for the energy-intensive processes. Each such mill once distinguished its paper products and branded and sold them directly to publishers.

As the industry matured, independent paper mills faced a variety of challenges that drove consolidation. Larger, more efficient machines were developed that gave a cost advantage to the larger facilities and to the companies with the economic scale to invest in such equipment. Distributors emerged, especially in the fine paper market, that had access to large markets and that had their own brand, rather than the individual mill's brand. The market standardized paper grades, reducing the ability of the individual mill to differentiate and thereby shifting pricing power to customers and distributors.

Compounding the need to consolidate was the highly cyclical nature of the paper market. In each down cycle of the economy, advertising markets collapsed and along with them the number of pages printed in newspapers and magazines. In the capital-intense paper industry, a severe drop in sales volume can be devastating, so competitors lowered prices to maintain volumes. Only the largest, most efficient operations could maintain positive cash flow in such an environment. The others became candidates for closure or acquisition.

The history of AbitibiBowater, now the largest newsprint producer in the world, illustrates this progression. Abitibi Pulp & Paper Company Limited was founded in 1912. It acquired extensive timber, waterpower, and mineral rights and became Abitibi Paper Company Ltd in 1965. It became Abitibi-Price in 1979 after acquiring controlling interest in the Price Company Ltd in 1974, a similar though smaller company by then also comprising numerous timber and paper operations. The combined company diversified downstream into a range of paper and wood products manufacturing and distribution operations, thereby controlling substantial market access.

In the recession of the early 1990s, Abitibi's profits were hit hard. While it had vast paper assets, it had not consolidated its operations and had not invested in the available efficient production technologies. In an oversupplied market, more efficient U.S. and European paper companies were keeping paper prices low.

Abitibi had to be restructured to remain competitive. Initially under the majority ownership of developer Olympia & York and later (when Olympia & York was bankrupted), under the control of a consortium of banks, Abitibi sold off downstream assets and sold or closed several mills to focus on newsprint production. By 1994, Abitibi was sufficiently profitable for the banks to divest it through a share offering.

However, international competition continued to put downward pressure on prices. Abitibi needed access to cheaper fiber, better scale economies, and access to international markets. In 1997, Abitibi-Price and Stone

Consolidated merged to form Abitibi Consolidated, and in 1999 Abitibi Consolidated announced the formation of the Pan Asian Paper Company (PAPCO), a joint venture with Norske Skog and Hansol Paper Company that combined the companies' Asian ventures.

The most recent cycle is being driven by retracting paper markets. The long-predicted impact of the Internet on paper has finally begun, with digital media taking share from print media. This is exacerbated by another economic downturn and the associated reduction in advertising. Abitibi merged with Bowater in 2007 to form AbitibiBowater, now the largest newsprint producer in the world, including 45 percent of North America's capacity.[1] And the weak mills continue to close, including a once flagship mill in Grand Falls, Newfoundland, closed in 2009.

In the course of these events, the North American newsprint industry has gone from being among the most fragmented to becoming the most concentrated. The product has commoditized, the economies of scale in equipment and distribution have become essential, and competition is international.

This industry life-cycle evolution has taken industry after industry from many to few players. These consolidated sectors include computer chip manufacturing, major appliances, and the automotive industry, among many others.

Where does it end? Are all industries subject to consolidation?

It depends, of course, on the industry and many other factors that can shape an industry, in addition to the forces of consolidation. For example, the economies of scale are so compelling in manufacturing that competing brands will source from the same factory in many industries (e.g., auto parts, home appliances, computer chips). Industries with expensive networks of infrastructure are natural monopolies, which is why regulators watch the consolidation of the railways and why AT&T once had to be broken up. Boston Consulting Group founder Bruce Henderson asserts that in most industries, three companies will eventually dominate.[2]

However, this is true mostly for industries that are capital intense—it takes considerable investment to launch and run them. In some other industries, such as consumer application software development, small, entrepreneurial upstarts have advantages and easy entry. While larger players will acquire and achieve some scale advantages, they are often acquiring for other reasons and such acquisitions will not result in the consolidation because of the constant entry and growth of new players. Other examples of industries not likely to consolidate are single-product or direct service providers such as home renovation or dry cleaning. Attempts to join the consolidation trend in such industries without adequate planning can be expensive strategic errors. Such ill-conceived consolidation attempts are frequently seen when new product markets develop adjacent to an old one.

The airline industry provides an instructive example. It is a very difficult industry to enter domestically and almost impossible globally. For this reason, international carriers are few in number. To be cost competitive on transoceanic flights requires large, expensive aircraft and passenger load factors that are difficult to achieve. Long-term contracts govern access to international gates, and these gates are in short supply in the most desirable destinations. Many international airlines are national flag carriers that benefit from direct or indirect support from national governments. The incumbents are also in a good position to defend these routes as they can maintain positive cash flow at price levels not sustainable for a new player. Moreover, international air travel is highly subject to consolidation; mergers and alliances have largely consolidated the industry within the limitations of national ownership and international cabotage restrictions.

However, short-haul regional air travel has substantially lower barriers to entry. Single-engine turbopropeller (turboprop) planes are much less expensive to buy or lease. Operating costs are also lower, and they require fewer passengers to break even. Gates and airports inaccessible to large aircraft are available to the smaller aircraft. Yet, in spite of the low entry barriers, the major airlines have repeatedly tried to consolidate these operations and eliminate the pesky competition on local short-haul routes. However, each time they are acquired they seem to reappear with a new name in the next economic cycle.

For example, Ontario regionals Great Lakes and Austin Airways were consolidated into a subsidiary of Air Canada in the late 1980s, eliminating a competitive problem in the Toronto short-haul markets. Renamed Air Ontario, service was expanded to offer turboprop service out of the convenient downtown Toronto Island airport to Montreal, Ottawa, New York, Washington, D.C., and other popular business destinations. In 2006, flights were consolidated into Pearson International, leaving an opening for a new regional to start offering service out of the Toronto Island airport, and Porter Airlines was launched.

The attraction of the downtown airport to customers remained, and the new Porter Airlines began offering flights to Montreal, then Ottawa, then New York, and so on, adding turboprop aircraft as demand warranted. Market entry with turboprop planes is much less expensive and less risky than acquiring a jet fleet, as noted earlier, and in this case was made even easier by the exclusive access to the Toronto Island airport.

And so the cycle repeats itself. Air Canada's attempt to consolidate the regionals didn't stick. It has had to negotiate access to the Toronto Island airport and is in fierce competition with Porter for the same routes it acquired 20 years earlier.

American Airlines took a different strategy with the development of American Eagle, the largest regional airline system in the world, with over 1,700 daily flights to more than 150 cities throughout the United States, Canada, the Bahamas, the Caribbean, and Mexico.[3]

However, it has been challenging for a major carrier to operate in this cost-competitive regional airline market. Independent regional airlines are lower cost and have been consolidating among themselves to reduce overhead so they can offer lower rates to their larger-airline partners. Major airlines are selling their feeder carriers to create a larger pool of smaller carriers with which to do business. American Airlines has tried several times in the last decade to shed its regional affiliate American Eagle. Airline consultant Robert Mann said American Eagle is a high-cost operation with no clients other than its parent, which could make it a tough sell.[4]

Moreover, acquisition of regional airlines by the major carriers at handsome premiums has produced fleeting benefits. Attempting the consolidation of an industry with relatively low entry barriers is expensive and a distraction from building the capabilities needed to compete in these markets.

What triggers consolidation among companies?

This question gets us closer to questions about competitive strategy, because knowing what may trigger consolidation or the next round of consolidation may put a company in a position to influence or anticipate the change. Here are several of the forces that can lead to consolidation.

The *economic cycle* is the main trigger of consolidation in the pulp and paper industry example cited earlier. That there would be another economic downturn was as certain as the next sunset, yet, when times were good, many players behaved as if high prices would last forever, failing to invest in production efficiencies and steadfastly independent. Those that planned for the next cycle and invested when they didn't have to achieved lower costs that would sustain them in the next downturn. These were the survivors and ultimately the buyers.

Change in the relevant market is another common trigger of consolidation and is often seen in the financial services industry. Markets can become larger as a result of market integration across product categories or across geographic borders. Banking and insurance provide a current example of market integration across products. The growth of the insurance market and the market demand for efficient distribution of financial services have effectively defined a "bancassurance" market in the European Union in which customers expect their financial institution to offer all financial services products. Regulators have accommodated the shared distribution, and most banks have acquired, or in some cases been acquired by, insurers.

Changes in regulation have been another important trigger of consolidation. The U.S. financial services market had been divided by state and product lines, but two laws changed that. First, the Interstate Banking and Branching Efficiency Act of 1994, known as the Riegle-Neal Act after its sponsors, allowed banks to operate across state lines and triggered a consolidation that is continuing today. There were over 15,000 banks in 1990. These have consolidated to under 8,000, with almost 80 percent of assets held by the top 100.[5]

In addition, the Financial Services Modernization Act of 1999, known as the Gramm-Leach-Bliley Act, opened up a merger boom across the traditional pillars in financial services of banks, insurers, trusts, and brokerages by repealing the Banking Act of 1933 known as the Glass-Steagall Act. This Depression-era law separated commercial banking, investment banking, securities brokerage, and insurance. In the United States, the repeal of the Glass-Steagall Act of 1933 permitted integration of banking, stock brokerage firms, and insurance. This led to the creation of large, diversified financial firms—the ones many blame for the financial crisis, sparking attempts to restore the Depression-era law.[6]

Market integration across geographies also motivates consolidation as globalization is expanding the relevant market for most industries today. As the relevant market is redefined, so is the standard for competitive scale and scope. The auto industry has exploited larger geographic markets and has developed international supply chains and global-scale parts manufacturing. Branded consumer goods such as automobiles and packaged goods can leverage product development, brand development, and even international advertising. As brands become global and the middle class grows in developing countries, global scale and scope become more important. Companies like Kraft are the product of multiple international acquisitions, the most recent being Cadbury of the United Kingdom, itself a product of several international mergers.

What's an example of consolidation occurring due to globalization?

Globalization is a trend affecting most industries, so this is a particularly important question. The telecommunications industry provides a rich example that highlights the importance of having a strategy to win in a redefined global industry.

When communications ran on landlines and simple hardware, it was very much a domestic industry. In fact, due to the strategic importance of communications, it was often a protected industry and still is in some jurisdictions. In such a capital-intensive, infrastructure-dependent industry, there was great benefit to domestic consolidation—so much so that some countries, such as Germany and the United Kingdom, ran the phone system as a public utility. Others, like Canada, granted regulated monopolies to private enterprises. In the United States, a natural monopoly developed in AT&T, which was eventually broken up through legislation.

Three main factors have redefined the telecommunications market as a global market: globalization of the industry's customer markets, increased demand for international communications, and the development of the Internet. There is plenty of evidence now with the global penetration of the BlackBerry network and other internationally available hardware and services, and with the presence of foreign carriers, such as Virgin, Deutsche Telekom, and France Telecom, in the U.S. market.

Those that anticipated this redefinition of the relevant market are emerging as the global consolidators. Deutsche Telekom was a state-owned monopoly in Germany until the 1980s, similar to those in other telephony markets. After 1987, the EU policy was adjusted to promote quality, choice, and low prices through greater competition and harmonization across EU countries. European telecom markets were thus gradually liberalized until 1998. Since market liberalization, European incumbents (often formerly state owned) continued to grow and managed to outperform the telecommunications industry globally in terms of revenues.

After 1996, the growth of European telecom incumbents was fueled, for the most part, by foreign acquisitions. For example, between 1999 and 2001 Deutsche Telekom made more than $40 billion worth of cross-border acquisitions, focusing on gaining critical mass and differentiation in the UK and U.S. mobile markets, respectively. The company was driven to gain scale internationally but simultaneously maintained a leading market share in both fixed-line and mobile telephony in its domestic market.

As Deutsche Telekom was under development, the company benefited from regulatory tolerance in the German domestic market. The regulator protected the company at home while it developed the strength to compete internationally. For example, Germany offered carrier selection only in late 2003, more than three years after it should have been available according to EU regulations, thus maintaining heightened entry barriers for as long as possible.[7]

Those who did not anticipate globalization of the industry, or whose regulators did not, have been caught subscale and uncompetitive in the new market. Telecom regulators in Canada, for example, have traditionally defined the telecom market as domestic and have restricted mergers in order to provide sufficient competition within Canada. Regulators are reviewing these restrictions with an eye to globalization now, but it may be too little too late. As the industry opens up, the companies that have been the largest within Canada have few or no international operations and will likely be uncompetitive and easy targets in the global market.

VALUE CREATION

How can consolidation create value?

Consolidation opportunities can be classified as follows, based on the part of the value chain that offers the consolidation benefit:

- In *research and product development*, the synergies usually relate to the ability to better diversify risks and optimize the development process across a broader research and development portfolio.

- In *operations*, the major cost savings are usually found in larger purchasing scale, the elimination of manufacturing and distribution redundancies, and the consolidation of corporate headquarters.
- In *sales and marketing*, the cost-savings potential is usually less important than the revenue potential afforded by brand and marketing scale and scope.

Each of these three key areas warrants careful strategic consideration.

How can consolidation create value in research and development?

Obviously, combining research and development functions across two companies reduces the cost of overhead in the short term. However, in the long term, mere cost reduction is not enough to create sustainable value if the combination causes a loss in research quality. Therefore, more significant benefits often come from managing R&D effectively across a larger, more diversified portfolio. This is best exemplified in the consolidation of pharmaceutical companies. In fact, strengthening the R&D pipeline has often been a primary motivator for mergers in that industry.

The first and most socially important benefit in the consolidation of R&D in the pharmaceutical industry is potential integration of good science to advance development. In addition to good science, however, there are several components of effective R&D management that can provide the strategic rationale for consolidation. There is first the opportunity to have a more proportional number of drugs at every stage of the pipeline. If one company has gaps in the R&D pipeline, then it cannot achieve a consistent pattern of revenue growth longer term. This clearly diminishes the net present value of that company through a lower growth rate and higher volatility (or beta) in future cash flows, and therefore a higher (less desirable) discount rate when projecting future cash flows. However, if the company combines with one that has drugs at complementary stages of the R&D pipeline, then the combined pipeline provides for both higher growth and a lower beta based on more reliable estimated future revenues, hence a lower discount rate for future cash flows. So complementary drug pipelines have more than an additive affect on value: 1 + 1 = 3.

The second R&D consolidation benefit lies in the fact that a larger laboratory provides more degrees of freedom for R&D optimization. One of the core competencies of R&D management is the ability to stop probable failures early and redeploy resources to higher-probability products. The larger the lab, the more opportunities there are for effective redeployment—this being far more efficient than severing staff and having to rehire and retrain scientists and technicians for the next project when it comes. So again, the combined value is more than the sum of the parts—all other things being equal, a larger lab, managed well, is more efficient.

The third R&D consolidation benefit is to achieve greater diversification of risk across the R&D portfolio. This is equivalent to the management of stock market portfolios. The potential value of future successes (e.g., blockbusters) is additive but at a lower beta if across a more diverse portfolio, so again 1 + 1 = 3.

There are other strategic considerations. For example, if one company's R&D function is more effectively managed with regard to the foregoing factors, then best practices in pipeline optimization and management can be applied. There may also be opportunities to rationalize lab infrastructure, such as buildings and equipment, or to improve the use of specialized equipment or staff in a larger-scale environment.

Ultimately, the strategic opportunities in R&D consolidations relate to the ability to manage along a well-balanced pipeline, to better optimize deployment, and to diversify R&D risk. For example, the announcement of AstraZeneca's $1.3 billion acquisition of Cambridge Antibody Technology said the acquisition would allow AstraZeneca to enter new research areas after stopping work on several of its own medicines.[8]

When does R&D consolidation fail to deliver value?

Mergers that fail in R&D consolidation generally fall into two categories: poor skills in the fundamentals of R&D management or failures in effective integration.

The skills needed to be effective in the R&D management fundamentals noted earlier are certainly not present in every lab. Again, notwithstanding that great science is key to every lab, the larger the lab the more important the management effectiveness. Weak fundamentals on lab management applied to a larger combined R&D function will result in little or even negative synergy.

Effective management of the postmerger integration process is important in every function and is a particularly subtle task in R&D integration, where motivation is so fundamental to success. One pharmaceutical merger that illustrates how great potential can be squandered is that of Pharmacia and Upjohn, a cross-ocean and cross-culture deal infamous for its failure in cross-cultural integration. Alan Friedman wrote in the *New York Times* in 1997: "Indeed, Pharmacia & Upjohn has suffered enough clashes of management culture, style and approach to make a case study of what American executives should not do when they come to Europe."[9]

How can consolidation create value in operations integration? When does it fail?

Operations consolidation is usually about reducing unit costs through larger scale. Larger-scale operations can purchase more cheaply and benefit from scale economies in fixed manufacturing and distribution costs.

Cost synergies such as these are the most obvious and, ironically, the most illusive. The fundamental problem with operating cost synergies is that, especially in a consolidating industry, the cost-synergy potential is easy to calculate and thus transparent to all possible bidders. Since the market for corporate control is competitive (i.e., multiple companies will have interest in any valuable target), the value of these clear and calculable synergies will tend to be negotiated away in the bidding process. The "winning" bidder has often been the most aggressive about what synergies can be achieved and how quickly and has bid accordingly, thereby transferring much or all of the value of the synergies to the sellers and simultaneously setting savings goals that are nearly impossible to achieve as quickly as estimated.

A look back at the consolidation of U.S. banking can be used to illustrate the great value in operating cost synergies and the propensity to transfer the value to the sellers. In-market bank deals have generally resulted in poor returns for shareholders. A 2003 study by SECOR Consulting of 10 years of bank deals in the United States and European Union[10] during a peak consolidation period found that 69 percent of domestic bank-to-bank deals failed for shareholders, resulting in total returns less than industry average during the three years following.

Starting with the branch networks, every bank has been optimizing its branch networks for decades. There are, in fact, decision support systems to estimate branch volumes based on the surrounding sociodemographics, foot traffic, car traffic, and so forth, and there are related decision support tools to optimize a network of branches. Many of the banks use the same third-party decision support algorithms for branch placement and branch network optimization.

Information on the locations and sizes of all bank branches is readily available (i.e., branches are highly visible on the real estate they occupy). So when Bank A considers the acquisition of Bank B, it can calculate with reasonable accuracy the potential savings achievable through branch network consolidation. In fact, Bank A can even identify the branches it could close and the effect of those closures on the network.

The problem is, Bank B could also do this calculation and so could Bank C, another interested buyer. If the offer to purchase leaves too big a gap between the price offered and the potential savings through network consolidation, then Bank B will be talking to Bank C.

Another large cost center for banks is purchased goods and services (e.g., office supplies, computer equipment and software, professional services, etc.). During the 1990s, many of the large banks adopted new approaches to purchasing of goods and services, often referred to as strategic sourcing. As the industry and its consultants gained experience in strategic sourcing, standards emerged as to the saving potential available in banks, usually around 15 to 20 percent savings potential.

Not surprisingly, scale matters. Larger banks could negotiate better prices, so purchasing of goods and services was a consolidation rationale. The potential was even greater if the target bank had not gone through a strategic sourcing process itself. However, while there was great potential value to be achieved by applying strategic sourcing to the combined spending of the merging banks, the seller and each of the potential buyers knew about it and they could calculate the savings with reasonable accuracy. Once again, much of the value was subject to the bidding process and was ultimately built into the price paid.

The third large cost savings benefit for merging banks is information technology (IT). IT consolidation has potentially large savings potential in a merger because the fixed costs of hardware and software far exceed the costs that vary based on transaction volumes. IT costs are somewhat less transparent than branch and purchasing costs, but given the frequent movement of IT professionals between banks and the heavy use of (often the same) third party providers, reasonable estimates can be made.

The additional problem associated with merger savings in IT is that achieving the savings is difficult, costly, and takes years of effort. Estimates of IT savings in mergers are invariably high and contribute to the tendency to overpay, as noted earlier, and estimates of the cost and time to achieve the savings are invariably low.

Moreover, the relative transparency of operations synergies usually results in deal pricing that reflects the potential, especially in a consolidating industry in which multiple buyers are available for every good asset. The cost structures of companies in other industries may be somewhat less transparent, but many companies have used third-party benchmarking to estimate competitive cost structures with reasonable accuracy.

With such transparency on savings available through operations consolidation, it is clearly a seller's market. However, there are three winning strategies to consider as a buyer. First, have such accurate and realistic estimates of savings potential that you know when to stop bidding (i.e., you will often win by losing, letting competitors destroy shareholder value as they outbid you). Second, have superior execution skills so that the cost and timing of savings that you can achieve are superior to competitors' and therefore exceed the price you will have to pay. Part III of this book examines the competencies of experienced consolidators that can beat the odds and create value far in excess of the gain of the seller on a single deal.

How can consolidation create value in marketing and sales? When does it fail?

The cost synergies in marketing start with elimination of redundancies in the organization as the two organizations combine sales staffs. The savings in sales staff can be very substantial if there is a large sales force, whether it is a company sales force or is outsourced. Mergers of consumer goods companies illustrate this well. For example, if both companies market confectionary products, even if these products are not directly competitive, the merger can reduce sales calls by up to 50 percent because one visit to each retailer replaces what were two visits when the companies were separate.

There are also savings in marketing costs from consolidation of advertising agencies and, depending on how much the products were competing with each other, savings in advertising.

Finally, there can be improvements in market pricing if a merger changes the competitive dynamics that were setting price.

When the products and markets of the merging companies are complementary rather than overlapping, there are fewer cost synergies but the revenue synergies can be substantial. The globalization of consumer goods markets provides many opportunities for merging companies with complementary product and geographic strengths to use each others' marketing and sales channels to sell each others' products, resulting in better penetration in some markets and low cost entry into some new markets. This has been one of the principal motivations in the global consolidation of the consumer goods industry as discussed earlier. For example, the reach of Adam's Brands expanded when Adam's Brands was acquired by Cadbury in 2002 and again when Kraft acquired Cadbury in 2010.

Note that this positive revenue synergy comes primarily because the companies' products and markets are somewhat different. In other words, this is not really a consolidation benefit per se. The next chapter explores acquisitions aimed more at growth and discusses the revenue benefits when product, channel, and geographic strengths are different but complementary. However, even in consolidating industries, merging companies' markets and products seldom overlap entirely, so such revenue synergies are available in most industry consolidations and should be an explicit part of the M&A strategy.

Referring back to the U.S. bank consolidation, it should be noted that many of the successful deals were acquisitions in adjacent markets, such as the TD acquisition of Bank North and then Commerce One. In fact, the success rate of cross-border bank acquisitions is twice that of in-market deals.[11]

Notwithstanding the generally positive revenue synergies in complementary product–market combinations, the sales and marketing synergies in consolidation plays often turn negative due to revenue losses. Unlike cost synergies, which are under the control of the merging companies, revenue synergies are ultimately under the control of the customer. Turning again to a banking example, customers have difficulty seeing any benefit upon the announcement of a bank-to-bank merger and are more likely to see the downsides: "They'll likely close my branch," "The fees will go up again," or "My sister-in-law working at that bank will probably lose her job."

The inevitable inconveniences to the customer resulting from merging operations and systems will cause some customers to leave. However, fearing customer losses, most merging banks have foregone or delayed the potential benefits of product rationalization. In reviewing rates and fees, they have frequently chosen the lowest of the two banks for fear of offending anyone with a price increase. As a result, what may have been touted in the deal proposal as a positive revenue synergy has more often resulted in loss of customers, reduced fees and lending rates, and complex product platforms.[12]

RISKS AND ALTERNATIVES

Since the risks of consolidation-based acquisitions are so high, what are the alternatives?

Companies can grow and prosper without acquiring or merging. McCain Foods Limited, Walmart, and Research In Motion Limited (RIM) have built leading international companies in food, retail, and technology, respectively, mostly organically. The industries in which they operate—food processing, department stores, and smart phones have undergone consolidation, and most competitors have grown by acquisition. However, each of these companies had a new and distinct product or business model and was prepared to invest heavily in expansion.

Companies in consolidating industries that lack such a distinct advantage must buy or they will eventually be targets. Selling into a consolidating industry is not necessarily a bad strategy if the company believes that it can capture more value by selling and if the company prepares to be an attractive target.

However, the companies that can lead consolidation have the potential to create more value than a single sale premium. In the consolidating mining sector, for example, handsome premiums were paid for Alcan, INCO, and Falconbridge, but these premiums pale in comparison to the value created in the development of mining consolidators such as Xstrata, BHP Billiton, and Barrick Gold.

What are some examples of companies that have been successful as consolidators?

Many consolidators grew from smaller companies than those they eventually acquired and multiplied shareholder value in the process. For example, Xstrata of Switzerland grew from $2 billion to $20 billion in the past 10 years, mostly through acquisitions, ultimately achieving the financial strength to outbid INCO, then the world's largest nickel company, for Falconbridge with whom INCO would have had large operations synergies with their reserves and operations side-by-side. The market capitalization of Xstrata went from a market cap of about $500 million in 2001 to $41 billion in 2011,[13] dwarfing INCO's one-time gain on its sale to Vale Resources of Brazil.

Similarly Belgium's InBev Brewing grew from $3 billion to $60 billion in the same period, eventually accumulating the financial strength to acquire America's brewing giant Anheuser-Busch for $52 billion.[14]

There are many other successful acquirers that have built shareholder value in a range of consolidating industries: BHP Billiton in diversified mining, Barrick in gold, R.R. Donnelley & Sons Company in graphics, Magna in automotive supply, Thomson-Reuters in information services, Deutsche Telekom in telecommunications, and others.

What are the risks of choosing not to play as a buyer or seller?

In a consolidating industry, the forces that are driving consolidation will ultimately put smaller companies at a disadvantage unless they can defend some small segment of the market. For example, some paper companies so cornered retreated to niches in fine paper to play in a smaller market that would be less subject to cost-based competition.

Such niches are harder to find in commodity products, such as in the mining industry. Some U.S. banks continue to hold out based on a dominant position in a local market. However, such companies are vulnerable to the eventual entry of a larger player with sufficient scale economies to "buy" the customers instead of the company.

The greatest risk for a company that chooses not to play is that the company becomes subscale in the consolidated industry and thus uncompetitive and ultimately unattractive as a target. For the company that has or can acquire the skills to be a successful acquirer, the value creation potential as a buyer in a consolidation industry is high. Alternatively, if a company can remain competitive, perhaps by making some acquisitions or by maintaining a valued market position, then eventual sale is an attractive option for shareholders.

Endnotes

1. Konrad Yadabuski, "Shrinking Giant," *Globe and Mail Report on Business*, March 28, 2008, page 1.
2. For a book devoted to this topic, see Jagdish Sheth and Rajendra Sisodia, *The Rule of Three:Surviving and Thriving in Competitive Markets* (New York: Free Press, 2002).
3. American Eagle data from American Airlines Company Website, http://www.aa.com/i18n/footer/eagleOverview.jsp, accessed October 9, 2011.
4. Karen Jacobs, "Regional Airlines Consolidating to Cut Costs," *Reuters Business Traveller*, August 30, 2010, http://uk.reuters.com/article/idUKTRE67T52Z20100830, accessed October 9, 2011.
5. Federal Deposit Insurance Corporation (FDIC). *FDIC Quarterly Banking Profile*. June 30, 2003, http://www2.fdic.gov/qbp/2010jun/qbp.pdf.
6. In 2009, Sen. Maria Cantwell (D-WA) and Sen. John McCain (R-AZ) introduced a bill that would bring back parts of Glass-Steagall, and Paul Volcker proposed a similar initiative in the administrative branch of government, dubbed the Volcker Rule. To date, none has been successful. See Alec Hamilton, "You Take That Back: The Challenge of Repealing Federal Law," January 18, 2011, accessed January 30, 2011, http://www.wnyc.org/articles/its-free-country/2011/jan/18/you-take-back/.
7. SECOR Consulting, "Positioning Canadian Firms in the Global Market for Corporate Control," Submission to the Federal Panel on Canadian Competitiveness, Government of Canada, 2008.
8. Christian Nordqvist, "AstraZeneca to Buy Cambridge Antibody Technology," *Medical News Today*, May 13, 2006, http://www.medicalnewstoday.com/articles/43423.php, accessed October 9, 2011.
9. Alan Friedman, "A Case of Culture Shock in the Global Arena," *New York Times,* April 23, 1997, from http://www.nytimes.com/1997/04/23/news/23iht-clash.t.html?pagewanted=all, accessed October 9, 2011.
10. Kenneth W. Smith and Eliza O'Neil, "Shareholder Value Created and Destroyed in Financial Services Mergers," *ABA Banking Journal*, December 2003, pp 7–10.
11. Ibid.
12. Kenneth W. Smith, "The Revenue Chase," *Banking Strategies*, March-April 1999, pp 58–64.
13. Xstrata stock price history from Bloomberg Financial, www.bloomberg.com/apps/quote?ticker=XTA:LN, accessed October 9, 2011.
14. Michael J. de la Merced, "Anheuser-Busch Agrees to Be Sold to InBev," *New York Times*, July 14, 2008, http://www.nytimes.com/2008/07/14/business/worldbusiness/14beer.html, accessed October 9, 2011.

CHAPTER 3

Expansion Strategy: Value in Revenue Growth

You can't shrink to greatness.

—*Grow to be Great*[1]

Revenue growth remains a key driver of strategy for most companies despite the challenges it brings. To be sure, bigger is not necessarily better, as the bankruptcies of titans have taught us in recent years. Yet growth in revenues does tend to be associated over time with growth in value—measured as returns to shareholders. In *Grow to be Great: Breaking the Downsizing Cycle*,[2] authors Dwight Gertz and João Baptista foresaw the limits of profit improvement without growth. When the book was written in the mid-1990s, many American corporations were obsessed with cost cutting to improve profits and boost stock performance. However, they were not seeing a commensurate improvement in shareholder value over time. The book demonstrated conclusively that the most successful companies achieve top-line as well as bottom-line growth, and the market disproportionately rewards growth in revenue over growth in profit.

This chapter looks briefly at why revenue growth is so important to shareholder value creation, and then examines the role of M&A in a range of growth strategies.

IMPORTANCE OF REVENUE GROWTH

Why are market valuations so sensitive to growth?

When the market values a company, it is valuing both its current performance and its future potential. Because the potential for cost cutting is finite (i.e., limited by the cost base), cost cutting offers at best a diminishing return without corporate growth. As Gertz and Baptista put it, "You can't shrink to greatness." However, as the top line grows so grows *the potential* for future returns.

This observation is borne out by the mathematics of valuation. While companies use a variety of approaches to valuing a company,[3] most valuation experts emphasize the net present value of future free cash flows.[4] Free cash flows (FCFs) are the cash a company will have left after debt payments, taxes paid, operating expenses, and capital expenditures.[5] While FCF is correlated with earnings in the long run, FCF is "real money," whereas earnings are based on the particular accounting applied to cash and noncash items such as deferred revenue and capital depreciation.

Intrinsic value is generally calculated based on a few years of known or predictable FCF performance, plus the *continuing value*, where continuing value is the present value of ongoing FCFs based on certain assumptions about sustainable growth and performance trends.

The standard formula for continuing value is $FCF/(WACC - g)$, where

- *FCF* is the first year FCF going forward
- *WACC* is the weighted average cost of capital (i.e., the discount rate to be applied in the net present value [NPV] calculation)
- *g* is the growth rate used to calculate the expected future FCF.

Note that FCF's relationship with continuing value is linear. For example, a 10 percent higher assumption on FCF yields a 10 percent higher continuing value. However, continuing value is affected geometrically by *g*.

Mathematics aside, this also makes intuitive sense. Potential returns are bounded by revenue. Growth in revenue releases that constraint. So an expectation of strong and continuing growth in revenue represents substantially more value creation potential, provided profitability is maintained.

Why isn't there more focus on revenue growth?

Many companies that have put growth ahead of profitability have failed. Indeed, bankruptcies have resulted when good ideas have grown the company beyond its financial capacity, whether organically or through acquisitions. To cite an old proverb, the companies' reach exceeded their grasp. Two examples will illustrate this point: Olympia & York and Allied–Federated.

Olympia & York

The Olympia & York Canary Wharf story illustrates the risks in organic growth. Olympia & York grew from a porcelain tile company in the 1960s into a highly successful commercial real estate developer by the late 1980s. It had major development projects in Toronto (First Canadian Place, the largest office development in Canada at the time); Manhattan (245 Park Avenue in midtown, three of the four towers of the World Financial Center, as well as One Liberty Plaza), and Boston (53 State Street). They also had corporate holdings, including controlling interest in Sante Fe Railroad and the pulp and paper company Abitibi-Price.

The next big project was the development of Canary Wharf in London, a well-conceived but ill-timed project. Olympia & York acquired 71 acres along the Thames to expand London's financial services industry beyond the City of London. The project was to build 9 million square feet of office space that would accommodate nearly 50,000 office workers.[6]

This strategy proved overly ambitious. First there came the recession in late 1989. Second, somewhat related to the recession, London delayed the development of the London Underground to Canary Wharf—postponing a public transit link that was critical to gaining advanced lease commitments from tenants. Third, the recession so affected the value of Olympia & York's other holdings that it could not access invested capital. Notwithstanding what has since proven to be truly visionary development of London's Canary Wharf, the company ran out of cash and had to file for bankruptcy protection in 1991. (The company has since reemerged as a smaller player in real estate development but no longer holds most of its earlier prized properties.)

Note that this was not a reckless company; it was an otherwise well-run company highly respected in the financial communities of Bay Street, Wall Street, and the City of London. However, any investment in growth comes with some risk, and in this case the company was bankrupted by a confluence of negative events its leaders failed to anticipate and plan for.

Allied–Federated

The Allied–Federated department store merger serves as one example among many of the risks of growth through M&A. Allied had been founded in 1935 to succeed Hahn Department Stores, Inc., a holding company that managed Boston's Jordan Marsh stores, among others. In 1950, Allied had been instrumental in the establishment of the first regional shopping center in the United States and had acquired the Stern Brothers and Block's department stores over the course of its history. Federated had also grown through acquisition. Founded in 1929, it subsequently acquired the Bloomingdales and Burdines chains.

In 1986, Campeau Corporation saw the opportunity to merge Allied with Federated Department Stores. Allied was acquired for $3.6 billion in a hostile, debt-financed takeover. The combined company then acquired Federated in 1988, also financed with debt. This created a massive retail conglomerate with opportunity for significant cost and revenue synergies. However, as already noted, in 1989 a recession cooled the retail market and depressed the cash flows intended to finance the debt. Federated and Allied filed the second-largest nonbank bankruptcy on record and entered the largest, most complex restructuring in the retail trade. Federated emerged from bankruptcy protection in 1992 and subsequently acquired Macy's, Broadway Stores, and Fingerhut. The company was renamed Macy's Inc. in 2007.[7]

While the circumstances of these two examples were very different, these bankruptcies have the following in common: (1) good concepts with high potential for value creation through growth, (2) large upfront investment required exposing the company to unforeseen circumstances, (3) a confluence of events delaying the cash flows.

Why is there such continuing focus on cost cutting over revenue growth?

With the constant pressure on CEOs to improve performance, cost cutting offers short-term results that can be directly achieved by management. Top-down direction can accomplish staff reduction and reductions in marketing and expense budgets almost immediately, whether or not such reductions are in the best interests of the corporation over the long term.

In contrast, revenue growth takes time and investment and usually introduces additional risks. Organic growth may require investment in new products or facilities, the launch of new marketing or branding initiatives, expansion of the sales force, or entry into new markets, all of which require time to make an impact and none of which are guaranteed to work. Even if successful, such initiatives often pay off for the successors of the current management team. For example, many of the CEOs who took their corporations into China in the 1990s, such as Jack Welch of GE in 2001 and Matt Barrett of Bank of Montreal in 1997, were well ahead of their competitors and the payoff. They knew they had little hope of a return on their watch, but these investments ultimately paid off handsomely for their successors or their successors' successors. Few leaders today take such a long-term view, due in part to the short-term nature of the markets.

Even in acquisitions that offer both revenue growth and cost reduction opportunities, the greater focus is usually put on the cost reduction opportunities introduced by the merger. The cost-reduction measures can be directed top down and have immediate impact. For the experienced acquirers in the U.S. bank consolidation, for example, postdeal staff reduction was down to a routine. Signet Bank employees were notified within 48 hours of the close of the acquisition by First Union in 1997 as to which day employees at each level of the hierarchy would find out their fates—top level week 1, second level week 2, and so forth; whereas the revenue synergies in these mergers were seldom achieved at all.

REVENUE GROWTH STRATEGIES

What are the growth strategies (of a single-business company) in which M&A can be deployed?

To look at the role of acquisitions in profitable growth, the following section examines four generic growth strategies or vectors for growth:

1. Growth within a current market with current product offerings
2. Growth within a current market with new products
3. Growth into a new market with current products
4. Growth into a new market with new products

In each case, there could be a make versus buy decision. That is, if there is growth potential available, is it best achieved organically or by acquisition? While most acquisitions cover more than one of these four vectors, this categorization provides a convenient framework for examining the unique issues associated with each.

Notwithstanding the range of new markets and new products that could be considered, the focus here is on acquisitions that are essentially in the same business. Holding companies that acquire, hold, and sell companies in different businesses were discussed in Chapter 1. This chapter assumes the case of a single-business company (even though some single-business companies will adopt a holding company structure to manage divisions in different markets or products).

What is the role of M&A in growth strategies within current markets and products?

If a company has growth potential within current markets and product categories, it is either because there is potential to expand the market (additional customers or increased consumption) with the products "as is," there is potential to expand the market with product improvements, or the potential new customers or consumption is currently being served by competitors.

In the first case, M&A likely has no role. For example, many people who could afford life insurance choose not to buy it, even though there are numerous product variations in the market. This is primarily a marketing and sales challenge to interest new customers in life insurance or to improve the coverage of existing customers.

In the second case, there is capacity for market expansion with product improvements. For example, you might use your favorite search engine more often if it were more effective for your purposes. In this case, there could be a make versus buy decision for the needed product improvements. For example, Google is constantly acquiring innovations to improve its core product, such as Deja.com in 2001 for search capabilities, Applied Semantics in 2003 for text processing for online advertising, and Picas in 2004 for photo recognition.[8] (Google uses acquisitions in all four generic growth strategies—discussed later in the chapter.)

In the third case, the make versus buy decision is between competing for the competitor's customers versus acquiring the competitor. In effect, this is in-market consolidation in which customer acquisition may be a primary motivator.

However, absent significant cost synergies or issues with market structure, an in-market acquisition for customers is unlikely to pay off. There are two problems with such an acquisition. First, the target's acquisition price will already factor in the net present value of the contribution of all of these customers (less fixed overhead, of course). Second, in this scenario, the buyer may not retain all the customers—these customers all bought from a competitor before, and nothing prevents them from doing so again. If there are other choices in the market, it is highly likely that at least some customers will go to them. (If there were no other choices in the market, there would be an antitrust problem.)

So the revenue synergies are negative, and the deal economics can't work on customer acquisition alone. The only way for such an acquisition to pay off, therefore, is if other synergies such as R&D, manufacturing, marketing, or corporate overhead are significant.

This theory was demonstrated in the in-market mergers during U.S. bank industry consolidation. As deal pricing ran up to and above the value of cost synergies, banks began identifying a range of revenue synergies in their deal proposals, including product growth and pricing synergies. However, when products unique to one bank were offered to the customers of the other, there was little uptake. For common products, when the teams sat down to decide pricing, product-by-product they chose the lowest price between the two banks for fear of losing customers to other banks in the market. As a result, the revenue synergies were negative. Throughout U.S. bank industry consolidation, the in-market deals performed worse than cross-market deals in which cost synergy was lower, but revenue synergy was positive. (More to come on this scenario.)

Moreover, M&A has a meaningful role in growth within current product markets only in the context of a make versus buy decision to advance product improvements or as part of a consolidation play. In the latter case, there must be compelling cost synergies as outlined in detail in Chapter 2.

What is the role of M&A in growth strategies adding new products in current markets?

This type of business combination is sometimes called related diversification. Related diversification transactions are in general more likely to create value than unrelated diversification or consolidation.[9] If such a merger can introduce a product to new markets, then substantial revenue growth can occur with little impact on total costs.

This type of transaction is well illustrated in the acquisition of Lotus Development Corporation by IBM in 1995, which was IBM's first large step from computer hardware into computer software. IBM acquired Lotus for $3.5 billion or $64 per share, double the trading value before the bid. In addition to the strategic imperative for IBM to diversify, the deal logic was to grow Lotus revenues by offering its products through the vast markets served by IBM.

Analysts were skeptical of the deal for three reasons—it was a diversification, the premium was high, and, at the time of the transaction, IBM had a history of crushing the entrepreneurial culture of the growth companies it acquired.

However, IBM carefully managed the integration issues and focused on achieving the product–market synergies. Protocols were established to keep the companies and cultures separate except for one thing—the IBM sales force was to sell the Lotus products. The number of Lotus "seats" (or desktops) was the measure of success, and "Get Lotus seats" became a rallying cry postdeal. The deal more than paid for itself and, in spite of the high premium paid, it created shareholder value and launched IBM successfully into software.

Such deals can be highly successful because they create new value, almost from nothing. Unlike consolidation synergies, these are not one-time revenue synergies but continue into the future. Such synergies are also less transparent and less transferable to other potential buyers, and hence less likely to get negotiated into the price of the deal.

Another domain of similar product–market combinations is the bancassurance market in Europe. Deals such as Credit Suisse–Winterthur, Lloyds TSB–Abbey Life, Banco Santander–Banco Hispano (BSBH), and Den Danske–Danika created value by offering the comprehensive channels of the banks for the marketing of insurance products. For example, 65 percent of BSBH's mortgage customers were acquiring life insurance from them when offered. While the famous acquisition of Travelers Insurance by Citibank in 1998 is often used as proof that such deals don't work, life insurance premiums were multiplied through Citibank channels, in spite of what many say was only a partially executed deal logic. The success rate of these so-called cross-pillar deals was over 70 percent versus the dismal 40 percent success rate of in-market bank mergers.[10] Over the past decade, banks remained one of the fastest-growing channels for insurance products in Europe, and in the years following the passage of the Gramm-Leach-Bliley Act in 1999, allowing bank-insurance integration in the United States, U.S. banks bought more insurance brokers than banks.[11]

In markets in which customers want end-to-end service, the acquisition of an additional piece of the offer can add value even beyond the growth of the new product by making the entire customer offering more complete and compelling.

For example, United Parcel Service has acquired various customs brokerage services. One such acquisition was Livingston Customs Brokerage in Canada in 2000.[12] Canada and the United States are each other's largest trading partners so the North–South lanes between Canada and the United States are strategically important to any freight transportation company. The services of Livingston were, of course, marketed across UPS's vast U.S. customer base achieving growth for the Livingston products through UPS channels, similar to the foregoing examples.

However, the benefit to UPS far exceeded the direct impact of brokerage sales growth. First, UPS could then offer to its U.S. shippers and Canadian consignees a simple, complete, and speedier service than if they used the Livingston brokerage directly. This was a competitive advantage over companies that did not offer a complete service of transportation and customs clearance. In addition, the economics of the Canadian lanes downstream from Livingston then benefited from greater route density—a key driver of courier economics.

Google acquires to offer new products to existing markets as well. The acquisition of Neotonic in 2003 led to the launch of a an e-mail platform with superior spam filters (Gmail), and Google's acquisition of YouTube in 2006 undoubtedly fueled growth of both the search engine and video sharing.[13]

However, while product–market combinations are strategically compelling, there are also many failures. Most of the failures are the result of trying to sell products through unsuitable channels. For example, many technology firms combined with strategy consulting firms in the 1990s and early 2000s believing that the strategy firms would offer channels to the senior executives that would help sell all of their products. In fact, the sales context and skills for strategy versus IT sales are very different, and the acquired channels did not work well. For example, McKinsey & Company acquired Information Consulting Group (ICG) in 1989, a 250-person information technology firm based in Washington, D.C. By 1993 half of the partners and more than half of the staff left.[14] Electronic Data Systems' acquisition of A.T. Kearney was eventually undone—long before EDS itself got acquired and renamed by HP. The US Web–Mitchell Madison Group combination later went bankrupt.[15] Accenture organically grew a large, top-tier strategy practice that disbanded within a few years (although Accenture has more recently reentered general management consulting).

The lesson of these failures is the lesson of all revenue-based M&A strategies: revenue synergies are earned when customers like the idea. So a product–market combination will have compelling deal logic if and only if it also presents a compelling value proposition to customers. Few clients would clamor for IT and strategy help in one basket, but many do want other kinds of combinations. For example, computer hardware with software that works is an attractive proposition. So is being able to insure your home where you get your mortgage (and have to provide proof of insurance), or being able to ship items using a complete, door-to-door, cross-border freight transportation service. In revenue synergies, the customer is always right.

What is the role of M&A in growth strategies taking existing products into new markets?

This is another type of M&A strategy with compelling logic for some of the same reasons. Successfully entering a new market segment or geography creates new value, whether done organically or by acquisition. It also carries substantial risk in either case.

There are many examples of geographic expansion through acquisition. For example, while Walmart developed across America organically, it chose to acquire in order to enter some international markets. While it initially opened new stores in Mexico and Hong Kong, it acquired 122 Woolco stores to enter Canada and 21 Wertkauf units in Germany, and it entered China and Korea through joint ventures.[16]

The advantages of using M&A in international expansion are speed and market knowledge. Walmart acquired complete chains in Canada and Germany that it then rebranded as Walmart. It brought instant value to these acquisitions by reducing the cost of goods, leveraging its buying power and vast supply network. In some cases, its selection, layout, operations, and brand added value through growth in same-store sales.

Opening stores in these markets one at a time clearly would have taken longer. An organic approach would have opened up additional costs and risks. First, there were loyalties to the incumbent discount operations that would have taken time and money to overcome. Second, as a new entrant, Walmart would have been more likely to miss the mark on selection and marketing. Third, the acquisition approach provided a local executive team and resources across each market, saving recruiting and training costs.

However, the acquisition approach also multiplies the consequences of getting it wrong. For example, in 1982, Canadian Tire Corporation, Canada's largest and most successful hard goods retailer, entered the U.S. market through the acquisition of White Stores, a chain of more than 400 automotive retail stores. Canadian Tire attempted to convert the stores into a format similar to that used by its Canadian stores. Unfortunately, this failed, and Canadian Tire took losses of over $300 million and faced a lawsuit of $400 million launched by dealers who had come south to start stores. In 1985, Canadian Tire exited.[17]

The successes outnumber the failures. Cross-border deals in Europe substantially outperform domestic deals. Only U.S. overseas transactions have a success rate below 50 percent, and this is due mainly to poor post-deal management failing to deliver on attractive potential.[18]

Among the many companies that have grown internationally by acquisition are Manulife in financial services (e.g., John Hancock in the United States, Daihyaku Mutual in Japan, and Pramercia Life in the Philippines), UPS in transportation (e.g., Alimondo in Italy and Germany and a number of freight airline services), and General Foods, now part of Kraft, in consumer goods (e.g., La India Company in Venezuela, Hostess in Canada, Kibon ice cream company in Brazil, and Krema Hollywood Chewing Gum in France), and Google (e.g., Chinese search engine Baidu in 2004), to name a few.

It should be noted that among the successful transactions during the U.S. bank consolidation were the cross-region deals.[19] It may seem counterintuitive that the less the overlap the more likely is success. However, as noted in Chapter 2, the cost synergies tended to be negotiated into the acquisition price of the U.S. banks, and the revenue synergies in in-market deals were negative, as noted earlier in this chapter. The cross-region deals averted the negative revenue synergies and in the best cases brought a better national brand, filled in product gaps, and introduced a superior operating approach to the acquired bank.

However, the magnitude of some of the failures is sobering. For example, the 1998 merger of Chrysler with Daimler-Benz, a $37 billion stock-swap deal, was the largest transatlantic merger to that day. The new company, with market capitalization approaching $100 billion, saw synergy potential in retail sales, purchasing, distribution, product design, and research and development. Three years later, DaimlerChrysler's market capitalization was $44 billion and its stock was dropped from the S&P 500, largely due to clashes of culture and mismanagement.[20]

Geographic expansion (even domestically) almost always crosses cultural borders, so in addition to the usual challenges of the integration of corporate cultures, these deals must manage across national or regional cultures and must do this across vast distances.

What is the role of M&A in growth strategies to enter new markets with new products?

On the face of it, this sounds like unrelated diversification. However, we refer here to situations in which there are product synergies and/or market synergies.

The growth strategy of Zwilling J.A. Henckels of Germany illustrates how M&A can facilitate growth across products and markets simultaneously. Zwilling is best known as the manufacturer of fine cooking knives under the brands Henckels and Zwilling. Over the past 10 years they have expanded into new segments of cooking knives as well as into cookware and beauty, each time through acquisitions in a new market.

The 2004 acquisition of Tweezerman International in the beauty segment significantly enhanced Zwilling's footprint in U.S. department stores while providing a new product line to market around the world. In 2008, Zwilling acquired Staub of France, a manufacturer of fine cast iron cookware. Staub is now marketed throughout Zwilling's international markets, and Zwilling cooking knives have enjoyed increased sales in France. Similarly, that same year the acquisition of Demeyere Cookware of Belgium, manufacturer of fine stainless steel cookware, added a product to market internationally while gaining better access in the Benelux countries.[21]

Moreover, with each of these acquisitions Zwilling was able to simultaneously take new products to its existing channels and take its current product lines to new markets, thus gaining the benefits of both the second and third types of growth strategies.

Like the foregoing strategies to use current markets for new products and to bring current products to new markets, this type of acquisition creates new revenue with little added cost, and hence can add significant value. (Zwilling is a private company and the actual value created in these deals is not available.)

Google's 2011 acquisition of Motorola Mobility Holdings for $12.5 billion was, among other things, a new product–new market acquisition. The Motorola deal may have been in some measure a defensive move in light of mounting patent infringement cases against Google's Android operating system used in 150 million mobile devices. However, the move simultaneously advanced Google in the telephony market with a leading smart-phone hardware product.[22]

Another company that executed multiple acquisitions of this type is Cisco Systems. Cisco grew to be a leader in digital network technologies through over 125 acquisitions from 1993 to 2010. Each acquisition added products to Cisco's offering, bringing Cisco closer to a "one stop shop" for network technologies.

Simultaneously, these acquisitions created a spider web of market channels, ideal for addressing its fragmented and entrepreneurial customer markets. Indeed, Cisco executed minimal integration, preferring to keep the market relationships of each acquired company. Yet it created substantial value for shareholders rising from its initial public offering (IPO) value in 1990 of $224 million to $84 billion in 2011. (At the height of the dot.com bubble, Cisco was the largest company in the world by market capitalization.)[23]

This type of growth is very difficult to achieve organically. Entering new products and markets simultaneously requires new resources and skills. Even if such investments can be made well, a new entrant must then win customers from existing competitors. So, at best, an organic approach to this type of growth strategy would take a much longer time to execute, and the probability of failure would be high.

However, it is also risky to execute such growth strategies through acquisition because diversification acquisitions have, in general, low success rates, and this type of revenue synergy can be a stretch—the deal logic is sometimes stretching reality, and, even when the deal logic is sound, the implementation can be a stretch of skills.

Keys to the success of the foregoing Zwilling and Cisco examples were excellent fit of new product lines, new channels highly suitable for a full range of products, and an implementation approach that preserved the strengths of the acquired companies.

COMMON RISKS AND SUCCESS FACTORS

Are there some common risks in these four M&A growth strategies?

More and more deal proposals are relying on revenue synergies. As consolidation progresses in industries such as banking and utilities, the cost synergies become transparent and get built into the acquisition price by the competitive bidding process. Deal makers are then forced to argue the revenue potential to get the deal done. In some cases the revenue potential is real, but even then the track record of achieving that potential is abysmal.

The main reason revenue synergies have proven to be elusive even to experienced acquirers is that success depends on the customer making the decision. Where cost synergies can be acted on directly by management, revenue synergies have to be earned through the retention, acquisition, and growth of customers that have a choice (unlike the terminated employees that make up the cost synergies).

How can the acquirer achieve revenue synergies to make growth-oriented M&A successful?

The key to achieving revenue synergies is development of the marketing strategy that will compel the customers to make the choices conceived in the deal logic. Marketing strategy is well summarized by the four Ps of marketing: promotion, place, price, and product, and we add a fifth: people.

Promotion: Segment First, Design for Growth Not Just Retention

A merger is an ideal time to re-segment and choose the ideal target customer mix for the new company. If the value proposition includes a better offer for the most attractive customers, they are less likely to leave. The idea of consolidating business, if properly presented, should increase business with customers well suited for the new company and its offer.

Many mergers could result in a better proposition for customers. The problem arises from lack of effective segmentation. Companies seldom have sufficient resources to reach all customers effectively. By identifying the most valuable customers—wholesale and retail—effort can be focused on marketing efforts that will really pay off.

Place: Leverage Coverage, Don't Slash Prematurely

Merger rationalization strategies often inadvertently close off opportunities for future growth. Distribution and sales force rationalization can be a tempting early cost saving. The models used for retail rationalization, for example, typically assess outlet profitability with great accuracy.

Customers don't like changing banks or clothing stores, for example, because of the inconvenience involved in changing and the trust they have in the brand or personnel. Considerable inertia, therefore, acts in favor of staying with the company after a merger. However, if the merged company puts a priority on rationalization of sales and distribution, then this inertia is upset and customers are forced to choose the new company or a competitor.

So, even if sales channel rationalization is compelling, it should often be delayed until after customer attrition stabilizes and the new combined channels have been exploited for new revenue.

Price: Optimize Price/Volume Trade-Offs

The typical process for integration of product pricing too often devolves to picking the lowest common denominator. Partly out of fear of customer attrition, marketers are very reluctant to raise prices for anyone after the merger. So for overlapping products when prices, service fees, and discount structures are compared product-by-product, the lower price of the two companies is often selected or the two marketers compromise simply to get closure. By settling for the lowest price of the two companies, they actually create negative revenue synergy and waste brand value.

Some merger strategies may recognize low price elasticity of demand for some services and brands and achieve large and immediate returns by raising prices in acquired companies. If such across-the-board opportunities are tapped out, more sophisticated differential pricing improvements may be possible using price elasticity–based segmentation.

Product: Sell the Full Product Line if Practical, Rationalize Later

In consolidation deals, proponents often strive to make the merger invisible to the customer. In fact, mergers cannot be invisible to the customer and still earn revenue synergies—by definition. Growth-oriented mergers capitalize on the combined product capabilities to grow new revenue.

Again, there can be a temptation to rationalize products to reduce costs. Even if product rationalization is warranted, a strategic approach is required to capitalize on revenue opportunities across the combined product set, before or while rationalizing.

People: Nurture the Acquired Growth Culture

Acquisitions of high-revenue growth companies fail most often. At first this seems counterintuitive. After all, buyers seek growth companies because of the high value placed on their future revenue growth.

However, higher-growth companies command a higher share price multiple and a higher acquisition premium. Typically, the market will make the buyer pay at least for the present value of the growth trajectory of the target. Unfortunately, the buyers can seldom sustain the acquired institution's internally generated growth. The culture of the larger acquirer tends to overwhelm the service-focused, entrepreneurial culture of the acquired. Some of the best people leave, more bureaucracy creeps in, and, particularly amid frequent acquisitions and restructurings, fear stifles creativity.

Consolidators need to go out of their way to nurture a creative, service-focused, entrepreneurial growth culture. They must express and demonstrate values of customer service and product development. They must carefully integrate work processes and decision processes to realize synergies without introducing unnecessary bureaucracy.

Even at the high acquisition prices in consolidating industries, acquirers can still create value in their deals. But with cost synergies already built into these prices, the only way to do that is to achieve revenue synergies, a difficult process that requires customers to make a decision in favor of the merging entity. Those companies that can demonstrate the value of the merger to their customers and earn additional revenue will create value for shareholders and emerge as leaders in the restructured industry.

Endnotes

1. Dwight Gertz and João P. A. Baptista, *Grow to be Great: Breaking the Downsizing Cycle* (New York: Free Press, 1995).
2. Ibid.
3. For an explanation of all the accepted approaches, see Robert A. G. Monks and Alexandra R. Lajoux, *Corporate Valuation for Portfolio Investment: Analyzing Assets, Earnings, Cash Flow, Market Value, Governance, and Special Situations* (New York: Bloomberg/Wiley, 2011). For data on prevalence of use among public companies, see the *2011 Public Company Governance Survey,* reporting the following usage of valuation techniques for 1,300 public companies (multiple choices allowed) for the purpose of compensation. The survey asked, "When linking pay to corporate performance, how do you define 'performance'?" The answers were as follows: profits 67.5 percent, sales

45.2 percent, ratios such as EPS 34.8 percent, cash flow 33.9 percent, stock price 30 percent, hybrid measures such as EVA or CFROI 16.1 percent, assets 11.3 percent, other 21.5 percent. The survey also reported on the prevalence of nonfinancial metrics such as customer satisfaction, employee morale, and diversity.

4. See Tom Copeland, Tim Koller, and Jack Murrin, *Valuation: Measuring and Managing the Value of Companies* (New York: Wiley, 2010). Valuation provides an explanation along with empirical evidence that market valuations correlate strongly with intrinsic value, calculated as NPV of future cash flows.
5. Of course, the challenge in valuing future cash flow lies in predicting the future in the first place. As William Phillips has observed, "Cash flow analysis is in essence discounting a series of known or estimated payments and receipts, ranged over a time scale, at interest either to obtain a present value (positive or negative) at a given interest rate, or valuing them at various rates to derive a yield that equates the present values of payments and receipts." Cited in Monks and Lajoux, op. cit, note 3.
6. "Olympia and York Moves into London," *New York Times*, July 18, 1987, accessed October 9, 2011, http://www.nytimes.com/1987/07/18/business/olympia-york-moves-into-london.html?scp=10&sq=Olympia%20and%20York&st=cse.
7. "Federated Shareholders Approve Name Change to Macy's Inc.," company press release May 18, 2007, accessed October 9, 2011, http://phx.corporate-ir.net/phoenix.zhtml?c=84477&p=irol-newsArticle&ID=1004322&highlight.
8. "Top 10 History of Google Acquisitions and Where They Are Today," *Lilo Magazine–Benny*, March 22, 2011, accessed October 9, 2011, http://lilomag.com/2011/03/22/top-10-history-of-google-acquisitions-and-where-they-are-today/.
9. Kenneth Smith and S. E. Hershman, "How M&A Fits Into a Real Growth Strategy," *Mergers & Acquisitions*, 32, no. 2 (1997).
10. SECOR Consulting, "Shareholder Value Created and Destroyed in Financial Services Mergers—Implications for Public Policy," report submitted to the Federal Consultation on Large Mergers in Financial Services, December 22, 2003, accessed October 9, 2011, http://www.fin.gc.ca/consultresp/mergersRespns_9-eng.asp.
11. "Banks in Insurance: A Five-Year Retrospective since the Passage of GLB," *Bank Director Magazine*, 2nd qtr. (2004).
12. "UPS Logistics Group to Acquire Livingston," Business Wire, August 30, 2000, accessed October 9, 2011, http://findarticles.com/p/articles/mi_m0EIN/is_2000_August_30/ai_64997242/.
13. "Top 10 History of Google Acquisitions" and "Where They Are Today" ibid.
14. *International Directory of Company Histories*, vol. 9 (St. James Press, Greenhaven, CT, 1994).
15. US Web acquired Mitchell Madison Group in 1999 and was subsequently acquired by Whittman Hart in 2000 and renamed MarchFirst; MarchFirst filed for bancruptcy protection in 2001, see *E-Commerce Times* April 13, 2001.

16. See the Walmart website at walmartstores.com at About Us - http://walmart stores.com/AboutUs/7603.aspx.
17. "Canadian Tire's Mistaken Leap in the U.S. Market," *Canadian Broadcasting Corporation*, broadcast December 8, 1985, accessed October 9, 2011, http://archives.cbc.ca/economy_business/consumer_goods/clips/16903/.
18. Ken Smith, "Losing (Ownership) Control," speech to the Canadian Consulate in New York, February 24, 2010.
19. See Kenneth W. Smith and Eliza O'Neil, "Bank-to-Bank Deals Seldom Add Value," *ABA Banking Journal*, December 2003, pp 7-10.
20. Sydney Finkelstein, "The Daimler-Chrysler Merger," a case history developed at Dartmouth College, http://mba.tuck.dartmouth.edu/pdf/2002-1-0071.pdf.
21. See the Zwilling website at http://www.zwilling.com/en-DK/Company-profile-company_profile/Chapter-kapitel/The-international-brand-policy-of-ZWILLING-J.A.-HENCKELS-1096.html, accessed October 9, 2011.
22. Omar El Akkad, "Google's Motorola Deal 'By and Large' a Defensive Play in Patent Wars," *Globe and Mail*, August 15, 2011, accessed October 9, 2011, http://www.theglobeandmail.com/globe-investor/googles-motorola-deal-by-and-large-a-defensive-play-in-patent-wars/article2129737/.
23. George Garza, "The History of Cisco," *Bright Hub,* January 9, 2011, accessed October 9, 2011, http://www.brighthub.com/computing/enterprise-security/articles/65663.aspx.

CHAPTER 4

Real Options in M&A

Back to the future.[1]

We discuss M&A as a tool of strategy throughout this book. Certainly any major deal will have strategic importance and will be accompanied by commensurate strategic risk. However, a single deal seldom comprises the entire strategy. Strategies usually involve several steps, often with each step depending on the one before. Such strategies can be further complicated if subsequent steps also depend on factors unknowable in advance.

In such cases, the strategic thinking moves from checkers to chess. Consider a simple example: the acquisition of land with precious metal deposits, say gold. The postdeal steps would be to fully assess the locations and richness of the deposits and then to develop the mine accordingly. However, the economics of each deposit depends on the sequence and timing of extraction and the market price at the time of extraction and sale. As a result, the value of the deposits—and the value of the acquisition itself—may be difficult to predict. They depend on future gold prices (which cannot be controlled) and the sequence and pace of future development (which cannot be decided in advance).

If at the time of acquisition the mine development would cost much more than gold prices would warrant, the whole deal could look quite foolish. However, if the company makes the subsequent investments in development only if and as prices warrant, then the *strategy* could create substantial value, and the acquisition will have been of *strategic value.*

The most important M&A value creation strategies may not be the most obvious. Indeed, some of the highest-value strategies may not create value directly but will rather position the company for possible subsequent steps that could create value depending on future circumstances. These possible subsequent steps can be considered as options. They are referred to as real options to distinguish them from stock options.[2]

DEFINITIONS

What are real options?

Real options[3] are similar to stock options, but instead of deriving from stock they derive from real capital assets. A stock option is a right that allows the holder to acquire a certain number of shares of a certain stock during a future period of time called the *exercise period*, at predetermined price called the *exercise price*. If the value of the stock goes higher than the exercise price during that period, then the holder is "in the money" and can choose to exercise the option. However, if the value of the stock is lower than the exercise price during the exercise period, the holder is "under water." The holder can then choose not to exercise. In this case the option becomes worthless, but at least the holder did not pay for actual stock that declined in value.

The situation with a real option is parallel. As mentioned, a real option is not a stock but a physical asset or a company. Like the stock option holder, the holder of the real option is in a position to make further investments in the future that could pay off under favorable circumstances. If the future circumstances are not favorable, the subsequent investments need not be made. However, the value of the original real asset may diminish and even become totally worthless, like the stock option, if the future is such that the further investments will not pay off.

Like the chess player, the acquirer of real options is thinking several steps ahead. The early moves create favorable positioning for future stages of the game. Whether or not these early moves pay off depends on subsequent actions and reactions of each player.

Returning to our precious metal example above, let's say that the gold mine will only be economic to develop at all if the price of gold goes up by 30 percent. The mine (as a "real option") is worth something today because there is a nonzero probability that the price of gold will go up by at least 30 percent. It will require further investment to develop the mine, but the cost of development, or "exercise price," depends on the sequence and pace of development and need only be paid if and when the mine will be "in the money."

Stock options have value because circumstances *may* be favorable in the future for exercise. Similarly, real options have value because they *may* provide a basis for additional value creation depending upon future circumstances.

Many acquisitions can incorporate real options. In fact, some of the most successful acquisition strategies create real options—options to take subsequent steps in the future that are of uncertain value at the time of the deal, but that would not be possible at all without the deal. The nature, value, and risks associated with real options in acquisitions are the subject of this chapter.

Is the "option value" the same as what acquirers refer to as "strategic value"?

We wish it were so. The option value of a deal is sometimes referred to as the strategic value, but the term *strategic value* is more often used as an excuse for weak deal logic.

Deal proposals usually justify the acquisition price in terms of the intrinsic value of the asset as is, plus quantifiable synergies. If this falls short, weak deal proposals will often try to explain away the shortfall on the basis of unquantifiable "strategic value," such as improved market position, acquired skills, or competitive advantage.

However, if such value is real, then it is in fact quantifiable. If improved market position will result in higher volumes or better pricing, then this can be quantified. If acquired skills allow the company to improve the R&D productivity, reduce cost, or gain market share, then these can be quantified. If the acquired competitive advantage will result in higher sales or lower costs, then these can be quantified.

Another explanation of the strategic value is when the deal helps the company do what it said it would do in a previously defined strategic plan. For example, if the strategic plan said the company would grow internationally, then the proposal of a cross-border deal might say that the deal had strategic value because it permits the company to fulfill the commitment in the strategy. However, an approved strategy should not be viewed as a license to destroy shareholder value. Even assuming that a particular strategy is right for the company (an assumption that senior management and the board should revisit as times change) this does not justify investments with no payoff. The pursuit of any strategy should be conducted in a value-enhancing manner.

In the best case, *strategic value* refers to specific steps the company could take in the future that would not be possible without this acquisition or that could have higher value with this acquisition. Such value is the value of the real options inherent in the deal.

Are real options quantifiable?

It is difficult to properly quantify the value of real options because of the combination of uncertainties. The standard method is to identify a security with parallel characteristics and to extrapolate the market's valuation of that security to a valuation of the real option.[4]

For most purposes, it suffices to identify and estimate the key variables (e.g., the exercise price/cost, the probability of a favorable outcome, and the return under a range of plausible future scenarios). This will often be enough information to put a range on the value, which may in turn be all the information needed to show that the value is sufficient to justify the price or not.

REAL OPTIONS IN M&A

What types of real options can be found in acquisitions?

The options that can be provided through an acquisition generally fall into one of three categories:

- Growth options, which provide the potential to pursue alternate markets in the future
- Flexibility options, which allow for different ways to exploit acquired assets in alternative future scenarios
- Divestiture options, which mitigate risk by enabling a company to "unacquire" all or part of an acquisition in the future.

What are some examples of options embedded in strategic acquisitions?

Growth options:

- A computer firm purchases a software startup company for its development capabilities in a target market rather than for its existing products.

- An overseas airline acquires a U.S. airline to break into the U.S. market and increase traffic on potential future routes.
- A large publishing firm buys a smaller, niche periodical firm, enabling launches of related periodicals in the future.

Flexibility options:

- A firm in the aggregates business buys undeveloped quarry sites that have future potential for municipal waste disposal.
- A retailer diversifies to facilitate switching formats among its leased spaces in shopping malls as market conditions for its retail formats vary over time.
- A newsprint maker with virgin fiber mills acquires a mill capable of using recycled fiber to have the ability to swing production as demand favors one or the other type.

Divestiture options:

- A company purchases a holding company whose real estate may in the future have a valuable alternative use.
- An airline purchases another airline recognizing that some routes or gates can be sold if they do not prove to be needed in the business.
- A company has the ability to sell acquisitions that do not meet growth targets, thereby truncating downside risk.

How do acquired growth options create value?

As mentioned, growth options provide the *potential to pursue alternate markets in the future*. A growth option is valuable because by not having to commit today to undertaking a future investment, a firm can temper its risk. Growth options are particularly valuable in high-tech or emerging industries, ranging from computer hardware and software to biotechnology, where there may be a very significant increase in future demand but where there is also considerable technological risk and uncertainty.

An acquisition can provide new growth options or enhance existing ones. A firm looking to enter a new market, for example, may find it cheaper or more expedient to purchase a growth option than to develop its own, especially when opportunities are near-term and development success is uncertain. The firm may acquire a smaller company that has developed an entrepreneurial concept and is looking to grow but lacks the infrastructure or capital it needs. By offering the acquired firm access to such resources, the firm probably will be able to pay less than the post-merger value of the company. Conversely, the purchaser may be having trouble exploiting a growth opportunity, and the acquired firm may provide the required technological skills or distribution channels.

Acquisitions also frequently involve the balancing or merging of the growth options of the purchasing and acquired firms. Firms that share opportunities for growth in an industry can, for example, derive considerable value from consolidating their growth options.

Consider the professional information and trade periodicals industry, which is characterized by frequent new product introductions and acquisitions. Publishers such as Thomson-Reuters, McGraw-Hill, and Reed Elsevier acquire many products, often in audience segments they already serve. Frequently in such transactions the acquirer not only receives the future cash flows of the product and the value of measurable physical synergies but also increases the value of its growth options in three ways:

- By combining the acquired products with its own products, it builds superior circulation lists and advertiser relationships, thereby enhancing the value of its options to invest subsequently in new magazine launches or other advertising products in this segment.
- The company further enhances the value of its options to acquire or launch other periodicals because the operational synergies with a subsequent, related periodical would be even greater than those gained with the current acquisition and would have a value magnified by the current acquisition.
- Furthermore, a real options perspective sheds light on the consequences of not doing such a deal. If the acquisition did *not* take place, the buyer and the seller would each continue to hold options to reposition products or launch line extensions to capture a share of the other's market. So the future without the deal could be worse than the status quo if the seller's options are considered. By acquiring the seller, the acquirer eliminates

the seller's option to grow into the market through new product launches or acquisitions pursued separately from the acquirer.

These points show why the status quo may not be a reliable base case for evaluating a potential acquisition. A firm must clearly recognize the cost of not reacting to changes in its competitive environment, and the value a potential acquisition can have in preserving competitive advantage.

What is an example of value created from growth options in an acquisition?

The following example will help to illustrate this. ABC Publishing is considering acquiring Tech Magazines for $100 million. ABC estimates the present value of Tech's cash flows at $90 million and projects that it will reduce costs by $5 million by consolidating operations. Based on these figures, the Tech purchase appears to have a net present value of negative $5 million and thus does not seem attractive.

The manager of ABC's technical publications division, however, points out that ABC and Tech are independently considering new digital magazines. The market for such publications seems promising but is untested. The ABC manager has determined that it is in the company's best interest to wait two years before deciding whether to launch the digital product. However, he also predicts that continued competition between ABC and Tech would lead both firms to launch their new digital products after only one year.

Based on the current market power of the two firms, the new publications would split the market equally. Obviously, acquiring Tech would provide additional value by enabling ABC to delay the launch of the new digital product and, once the launch had taken place, to gain the market share that would have been lost to Tech's publication.

How can the growth option value be quantified?

Table 4.1 compares the estimated cash flow resulting from ABC's expansion into the new market on its own and the cash flow resulting from ABC's

Table 4.1 Growth Option Valuation

Comparison of Launch of New Digital Product Alone or with Acquisition ($ millions)	ABC Proceeds Alone	ABC Acquires Tech
Present value of profits (*P*)	$10	$25
Present value of launching costs (*C*)	10	15
Net present value (*P* – *C*)	0	10
Option value*	$1.97	$11.82

*Option values provided; see note 4.

acquisition of Tech. Note that the present value of ABC's profits is more than double if ABC acquires Tech and thus gains greater economies of scale. By joining forces with Tech, ABC also can establish economies that reduce the fixed cost of launching the magazine by 25 percent. Instead of $20 million for two launches, the cost falls to $15 million for a single launch.

The last row of Table 4.1 shows the estimated value of ABC's growth option under both scenarios. The acquisition effectively increases the value by $9.85 million ($11.82 minus $1.97 million). Taking this into account, the net present value of the acquisition is $4.85 million rather than the negative $5 million derived through traditional cash flow valuation.

The $9.85 million increase in value can be traced to three sources. First, ABC purchases Tech's option to develop its half of the market. Second, economies of scale will be obtained from developing the larger-scale growth option, translating into lower costs for the launch and subsequent operation of the new publication. (Note that the actual gains would only be realized if ABC exercises its growth option.) Third, by avoiding a race with Tech to reach the market first, ABC is able to wait two years, rather than one, before deciding whether it should launch the new publication. This incremental value of waiting two years is $1.06 million ($11.82 minus $10.76, where $10.76 million is the value of the combined growth option with a one-year horizon).

This example shows how an acquisition can increase the value of a firm's growth options by decreasing the exercise price, increasing the present value of future profits earned upon exercise, and allowing greater flexibility in the timing of the exercise. In addition, each successful acquisition can enhance the value of the option to make further acquisitions by enlarging the synergies to be gained or by reducing the risk of being left out of an industry consolidation or being structurally disadvantaged in the future.

Many growth companies acquired real options in the early stages, some of which were exercised and some of which were not. For example, Xstrata's early acquisitions included substantial aluminum, zinc, coal, copper, lead, silver, and gold. It disposed of aluminum assets. In 2001 Xstrata acquired Asturiana de Zinc, a Spanish-listed zinc group, exercising the option to develop zinc. In 2002, Xstrata acquired Glencore's Australian (Enex) and South African (Duiker) coal assets for $2.5 billion, becoming the world's largest exporter of thermal coal.[5] And Xstrata referenced options in the announcement of the acquisition of nickel giant Falconbridge:

> More importantly, the Enlarged Group's new copper business will have exceptional flexibility to optimize product flows between operations and to extract real value from the expansion options inherent in the integrated copper operations. Our Latin American presence holds significant potential for integrating future Las Bambas, Collahuasi or Tintaya expansions through the Falconbridge processing facilities in either Chile or Canada.[6]

Ultimately, Xstrata acquired Falconbridge from under the nose of INCO, once the world's largest nickel producer with major operations adjacent to Falconbridge's.

How do acquired flexibility options create value?

As mentioned, flexibility options allow for different ways to exploit acquired assets in alternative future scenarios. This introduces needed realism into the planning process. All too often, the value of the synergies provided by an acquisition—consolidated administrative staffs, shared marketing distribution channels, reduced excess plant capacity—is estimated under a "static scenario" assumption. In other words, it is assumed that the markets in which the combined business units operate will not change after the acquisition. Given the uncertainties affecting virtually every market today, this assumption is unrealistic. If the effects of uncertainty are more carefully analyzed, however, many acquisitions can be seen to have additional value because they increase the acquirer's flexibility.

For example, a firm's existing flexibility in organization, manufacturing, distribution, or financing may be more fully exploited by diversifying across products or lines of business without highly correlated profitability.

This is strategic diversification and the distinction between it and financial diversification must be emphasized.

Financial diversification is sometimes defended as being a means of reducing business risk. However, critics of acquisitions undertaken purely for financial diversification rightly point out that the shareholders can usually diversify more efficiently on their own, and that it is the acquiring firm's managers, not its shareholders, who stand to gain the most from such reduction in risk. Besides, firms that don't "stick to their knitting" have a greater risk of investment, market, or operational errors.

However, strategic diversification cannot be criticized on these same grounds because it creates options not otherwise available to shareholders. Consider the following simplified example of how a company pursuing strategic diversification can enhance the value of its flexibility options through an acquisition. Company A, a manufacturer of luxury automobiles, has followed a strategy of maintaining flexible resources, including its distribution channels, labor force, and manufacturing facilities. It has recently modernized its production facilities and equipped them with flexible tooling for producing a wide variety of vehicles. These facilities have the capacity to produce 100,000 cars per year at an annual fixed operating cost ("fixed cost") of $80 million. Management forecasts demand over the next year to be either 95,000 or 75,000 cars, depending on whether the price of oil, currently $20 a barrel, falls to $15 or rises to $25, respectively. The profit per car (before the fixed cost is covered) is $1,000.

Company A's management is concerned about the possibility of incurring a $5 million loss next year should oil increase to $25 (see column A in Table 4.2) and is considering alternatives for using its excess production capacity. As Company A does not have any new lines to introduce over the next year, it is considering the purchase of one of two smaller automobile companies whose cars could be produced and sold using its flexible resources.

Company B sells only compact cars, the demand for which increases with the price of oil and is thus negatively correlated with the demand for Company A's luxury cars. Company C specializes in midsize vehicles, the demand for which is insensitive to the price of oil (and thus uncorrelated with that for Company A's cars). Companies B and C generate the same pre–fixed-cost profit per car as Company A ($1,000), and each has one manufacturing plant with a capacity of 25,000 cars and an annual fixed cost of $15,000. The cash flows for B and C are shown in Table 4.2.

Table 4.2 Flexibility Options

Scenarios for Auto Manufacturers Based on Range of Oil Prices	Company A Alone	Company B Alone	Company C Alone	A Acquires B	A Acquires C
Price of oil ($/barrel)	$15 to $25	$15 to $25	$15 to $25	$15 to $25	$15 to $25
Profit before fixed operating costs	95 to 75	5 to 25	20 to 20	100 to 100	100 to 95
Fixed operating costs	80 to 80	15 to 15	15 to 15	80 to 80	80 to 80
Net profit	15 to –5	–10 to 10	5 to 5	20 to 20	20 to 15
Present value	$2.86	$1.90	$4.76	$19.05	$16.19

$ millions, except as indicated.

The last two columns in the table show the combined cash flows of Company A if it acquires Company B or C. If B is purchased, the combined demand would be exactly 100,000 units (whether the price of oil goes up or down), and A's resources would be sufficient to manufacture and sell all the vehicles. Given that the fixed cost remains $80 million, A's profit would be $20 million, again regardless of the price of oil. If C is purchased instead, the demand for the merged company's cars would be either 115,000 or 95,000 units, depending on whether the price of oil goes down or up, respectively. If the price of oil decreases, A would choose to operate at full capacity, forgoing the revenue from 15,000 of C's cars rather than keeping C's plant open at a fixed cost of $15,000. Therefore, A's profit would be $20 million if the price of oil declines and $15 million if it rises.

The bottom row of Table 4.2 shows the present values for the independent companies and for the merged companies. (These values are obtained by using a one-period binomial option pricing model.) The values indicate that A would be better off acquiring B, assuming that it pays a fair current market price—$1.9 million for B or $4.76 million for C.

The incremental value from acquiring B is $14.29 million ($13.05 minus $2.86 minus $1.3) while that from acquiring C is only $8.57 million ($16.19 minus $2.86 minus $4.76). B is thus a better acquisition than C, even though C appears less risky and more valuable on its own. The critical difference between these purchases is that the demands for A's and B's cars complement each other in such a way that A's capacity is always fully used and overall demand is completely satisfied.

This example illustrates that flexible production capacity can be very valuable, particularly when a firm is able to create a portfolio of products whose cash flow streams are negatively correlated. The greater the uncertainty surrounding the demand for the firm's products and the lower the correlation among these product demands, the more valuable the combined benefits of flexibility and diversification will be. While a typical diversification program reduces risk by narrowing the distribution of cash flows, strategic diversification can truncate the downside risk while preserving the upside potential.

In many industries, corporate real estate is considered one of the most valuable assets, often because of its flexibility. Acquisitions can generate value by adding real estate that is flexible (due to its location or zoning) or by increasing the value of the acquiring company's real estate by creating a diversified portfolio of businesses that might exploit the real estate's flexibility in the future.

Companies in the aggregates business, for example, often own sites that have potential value not only for the extraction of sand and gravel but also for the disposal of municipal waste. Although the extraction and waste-disposal businesses serve different markets with entirely different products, the sites they require share special characteristics: they must be sufficiently close to a major city to have favorable transportation economies but far enough from local communities to offend as few people as possible.

At some stage in the development of these sites, the marginal value of further extraction may fall below the value of filling the hole with garbage, rendering the property more valuable as a landfill. Therefore, when an aggregates company purchases another aggregates business whose sites can later be used as landfills, it is also acquiring valuable flexibility options. When the extraction value of one of the sites dips below its value as a landfill, the company has the option of either converting the site on its own or selling it to a waste-disposal company.

The history of the Operating Industries Incorporated (OII) site in California demonstrates the option value. Prior to 1946, the OII property was a sand and gravel quarry. Waste disposal operations at the landfill began on 14 acres in October 1948 by Monterey Park Disposal Company. By 1958, the landfill had expanded to 218 acres. The size was later reduced to 190 acres when the State of California purchased 28 acres for construction of the Pomona Freeway.[7] In 1984, the State of California placed OII's landfill on the California Hazardous Waste Priority List, and the site shut down operations. Part of this site may soon become a new retail shopping area, bringing new business to the area. More than 20,000 people live within 3 miles of the 190-acre site now.[8]

Certain distribution assets incorporate flexibility options. For example, banking networks have been acquired in other markets with a view to expanding the financial services sold through these networks. The embedded real options of the bank networks in Canada, for example, include the option to sell insurance in the future, although currently sale of insurance through bank channels is not permitted. When TD Bank acquired Canada Trust it vastly increased the scope of its retail bank operations and, in the eyes of some critics, was seen as overinvested in the branch network. However, TD also has the largest home and auto insurance brokerage in

Canada. While insurance cannot be sold through its branches today, the value of the branch network is significantly enhanced by the possibility that such bancassurance will be permitted, as it has been in most other markets, and by the superior position this would give to TD as a major home and auto insurance distributor.

Another highly flexible resource is financial capital. A firm that can easily raise capital does not have to worry about integrating its various business units to ensure a balance of supply and demand for cash. Most firms, however, have constraints on their ability to raise capital, if only because of the costs associated with going into the financial markets. Recognizing that the expense of raising capital often varies by industry, many companies undertake acquisition programs to create a balanced portfolio of business units that enables cross-financing.

How do acquired divestiture options create value?

Divestiture options, as mentioned, mitigate risk by enabling a company to "unacquire" all or part of an acquisition in the future. Thus divestiture is, paradoxically, an important element in the value of many potential acquisitions. An acquiring firm will often retain the option of divesting an acquired business—in whole or in part—should that business's market price turn out to be higher than its actual value to the firm. For example, a company may acquire a business to realize synergistic gains that prove illusory and may find that divestment is the best way to cut losses.

The option to divest is a particularly important consideration in risky consolidation strategies. During the 1980s, for example, Maxwell Communications PLC bought several commercial printing businesses in the United Kingdom and North America. It subsequently divested all of them (well before the death of the founder and demise of the empire). Whatever Maxwell's original strategy and regardless of its effectiveness, the ability to divest the acquisitions substantially reduced the risk of acquiring them.

Companies often purchase other firms with the intent of selling off some units but hold the divestiture option until the businesses in question develop further or until the industry consolidates to the point that it becomes a seller's market. Consider the hypothetical case of PJP, a large conglomerate contemplating the acquisition of another firm with substantial real estate holdings. If the acquisition goes through, PJP plans to develop a particular piece of centrally located real estate for a distribution facility in two years. Based on its projected use, PJP has valued this piece at $20 million. Market conditions will of course cause the value of this real estate to fluctuate over the next two years. However, if the firm's business outlook turns sour and the distribution facility is projected to be unprofitable, the firm would be able to sell off this land quickly for at least $15 million.

To account for the value of this divestiture option in its valuation of the acquisition, PJP's management uses a simple two-year binomial model. Management assumes that the value of the real estate to the firm (without taking into account the divestiture option) will either appreciate by 50 percent or depreciate by 40 percent each year. In the worst-case scenario, the land would be worth only $7.2 million to the company after two years. In effect, the divestiture option established a $15 million floor for the value of the real estate after two years, thus mitigating the risk of the acquisition.

Even though the value to PJP of the real estate as a site for its distribution facility may be only $12 million at the end of the first year, it is still not optimal for the firm to sell it at that time for $15 million if it can sell it for that price at the end of the second year. The firm would prefer to retain the option to develop the land at the end of the second year should business conditions improve (at which point the value of the land as a distribution facility site would rise to $18 million).

The incremental value of waiting to divest amounts to $710,000 at the end of the first year. Overall, the divestiture option increases the current value of the land from $20 million to $21.77 million. Thus the value of the option is $1.77 million. In practice, of course, the resale price of an asset is not guaranteed, and more sophisticated option pricing techniques would be required. The logic behind the valuation and exercise of a divestiture option, however, is still instructive.

There are many real examples. Southam Inc., a predecessor of Canadian media conglomerate CanWest, bought Murray Printing & Gravure for $700,000 in the 1960s. The Murray plant increased Southam's printing capacity, but it also sat on real estate sure to be engulfed by the growth of Toronto. Around 1990, a plan was developed to consolidate operations into other plants, freeing up the real estate under the Murray plant. The entire modernized printing operation was then sold to Transcontinental, and the real estate sold for development.[9]

It may seem obvious in hindsight that the development potential of real estate should be a consideration in the location and development of corporate assets. However, it is seldom considered. In fact, the option value of most corporate assets is seldom considered until someone actually comes calling, such as when the railroads all discovered that their uninterrupted ground-based infrastructure was coveted for laying fiber-optic cables, the port lands became sought-after condominium sites, and downtown churches discovered that they could build their endowments by selling air rights to neighboring high-rise developers.

IMPLICATIONS AND RISKS

Are real options an important consideration in the development of M&A strategy?

As noted earlier, global restructuring is well under way in many industries. Freer trade and the growth of developing economies have created large global markets for many raw materials, products, and services.

Participating in the global restructuring of an industry requires acquisitions that may not pay off by themselves. The first acquisition in a new market will offer little or no synergies. However, it can establish a base on which to build. The value of this base is the value of the options to grow the business, to repurpose the assets, or to divest if it comes to that. Without attributing value to these real options, the important initial steps internationally may not appear justified.

Furthermore, standing still as an industry changes is not "business as usual." Some of the value of the company that chooses not to grow internationally is being eroded by benefits of international growth accrued by competitors that may be relevant in the home market. For example, if competitors gain access to economies of scale and scope, to new products and production options, or to experiences and skills, they could gain a competitive advantage in the home market in due course. Consider, for example, HSBC, Manulife, and Toyota, which dominate their home markets in part thanks to their international positions. In other words, some of the value in the options acquired by others will be at the expense of the companies that choose to stay home.

The same is true of industries subject to significant change of any kind. For example, the computer hardware competitors that diversified into software and services, such as IBM with its acquisitions of Lotus and PwC, were in a position to benefit from the shift in value chain economics at the expense of competitors that had not diversified and lacked such flexibility options, like the former hardware juggernaut Wang Laboratories.

Moreover, consideration of the longer-term, game-changing opportunities requires consideration of real options because there are simply insufficient facts about the future to move with certainty down any one path. The superior strategist will have multiple options, either acquired or otherwise developed. The company with a linear strategy (i.e., a strategy without options), is only as good as its ability to predict the future, which in most cases is poor.

Why are real options so valuable?

Recall Exhibit I.1 in which the value potential of financial, consolidation, growth, and real options transactions was distinguished by the size of the gap between the buyers' and the sellers' perceptions of the value. We said there that these four roles for M&A represent successively more complex as well as higher-potential M&A strategies. Part I of this book was organized to walk through these four roles in succession.

In a change of ownership alone, such excess must all be found in the new owner's ability to foresee or extract better performance from the business. In business combinations that offer cost synergies between the businesses, there is potentially much greater value at stake, but the transparency of the cost savings potential tends to result in deal pricing that shares much of the value with the seller. The value potential of revenue synergies tends to be more unique to the individual buyer and also more difficult to achieve, so less of the value in revenue synergies is negotiated away in the price. In addition, revenue synergies represent top-line growth that creates more value for shareholders in the long run than one-time cost savings.

Finally, we said that the most strategic deals take many steps to implement and require placing bets on future circumstances. The value of these deals may be unique to the buyer and may also be hidden, so the difference in the assessment by the buyer and seller is greater than revenue, cost or financial synergies. Thinking of the value as option value helps acquirers account for the value and ultimately realize its optimum potential.

Does the market appreciate the value of real options?

Not always. When acquirers pay for options, they can be criticized. Acquisitions of growth options, such as the first acquisitions in a new market, are a case in point. The analysts are more likely to criticize the first movers into new markets, and the stock market may devalue the shares of the pioneer.

Similarly, the market is unlikely to credit the potential offered by flexibility options. Bancassurance potential is not a factor in Canadian bank valuations because neither analysts nor executives are likely to look beyond current regulations, let alone bet on a change.

The market does value divestiture options at some level. For example, it is common practice in valuations to consider the intrinsic value of acquired assets and comparables of a corporate division with valuations of its peers, effectively, the sale value. However, if the divestiture potential is hidden in real estate or other assets outside of business as usual, then it is less likely that it will be valued by the market.

If the market fails to appreciate the value of real options, what does this mean to the acquirer?

Prior to an acquisition, it can be a positive thing. Because the value of real options is typically less apparent than other assets or uniquely available to the buyer, it can be fully captured by the buyer. The existence of the options typically won't cause the seller or the market to increase the price of the company. If the options were fully understood, then the targets holding options would be more expensive to buy.

What are the risks inherent in the acquisition of real options?

These acquisitions are all about the risks. If there were certainty, there would be no real options. The greatest risk in looking for the real option potential in M&A is that the potential is either not considered carefully enough or it is considered too carefully.

In the first case, and as mentioned earlier in the chapter, such strategic deals or real option potential can be seen as an excuse for otherwise weak deal logic. When and how the options can be exercised and at what cost are essential considerations. For example, if the anticipated change in regulation that will make bancassurance a reality in Canada requires a change in the Bank Act, and if such a change is unlikely under the current government or its opposition, the value of holding a bancassurance option has to be significantly discounted. There may need to be nearer-term and more certain opportunities to justify a bank–insurance merger.

In the second case, *too carefully* refers to the risk of getting lost in the technical details. Some very complex probabilistic models can be used to portray potential scenarios and estimate the impact of a sequence of decisions, but such models are no replacement for the mind of the strategist.

What are the implications for acquirers?

There are implications for the tool kit, but more importantly for the mindset of decision makers.

For the tool kit, it is clear that net present value and market multiples are inadequate valuation tools in restructuring industries. Failing to value the real options could result in the buyer walking away from a good opportunity or a seller taking too little. It may be most critical for a reluctant seller to do the math because a corporate board can be liable for turning down an attractive deal premium without a good rationale. The option value could provide the needed justification to resist the takeover or to hold out for more.

For the mindset of decision makers, first note, this is no substitute for brilliant strategists, who likely have the chess game in their heads and are considering the real options but not calling them so. There is more intuition than mathematics in the stories of great deals and great deal makers, along with ambition and good luck. However, there are an equal number of corporate disasters based on intuition, ambition, and luck. Identification and consideration of real options, even without the math, will make for more sound and well-considered strategy in restructuring industries, whether the decision is to be a buyer or a seller. At times the more sophisticated analysis of option value will add needed precision to good judgment to close the right deal or to pass.

Endnotes

1. *Back to the Future*, Universal Pictures, 1985.
2. The application of real options in M&A valuation was first proposed by Alexander J. Triantis and Kenneth W. Smith (coauthor of this book) in Lenos

Trigeorgis, ed., *Real Options in Capital Investment* (Westport, CT: Praeger, 1995). Chapter 4 draws on this work as well as on Smith and Triantis, "Untapped Options for Creating Value in Acquisitions," *Mergers & Acquisitions* 29, no. 3, pp 17–22 (1994).

3. See also Martha Amram and Nalin Kulatilaka, *Real Options* (Boston, MA: Harvard Business School Press, 1999) and Timothy Luehrman, "Strategy as a Portfolio of Real Options," *Harvard Business Review* (September 1998).
4. See Trigeorgis, *Real Options in Capital Investment* for a more detailed explanation of the valuation of real options.
5. See the Xstrata company website at http://www.xstrata.com/about/history/.
6. See the Xstrata company website at http://www.xstrata.com/assets/pdf/falconbridge_offer.pdf.
7. EPA Superfund Record of Decision: OPERATING INDUSTRIES, INC., LANDFILL EPA ID: CAT080012024 OU 01 MONTEREY PARK, CA, September 30, 1996, accessed October 14, 2011, http://www.epa.gov/superfund/sites/rods/fulltext/r0996152.pdf.
8. United States Environmental Protection Agency, "Operating Industries Inc. Landfill: In California, Many Hands Make Greener Work," http://www.epa.gov/superfund/accomp/success/oii.htm.
9. See the Transcontinental company website at http://www.transcontinental.com/en/3-who-we-are/3-5-history1.html.

PART II

Development and Execution of M&A Strategy

In Part I of this book we outlined four broad roles of M&A in strategy: developing the business portfolio, consolidating an industry, acquiring for growth, and developing real options. While it was noted that some deals could play multiple roles, usually one role will predominate, based on the nature of the company (e.g., holding company or operating company) and the industry situation (e.g., consolidating or growing).

We also noted how value can be created in each case and cited numerous examples of companies that have successfully created value using M&A to build business portfolios, consolidate industries, grow new global corporations, and exploit uncertainties with the acquisition of real options.

However, notwithstanding the demonstrated potential of M&A to create value, most deals fail. An examination of two decades of large transactions has revealed that many of the commonly held beliefs about M&A success and failure are myths.[1] The following list describes five of the most common myths:

* *American companies are superior acquirers.* While American companies have been active acquirers at home and abroad, they have a poor track record for value creation in domestic and especially cross-border deals. The best acquirers in the past two decades have come from Europe.

* *Growth companies are the best targets.* Large, mature companies often seek to stimulate innovation and growth by acquiring smaller, high-growth companies. Such deals typically fail for two reasons. First, the market price of the target fully incorporates the growth rate. Second, the

buyer can't sustain the growth because the larger company's culture tends to prevail over the smaller firm's entrepreneurial culture that was responsible for the growth in the first place.

* *The failures paid too much.* There is in fact almost no correlation between deal success and price premium paid. The biggest determinant of price is the market—you have to pay what you have to pay. It is therefore not the price that determines success, but rather the ability to earn back the price premium and more.

* *There were not enough savings available.* As noted in Part I of this book, many of the most successful deals are not based on cost-savings at all. The consolidation deals that are principally based on cost-savings typically fail because the savings were accounted for in the market price and were not achieved fully or fast enough.

* *The strategy was flawed.* Postdeal audits that review the strategy outlined in the deal proposal versus achievement seldom find that the strategy was at fault. Rather, deals that have failed have typically not executed much of what was in the proposal. Among the reasons for this costly lack of follow-through are ambiguity in required action steps, weak postmerger project management, and lack of organizational alignment.

Rather, the most common elements in deal success are independent of the particular strategy, target, or price:

1. *Clear and compelling deal logic*. Whether the potential lies in performance improvement, cost savings, revenue growth, or real options, neither the price justification nor the implementation plan can be sound if the deal logic is ambiguous.
2. *Alignment of organization cultures.* We emphasize *alignment* versus *fit*. The merged company must be able to align the organization with the deal logic. This is an active process, not a passive examination of similarities and differences.
3. *An actionable postdeal plan.* The right postdeal actions are determined from the deal logic. If the key steps are not sufficiently clear and agreed to before the deal, then, at best, valuable time will be lost and, at worst, the postdeal energy will be consumed by other matters.

Note that all three are rooted in the strategy through the deal logic. Therefore, Part II provides guidance on the development and execution of successful M&A strategies that incorporate sound deal logic in the context of strategy and that anticipate organizational and postdeal planning challenges. In Chapter 5, we examine how to determine the role of M&A in the company strategy in consideration of industry imperatives and the nature and skills of the company. This requires a review of strategic planning, but we restrict this chapter to the aspects of strategic planning most relevant in the M&A context.

Chapter 6 outlines a step-by-step approach to the search for a suitable partner. Many companies simply react to opportunities. The corporate development department is approached regularly with deal opportunities, and deal screening can be simply a matter of selection from among the opportunities presented. However, this falls well short of strategy by any definition and is a contributing factor to the low success rates. The approach presented is proactive and strategy driven and includes postdeal implementation considerations.

Most M&A strategies consider the sale option only when in trouble or when approached by a buyer. The M&A strategy is otherwise assumed to be all about what to buy. Yet, in a restructuring industry (and most industries are restructuring in one way or another), more companies will ultimately be sellers than buyers, of parts or of the whole. Chapter 7 makes the case that the buy or sell option should be considered proactively and provides a basis for weighing buy versus sell options, both as part of M&A strategy development and execution, and in the event of a surprise takeover offer.

Chapter 8 looks at the role of the board of directors. When on the buy side, the board usually delegates the M&A strategy and search to management but then often lacks sufficient context and engagement to properly review proposals once presented. When on the sell side, the board is thrust to center stage—the sale of the company is one of the few things that the board cannot delegate. In either case, the stakes are high, and boards should be well prepared and properly engaged in M&A decisions.

Endnote

1. See Appendix to Part I for explanation of the deal assessments and sample analysis.

CHAPTER 5

M&A in Strategic Planning

If one does not know to which port one is sailing, no wind is favorable.

—*Seneca*

M&A strategy must advance the strategy of the corporation—as noted throughout this book, from our opening chapter on holding company portfolios to the previous chapter on real options. Successful companies—even holding companies—need a strategy for what type of assets they will acquire and how they will add value. Sometimes the value is in the selection and stewardship alone (e.g., some holding company models); other times the value is created in integration (e.g., value in consolidation) or in the ongoing growth and development (e.g., value in revenue growth); and sometimes the value will depend on circumstances requiring some future steps (e.g., value in real options).

However, the converse is not true. The strategic plan need not incorporate M&A strategy. First, M&A may not be needed if there are internal options to grow and remain competitive. Many companies have grown successfully without M&A. Second, even if M&A is a strategic option, it may not be possible to outline the M&A strategy at the time of strategic planning. It may also be imprudent to include M&A considerations in formal company plans. For example, while IBM clearly had the intention of moving downstream from hardware to software in the early 1990s, if the idea of a major acquisition had been part of a formal plan this could have leaked to the market. Even if the targets were not specified, such information could have materially affected the price of potential targets, such as Lotus.

Finally, M&A opportunities may arise that were not contemplated at the time of strategy development. For example, Reuters PLC was not looking for an information services partner when Thomson Corporation came calling in 2007. However, the idea of creating with Thomson the world leader in information services was compelling. Furthermore, through a lengthy series of confidential discussions, directors at Reuters and Thomson Corporation learned that they were very much aligned in corporate culture and customer service values, and they soon developed a shared vision for Thomson Reuters.[1]

So the strategy supersedes M&A strategy, but it must be dynamic. A strategic plan is a roadmap and should not be regarded as step-by-step directions. Yet there can be no *change* in direction if there is no direction in the first place—this is the kind of random development that has led to acquisition disasters, to the market discounts applied to low-value-added conglomerates, and to companies left behind while others led the restructuring of their industry. Strategy is the basis to assess opportunities, especially when such opportunities challenge the strategy and force hard thinking. A strategic plan should guide the company's proactive decisions while adjusting to new information and unexpected challenges or opportunities.

This chapter reviews the essential elements of strategy as the required context for M&A strategy. It references standard strategy texts and frameworks that the reader can pursue further to study strategy and strategic planning in general. The priority here is showing how to incorporate M&A into strategy considerations, both as a tool for pursuing a range of business goals and as the central strategy in some circumstances, including, but not limited to, holding companies.

STRATEGIC PLANNING AND THE RELEVANCE OF M&A

What makes planning strategic?

Planning means thinking ahead about how to accomplish a goal. To say that a plan is strategic implies that it is of importance, it is coordinated, and it is competitive. (As mentioned earlier, the Greek root, *strategein*, means to lead an army in battle.)

A strategic plan is typically based in a study of the situation, and a direction that is understood by the key actors and that will require coordinated actions over time. The situation analysis includes an understanding of the industry environment, customers, and competitors. Most strategies consider the particular position and competencies of the company to identify the bases of competitive advantage—the means to do better, to gain ground or to capture new opportunities, whether by having lower costs, developing a better product or service, or providing the product or service in a superior way. These are the three generic strategies identified by Michael Porter in his classic book *Competitive Strategy*.[2]

What is the relevance of the strategic plan to M&A opportunities?

The question really should be asked the other way around: How can M&A help to fulfill the strategy? Before pursuing any strategy, decision makers should recognize an organization's mission (why it exists) and vision (what it is striving to become). Strategy is the path toward fulfilling the mission and reaching a vision. M&A is sometimes a tool that can be used along the way, sometimes it is an essential tool, and sometimes the M&A strategy *is* the strategy.

For example, if the company determines that it has superior growth opportunities internationally, the company may decide to enter new international markets with "greenfield" operations, as did McDonald's, or with the acquisition of local competitors, as Walmart did in Germany with the acquisition of 21 Wertkauf units and in Canada with the acquisition of 122 Woolco stores.[3] The strategy in each case was international expansion. M&A was one means but not the only means to pursue the strategy.

By contrast, in some situations M&A is *essential* to competitive strategy. The most obvious example would be holding companies, where the strategy is often dominated by the company's buy-and-sell criteria and asset selection. However, as outlined in Chapter 1, there is a range of M&A strategies among successful holding companies, each based on specific competencies with distinct strategic goals. That is, even in holding companies, M&A is guided by strategy.

M&A is also a necessary part of strategy for companies that operate in or supply to industries that are undergoing consolidation. For example, in the consolidation of the newsprint industry outlined in Chapter 2, paper mills that remained independent could not maintain competitive costs and market access. Some chose instead to switch production to niche products, but none were able to compete in the commodity newsprint business without scale, and it was not practical to develop scale with new greenfield operations in this mature business.

In all cases, armed with a strategic plan, the corporate development staff can become highly selective, pursuing only those opportunities that will fit with its chosen strategy. This greatly reduces the cost of analyzing random opportunities presented by sellers or investment banks.

More importantly, in the absence of a well-considered strategic plan, there is great risk of closing on an opportunistic deal that won't work or passing on an opportunity for which the strategic importance was not understood. There are many examples of the former among the famous failures, bankruptcies, and deals eventually undone. However, the missed opportunities don't make the press. For example, companies such as Anheuser-Busch, INCO, and Duane Reade each had the potential to lead their respective industry's restructuring but wound up targets instead, at least in part due to lack of foresight into the restructuring of their industries and insufficiently ambitious M&A strategies.

But wasn't it strategic planning that led to the misguided diversification strategies of previous decades?

Actually, it was the other way around. Diversification and the development of corporate holding companies grew in the absence of strategic planning as we now know it. In some cases, diversification *was* the strategy. A classic example of this was LTV. Looking back on the life of Jimmy Ling, a writer for the *New York Times* noted that "Mr. Ling, known as Jimmy, collected companies the way boys collect baseball cards as he built the nation's 14th-biggest company, LTV, in just 14 years."[4] This is not to say that Jimmy Ling lacked any concept of value. On the contrary, the 1966 LTV annual report said the firm's acquisitions "must meet the test of the 2 plus 2 equals 5 (or 6) formula."[5]

Other conglomerators included Harold Geneen of International Telephone and Telegraph and Charles G. Bluhdorn of Gulf & Western Industries, who "engaged in relentless pursuit of ever more sweeping conglomerates."[6]

In other cases, the conglomerates arose from lack of alternatives for investment of cash flows from successful core businesses, and a lack of understanding of how corporate centers could add value. From the cash generated by railroads, newspapers, real estate, water, and brewing, for example, grew seemingly random collections of holdings of companies like CP Limited (once 160 companies including railways, hotels, airlines, coal, oil and gas, shipping, telecommunications, commercial real estate, and others),[7] the earlier Thomson Corporation (newspapers, department stores, oil and gas, travel),[8] Olympia & York (real estate, railroads, newsprint, forest products, spirits, oil and gas),[9] Compagnie General des Eaux (waste management, energy, transport services, construction, property, automobiles, and eventually media, which led to the company Vivendi),[10] and Anheuser-Busch (brewing, sports and entertainment, baking, food distribution, theme parks),[11] respectively, although in the last case it is argued that it was all related to beer marketing.

Strategic planning, while an old concept, became popularized as a means to cope with these diversified morasses. Some prepackaged approaches segmented a company's operations into market-share/market-growth categories and yielded such classifications as *star* for high-growth/high-share, *dog* for low-growth/low-share, *cash cow* for high-share/low-growth, and *wildcat* for low-share/high-growth. The "strategy" was to redeploy revenues from cash cows to wildcats.

These concepts were originally developed and successfully promulgated worldwide by the Boston Consulting Group (BCG). There were as many variations as there were consulting firms, and many have now been widely taught and used. While simple, these tools were an improvement on how many conglomerates had been built—on hunches, egos, friendships, or family ties.

Strategic planning also helped in the divestiture process—the ultimate opportunity to redeploy resources. Most of the old conglomerates ultimately refocused or were broken up, as the value of the assets to alternate owners was weighed against the conglomerate discount.

Now these simple tools have been supplanted by more comprehensive analyses that pay more attention to competitive factors, corporate competencies, and opportunity inventories, and usually consider choices and priorities based on shareholder value. In addition, strategic planning has become a standard for single-business companies or business units, not just holding companies. While the quality of planning varies widely, there are few large companies now operating in the absence of a strategic plan.

IMPLICATIONS FOR THE PLANNING PROCESS

What is the difference between a strategic vision and a strategic plan? Is M&A relevant to both?

The strategic vision is a descriptive goal for a company in the context of a view of the future environment of the company, the defined markets or arenas in which the company will compete, and the basis of the advantage it will need to compete in those markets. M&A can be an important consideration at this level of thinking as it can be used to enter or exit markets or to acquire needed scale, scope, or skills to compete. So it is particularly important to consider the strategic vision first when M&A could be part of the strategy.

The strategic vision answers *where* the company will compete, *why* it chooses to compete there, and *on what basis* it will compete. However, it need not answer *how*.

For illustration, IBM may have defined its strategic vision in the late 1990s as follows:

> IBM will transform from a hardware manufacturer to become the world leader in business software and services. This is based on:
>
> - View of the future: There will be continued growth of information technology, but with greater competition and lower margins in hardware manufacturing.
> - Arenas of competition: IBM will use its understanding of customers and their markets to develop new and better applications, and will use its R&D capability to advance technology. IBM will increasingly outsource manufacturing.
> - Sources of competitive advantage: Maintain superior customer relationships and knowledge, and superior applied R&D capabilities; develop new capabilities to become a skilled acquirer and to partner in the supply chain.

The strategic plan or competitive strategy defines *how* the organization will compete in the chosen markets to win. It comprises the integrated set of actions, including M&A, that will be taken to achieve specific goals in a competitive environment. It may include the competitive strategy for a single-business or business unit for which the relevant markets and competitors can be identified. Pursuing the earlier IBM illustration, the competitive strategy would define how it would achieve the stated position in software and services (which included M&A among other initiatives) and reduce exposure to manufacturing (which included divestments).

Strategic planning can also be applied at different levels, from the overall enterprise strategy to functional strategies.

What are the levels of planning in which M&A is relevant?

Actually, strategic planning can be useful at many levels, depending on how the company is organized. A simple, single-business company may only require one level of planning, while larger, more mature companies may be organized by divisions and have as many as six levels for planning. M&A can be relevant at every level.

Enterprise strategy applies only when investors own several companies not under common management and so is developed at the board-of-director level. The strategic decisions involve industry focus and acquisitions and divestitures.

Corporate strategy is most commonly the highest level of strategy for businesses under common management. Under the corporate center the holdings may be organized into groups of companies that have common operating elements—technology, marketing, geographic location, and so on. For example, General Electric is organized into five groups—Energy, Technology Infrastructure, GE Capital, Home and Business Solutions, and NBC Universal.[12] Each group in turn comprises numerous companies. Strategy at the corporate level is primarily concerned with investment criteria and reallocation of resources among the groups to maximize long-term return. Each group may be seeking new investment opportunities that fit with the group's commonalities and the corporate criteria. In some decentralized companies, the group may administer its own M&A activity independent of the corporate center.

(Note that the term *corporate strategy* is also used in single-business companies to define the aspects of strategy that involve external solutions, such as mergers, acquisitions, partnerships, and divestitures. This is typically the realm of the corporate development function as distinct from the line management task of competitive strategy. The two uses of the term are not inconsistent if you regard the general management and staff of a single-business company as the corporate center.)

Sector or group strategy calls for assembling, under one corporate or operating group, strategic business units (SBUs) that have some commonality or synergies. Then, as in the corporate strategy, cash flows are allocated and reallocated back out to the individual business units or into new internal or external investments, including acquisitions. Note that the corporate level and the group level are as one in all but the largest multibusiness corporations.

Business unit strategy is the first level of single-business strategy. Business units typically have under common management those product lines that have some commonalities—most often manufacturing or marketing. At this level, strategic planning is not just about the portfolio and M&A. The business unit requires competitive strategy—that is, a plan to leverage its position and strengths to win in a competitive market. At this level, M&A is one among many strategic tools.

Functional strategies deal with the strategic aspects at each stage of the value chain. For example, the product development strategy is concerned with product life cycles and the project portfolio in the lab. Strategic planning will be concerned with which projects to abort and which ones to accelerate. Acquisitions of products or intellectual property (IP) at various stages of development are often used to strategically match the development pipeline with anticipated market needs.

The functional strategy for manufacturing will be concerned with capital equipment investments, manufacturing locations, outsourcing, costs, and quality. M&A can play a role in expansion of manufacturing capacity, and sometimes unneeded facilities can be sold for noncompetitive purposes rather than being shut down.

Similarly, there are important investment questions to be addressed in distribution and marketing strategies. M&A can again play a role; for example, in the ongoing acquisitions by insurers and banks of independent brokers.

Geographic strategy can cut across the five levels described here. This is increasingly important in international companies in which some local investment in R&D and manufacturing is economical or a condition imposed on foreign operators. The geographic strategies may impact multiple groups, business units, or functions. Therefore, geographic strategies must be consistent with functional, businesses unit, group, and corporate strategies.

In the best cases, the planning process allows each to complement the others. In particular, the geographic strategies are developed through a different lens, concerned with a local market with local competitors.

Considering this view from across a number of geographies can provide insights relevant at every planning level.

Again, M&A can be used to achieve better competitive position or acquire relevant capabilities in the local market, which sometimes will in turn have value elsewhere in the organization.

Given the role of M&A in strategy, who should be involved in strategic planning at the various levels?

Whether or not M&A is a consideration, the strategic planning process should ideally engage all levels of management and the board. In particular, the board's involvement is essential if significant M&A activity is being or should be considered.

Broad management involvement in the planning processes serves three purposes. First, management across the company may be aware of threats and opportunities in their respective areas of responsibility, from supplier pressures at one extreme to competitive pricing pressures at the other. The perspectives of operating management can serve as early warnings to changes in the competitive environment that need to be considered in the strategic plan. For example, the supply chain managers have front row seats on developments of the industry supply structure as they receive sales calls from current and prospective domestic and international suppliers. Similarly, sales management will hear of new entrants and competitive price pressures that could indicate changes in market structure.

Second, operating management can contribute to solution ideas, including M&A opportunities. For example, the supply chain management could have insights on offshore manufacturing opportunities. Sales management could highlight a new entrant as a possible acquisition target or could point to the need to consider industry consolidation to lower fixed costs to compete with a larger low-cost competitor.

Finally, involvement in the process results in a better understanding of the findings and more likely commitment to the chosen solutions. So those that are key to effective implementation of the plan would ideally be part of its development.

This applies to members of the board of directors. The board is responsible for the strategic direction of the company and must ultimately approve the strategic plan. In particular, when their approval and support will be required for a major strategic initiative, such as an M&A decision, their involvement will put them in a better position to understand the issues and weigh the options. (Chapter 8 discusses in-depth the board's role in M&A.)

What kind of strategic planning process should be used to get appropriate involvement in M&A considerations?

There are many effective strategic planning processes in use, some proprietary and some available from consultants. The best processes engage the various planning levels iteratively. SECOR Consulting defines a process that follows a "W" pattern[13] whereby the process moves down and then up the levels in two iterations (Exhibit 5.1).

The start of the first "V" is the board's launch of the process. The board should set out the key issues to be resolved, the ambition, and the tolerance for risk. In particular, if the industry is restructuring or there is an opportunity for growth through acquisition, the board should indicate its expectations.

With this guidance from the board, the diagnostic work should cascade down through each level, adding as necessary to the issue list and identifying options for the resolution of strategic issues, including acquisition options as relevant at each level. For example, the board may raise the issue of globalization. Corporate management may in turn ask if the businesses will be

Exhibit 5.1. SECOR's "W" framework for strategic planning.

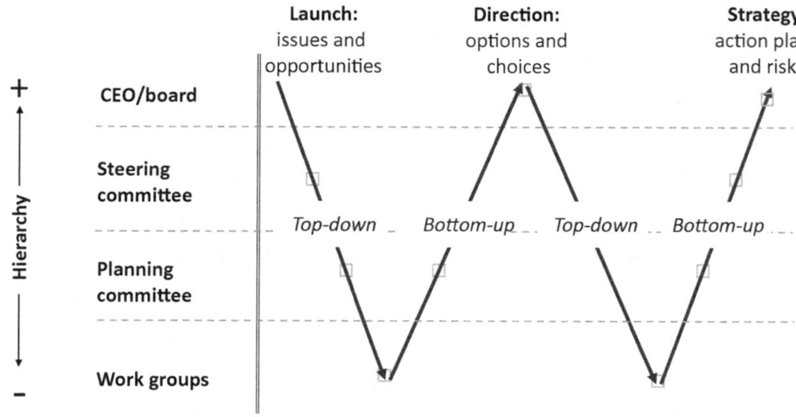

competitive on a global stage. This question may lead the SBUs to question scale economies and international marketing capabilities. Function management might then provide manufacturing cost comparisons and benchmarking of international sales organizations.

The analysis of options then works its way up through the planning levels, identifying common themes, consolidating ideas, and addressing the higher-level issues. Following the foregoing example, function management may analyze both acquisition and organic options to achieve globally competitive scale and scope. Business unit management may provide analysis of competitive competencies and may add organic and acquisition solution options that would achieve scale and scope objectives noted by the functions but also add new products or capabilities. Group or corporate management might then weigh these options against exit or sale of the business line.

At the middle peak of the "W," the board is then presented with a proposed strategic direction, options, risks, and implementation challenges. Some decisions are confirmed; some questions are raised about issues, options, or risks; and some parameters are discussed for implementation planning. In the case of M&A solutions, for example, criteria may be set on the nature and size of transactions to be considered.

The second "V" is about translating the agreed upon direction or strategic intent into action plans. The strategies and remaining questions are delegated to the appropriate level for planning. The task to define the search criteria for acquisitions, for example, would go to the corporate level if large in size or business scope, or it could go to the business unit and involve the functions if smaller and specific to a business or function.

The final trip up the second "V" is the integration of the plans into a single coherent strategic plan including key steps for each strategic issue or opportunity, responsibilities, milestones, and metrics. Ideally, the plans will also indicate key external factors to watch that could affect the plan positively or negatively. In the case of M&A, plans would include the purpose, criteria, team, and approach for screening and selection. Plans would not typically include specific partner candidates, except perhaps as examples.

Again this particular approach is for illustration. The key characteristics of this approach that are common to most effective strategic planning processes are board involvement in setting the direction, ambition, and risk tolerance; a fact-base on which to make decisions, including relevant data and analysis on the markets, competitors, and competitive position of each unit; appropriately deep and broad involvement in plan development, ensuring diverse perspectives on the challenges and opportunities; iteration of thinking that enables alternative perspectives to be considered and integrated; a coherent plan in sufficient detail to be actionable and measurable; and flexibility with an eye to the external factors that could impact the direction.

DETERMINING ROLE OF M&A IN STRATEGY

How is the role of M&A in the strategy determined?

Choice of the M&A option should be viewed differently depending on the nature of the issue. For example, at the functional level the strategic issues that lend themselves to M&A solutions usually involve a competitive gap or an opportunity unaddressed. In most cases there are internal options as well, so the acquisition decision amounts to a "make versus buy" decision.

However, at the corporate or enterprise level many M&A decisions are essentially portfolio investment decisions. There is no question of make versus buy, and the individual business unit strategies may or may not be a factor, depending on the role of the corporate center.

Moreover, the considerations vary depending on the level, the strategy, and the options. Since the strategy is ideally developed bottom-up (see "W" approach just described), we will start at the functional level and work our way up to the enterprise level.

How is the role of M&A determined in functional strategy?

At the functional level, there is usually an internal (organic or greenfield) option to deal with the issue or opportunity at hand. Therefore, an acquisition option can be compared with the internal option on the basis of costs, benefits, and risks.

Consider the R&D strategy of a pharmaceutical company, for example. Pharmaceutical companies are constantly monitoring their development pipelines to ensure that there are enough drugs at each stage of development to keep the company going when current drugs go off patent or decline in use. When there is a gap at one stage of development, they look upstream to determine if there are earlier-stage drugs that can be accelerated to market through investment. Acquisition of a smaller biotech firm can be an option to such in-house investments.

The strategic context is essential here. In the context of the drug development strategy, such an acquisition is an alternative to the internal options and should therefore be assessed in comparison with internal options (including, of course, the do nothing option that could result in the company's future exposure to a period of insufficient cash flows to sustain the business). This is an important point often missed in valuations—the valuation in such circumstances is not just about the target company and potential synergies but must be compared to alternative courses of action.

The drug potential, investment costs, and risks associated with the internal and external options can ideally be assessed "apples to apples." It is seldom the case, however, as there will be multiple drugs, IP, facilities, staff, and other assets to consider. Nevertheless, the comparison with the internal development option is the beginning of a product-based acquisition decision.

Similarly, M&A often comes into manufacturing strategy as an option to gain more or better capacity. (We differentiate this from the acquisition of, or merger with, a competitor for which there can be a range of objectives. Such transactions are at the SBU or corporate level and will be discussed later.) An example would be the acquisition by Alon USA Energy of Edgington Oil Company and Paramount Petroleum Corporation and the merger of their Long Beach, California refineries. The western crude mix is increasingly heavy as the sweet light crudes are depleted and production of heavy crude from the oil sands increases. Refiners of North American crude have to either draw from the depleting supply of light crudes or invest in capacity to refine heavier crudes. Alon has made capital investments (e.g., catalytic cracker capacity) and acquired Edgington and Paramount (both heavy oil refiners) in 2006, and as a result was able to shift its mix in California from under 40 percent heavy crude to over 70 percent heavy crude in three years.[14]

As in the preceding product example, Alon needed more heavy oil refining capacity. The alternatives to acquisition were to further invest in existing refineries, build a new one, or do nothing—that would lead to the pursuit of lighter crudes and would require changes in product–market focus as well. The right strategic analysis was to compare the acquisition with other options.

Examples of marketing and distribution strategies in which M&A is considered can be found among bank acquisitions of insurance brokerages in the United States. Many U.S. banks are developing insurance products and are permitted to sell them through bank channels by U.S. regulators. However, the broker channel is well established and dominates U.S. insurance sales. While some insurance is sold through bank channels (branches, financial advisors, and online), it may take years for consumers to shift substantial sales volumes from broker to bank channels.

A bank that sees opportunity to grow share through the brokerage channel has several options: build its own dedicated broker, which will require investment and will lose time in the market; use independent brokers, which requires little investment but sacrifices margin; acquire one or more independent brokers; or be content with the volumes it can sell through bank channels. Once again, the strategic context puts the acquisition decision as one choice among several. To decide upon the acquisition in isolation in this case could lead to undervaluing the option and potentially rejecting deals that would have, in fact, been the superior option.

How is the role of M&A determined for the strategy of an SBU or single-business company?

At the single-business SBU level, the strategy is primarily about competition and the means to do better, to gain ground, or to capture new opportunities, whether by having lower costs, developing a better product or service, or providing the product or service in a superior way.[15]

The industry context is highly relevant to where and how M&A should be considered in competitive strategy. For example, if the industry has scale economies but has not been consolidated, then mergers of competitors will likely be occurring, and the company's merger strategy will be central to its business strategy. Other elements of competitive strategy will complement the merger strategy.

The U.S. bank consolidation provides a clear example. Since the restrictions on interstate bank mergers were lifted in 1994,[16] the industry has been consolidating, excepting for a pause to cope with the current financial crisis. The potential to lower costs through branch rationalization and the consolidation of back office and headquarters' functions and systems is compelling. In addition, if competitors achieve lower costs through mergers, a company can be left behind if it doesn't participate, unless perhaps it has a defendable niche of some kind.

However, as noted in Chapter 2, many bank mergers fail to create value. In the context of consolidation the potential benefits are known to all, and the acquisition prices tend to be bid up to include much of the cost synergy potential.

The M&A strategy in this context is not just about what to buy. Rather, the company must set a path to become a superior acquirer or, failing that, determine when to sell (the subject of Chapter 7). To become a superior acquirer requires model cost structures to begin with and a well-defined process to integrate new operations. The former is a valid strategic objective in any case and will serve shareholders well as part of the internal business strategy, assuming it is complementary to good products and service for customers. The latter requires investment to develop and gain experience in postmerger integration.

Moreover, the M&A strategy of the consolidator requires five components in total:

1. A defined view of the future industry environment, structure, and key success factors. (Note that the companies that have this view early and choose to pursue a leadership position have a great advantage. Many companies have come to this view of their industry too late and then can't compete with more experienced and more confident acquirers and ultimately become targets. Consider the mining industry as discussed in Chapter 2, for example.)
2. A strategic vision for the business, considering the scale and scope that will be required to compete in the future.
3. The internal actions to develop low-cost but scalable operating models for operations, headquarters, and back-office functions. (We refer the reader to the extensive literature on cost benchmarking,[17] requisite organization theory,[18] process reengineering,[19] sourcing,[20] and outsourcing[21] for further reading on low-cost operating models and cost-reduction strategies.)
4. A well-defined and practiced process for integration. This includes a process to achieve cost synergies with superior effectiveness and speed. It must also include solutions to other integration challenges: avoiding or minimizing value risks such as the revenue losses associated with pricing and product integration as discussed in Chapters 2 and 3; and capitalizing on revenue growth opportunities that may be available in cross-market deals as discussed in Chapter 3. (We refer the reader to *The Art*

of M&A Integration[22] for a full discussion of postmerger integration approaches.)

5. A process to identify, screen, and attract merger partners. (We address this process in the next chapter.)

Another industry context that places distinct focus on the role of M&A in competitive strategy is a change in the relevant scope or definition of the industry. Examples include the globalization of the brewing industry (redefined geographic market scope); the convergence of telecommunications, media, and entertainment (redefined product market scope); or the emergence of monoline banks and outsourced back-office services (redefined value chain).

In the first example, there was a range of strategies. Heineken[23] developed a global brand, developing the global recognition and distribution capabilities for Heineken largely organically. (Heineken was recognized as the Brand of the Century by the Dutch business community in 1999.) The international development of the Heineken brand predated the acquisitions in the last decade of a number of local brands and other global brands, such as Amstel, Newcastle, and Sol. Heineken's brand strength and distribution can now carry other brands into its vast premium retail and restaurant channels.

Other companies acquired their way to the creation of international brewing companies such as Interbrew of the Netherlands, now known as AB Inbev. Interbrew's global strategy was to acquire leading national or regional brands and then expand the markets for these brands. Interbrew acquired Hungary's Borsodi Sör, Mexico's Dos Equis, the United States's Rolling Rock, Canada's Labatt's, the UK's Bass and Whitbread, and Germany's Beck's. This all predated the acquisition of Anheuser-Busch in 2004 to form AB Inbev.[24] Small local brewers remain and indeed the microbreweries have found a defendable niche.

In the second example, organic development is unlikely. Technology and regulatory changes created the convergence opportunity somewhat suddenly, and there were and are in most such cases existing players in each of the new product–market segments. The strategic choices are to acquire in the new product–market segments, to define and defend a niche related to current competencies, or to sell at some point. This story continues to unfold as the services of cable, telecommunications, media, entertainment, and Internet companies increasingly overlap and the major players weigh merger alternatives.

The third example is similar to the second in that the defined boundaries of the industry changed, but instead of convergence the industry disaggregated. In this case, the industry has segmented along the value chain with the emergence and growth of single-product companies like Capital One in credit cards or USA Mortgage in mortgages, or service companies such as the custodial bank Bank of New York Mellon or the back-office services company First Data. This changes the context for formerly integrated operations of the incumbent competitors. In their market-facing businesses, such as credit cards and mortgages, they have new competitors and must reconsider their competitive position. For example, there became a need for a strategic view of the industry and a competitive strategy for the credit card divisions, including consideration of acquisition and divestiture options. On the one hand, First Union sold its credit card portfolio to monoline MBNA in 2000. On the other hand, Bank of America chose to grow its credit card business and acquired MBNA in 2005.

For the back office, these considerations have been referred to as outsourcing options. However, choosing to outsource a function is really the acknowledgment of a new industry competing in that space. It requires restructuring the company to isolate the function and a decision not to participate in that new industry (i.e., to divest the function). Not only do the new service providers offer the outsourcing alternative but the alternative offered also provides a benchmark for cost and quality. Some companies continue to choose to keep these services in house and focus on performance improvement to achieve benchmark performance. However, as evident in the growth of companies like Bank of New York Mellon, many are taking advantage of the new industry structure and exiting.

In such cases, the M&A option, if chosen, is about growth in new product–markets or exit from a newly formed product–market sector. This is distinct from the goals and value creation opportunities for the consolidator discussed earlier. Accordingly, the M&A strategy has some different components:

1. A defined view of the future industry environment, structure, arenas of competition, and key success factors. (Again, note that the companies that have this view early and choose to pursue a leadership position have a great advantage.)
2. A strategic vision for the new business considering in what arenas to compete and the company's basis of competitive advantage. It is a legitimate option to wait and sell. However, it is not a

legitimate option to ignore the changes or likely changes in the industry—it is poor strategic planning that fails to recognize and deal with conditions that could lead to industry change.

3. The internal actions to reorient the business functions and build the competencies that will be needed in the new industry as it is formed. While much of the new product market knowledge will be acquired along the way, there will also be new skills required to compete in a newly defined industry, and the organization structure will likely need to be reoriented to align with how the company will compete in a changed industry.
4. The integration strategy. This is not the postmerger integration strategy per se, but rather the defined model for value creation in newly defined product markets. In the case of telecommunications, media, entertainment convergence, for example, this was the step many forgot. AOL–Time Warner was a convergence play in name only; what they intended to do together remains a mystery, especially to shareholders.
5. A process to select, screen, and attract the right partners (again, to be discussed in the next chapter).

The first three components essentially constitute "Competitive Strategy 101" but on a newly defined market.

How is the role of M&A determined for the strategy of a geographic division?

As noted earlier in this chapter, geographic strategies often cut across product, function, SBU, group, and corporate strategies. For a group or corporate holding company, we will deal with geographic strategy in the next section. However, for the single-business company, the development of the geographic strategy and the role of M&A are straightforward (which doesn't mean easy) and a variation on processes described earlier for product, functional, or SBU M&A strategy.

There are three key points in the development of the strategy, and the M&A strategy in particular, for the geography:

1. Since the market and competitors are likely distinct, the analysis of all aspects of competitive strategy should be robust.

2. However, product and functional development and a change in strategic direction in one market can affect the market positioning, scale economies, and resources available across international operations.
3. Therefore, decisions need to be made in the context of international strategies and investment priorities.

An international courier company, such as UPS, can be used to illustrate these points. While UPS has been the dominant provider in the United States for many years, its position and strategic challenges vary greatly across other markets around the world. UPS has entered some of these markets by acquisition, and each country management team advances its own ideas to compete effectively within its market. However, a process to integrate these ideas with company-wide strategy is essential.

For example, if the UK product/pricing strategy were to promote domestic lanes at the expense of international lanes, it may be a valid strategy against local competitors but it could be detrimental to system profitability.

UPS faced a dominant and sophisticated local competitor when it entered Canada. Purolator Courier had superior product offerings (e.g., multiple delivery times with guarantees not common in the industry at that time). To match Purolator offerings in Canada, UPS would have had to consider the implications for the system. Ultimately, UPS matched offerings in Canada and exported many of the ideas for the system.

Most of the major international couriers have considered the acquisition of Purolator at some point. However, while a valid strategy for Canada, this size of investment has to be considered in the context of global operations, and the relatively small Canadian market has not yet won the support of corporate management against other international priorities. Again, this demonstrates the local nature of the challenges and M&A opportunities, but decisions must be made in the context of international strategies and priorities.

How is the role of M&A determined for the strategy of a group or corporate holding company?

At the corporate level of a multibusiness company or at the group level of a large holding company, the business strategy is in general to assemble assets to which the corporation or group can add value. The corporation's strategy for adding value determines the kinds of companies to be held and the M&A strategy.

In Chapter 1, we noted three alternate roles for holding companies that "manage" assets: controller, coach, and orchestrator. The strategies and associated competencies to add value to acquired assets vary across these models, but in each case the M&A strategy must accomplish two broad goals: the first is to develop the portfolio of assets to which the parent's strategies and competencies will be relevant and will create value; the second is to meet the M&A needs of the product, function, SBU, and geographic strategies of the group, as outlined earlier.

Developing M&A strategy for such a portfolio is multidimensional and requires an organized way to examine the current portfolio's strengths and weaknesses, and then to determine how best to develop the portfolio, considering each business. The overall process to engage the various levels can follow the "W" as already outlined. However, in the case of such a portfolio of businesses, the process is so much about M&A opportunities that a tool specifically designed to generate and screen M&A opportunities may be useful.

The Art of M&A[25] introduces the wheel of opportunity/fit chart (WOFC) that can be helpful in developing M&A opportunities for a large managed portfolio. The WOFC is a method with which to engage the various levels of a multibusiness corporation in generating and screening acquisition needs and opportunities toward creating an M&A strategy. (See Exhibit 5.2.)

The M&A strategy is the strategy for the most part at the portfolio level for this type of company. The WOFC or a similar process can be used to define the strengths, weaknesses, and needs of the current portfolio and delineate the opportunities in a robust and disciplined way. In a large portfolio, a high involvement process can be useful to get the necessary input on needs and opportunities from the perspective of each business. The product, functional, SBU, and geographic M&A issues and opportunities at each level can be relevant to the M&A strategy, as outlined in the previous sections. Having used a common framework at each level, an overall corporate view of the WOFC can then be amalgamated and the corporate perspective added.

At the corporate level, the M&A role and strategy can then be determined in three steps:

1. From files of "opportunities" that have been assembled for evaluation, candidates are entered on the wheel of opportunity.
2. Criteria are adopted for selecting between these and future alternative acquisition opportunities, using the strength and weakness

Exhibit 5.2. Wheel of opportunity/fit chart (with illustrative example and notes provided in Appendix II.2).

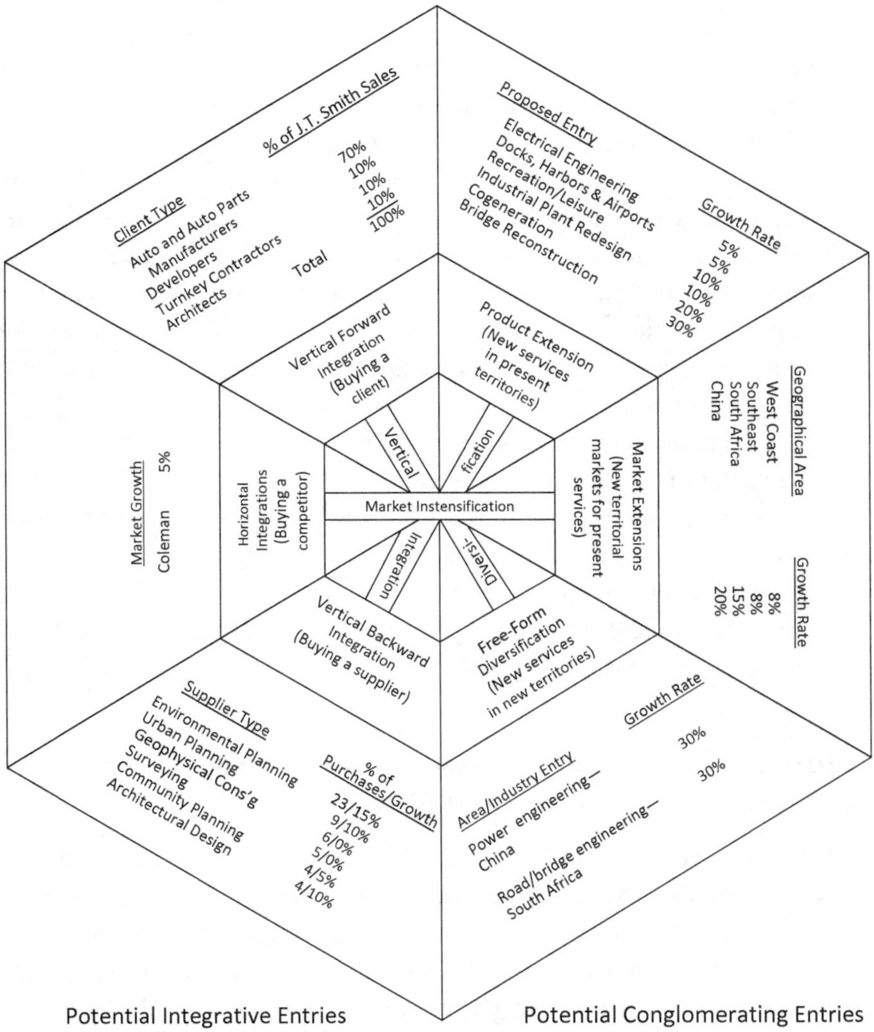

analysis developed by the fit chart and a view of the key external factors that may affect one or more of the businesses.

3. The alternative acquisitions on the wheel are rated against each other using the scoring criteria developed in the fit chart.

This prioritizes the search process and helps identify where acquisition solutions at one level may provide solutions to needs at other levels. Ideally, this is a consensus process. However, corporate priorities may trump investment opportunities as seen from the perspective of other levels.

In order to be comprehensive, a 360-degree approach can be used to look at horizontal, vertical and diagonal opportunities. Horizontal opportunities are the direct competitors or companies in the same business in another market. As already noted, these are most relevant in an industry that has or may have conditions for consolidation as discussed in Chapter 2.

Vertical opportunities are up and down the value chain from the company. It is especially important to look here if the relevant competitive scope of the industry is changing or if there are supply chain or market channel constraints, as we earlier observed in the heavy oil refinery and insurance distribution examples. Diagonal opportunities include the product and market extensions outlined in Chapter 3—new products for existing markets or new markets for existing products.

In all cases, it is important to refer back to the view of future industry and consider the 360 in the future context. This will also facilitate consideration of real options (see Chapter 4) whereby the opportunities are not of certain strategic value but may position the company for future opportunities depending on how the industry develops.

(Sample checklists for strengths and weaknesses and for assets to consider in complementary analysis can be found in the Appendix to Part II.)

How does the role of M&A change if the company requires transformational change?

There are three situations to consider. In Chapter 1, we referenced the surgeon and architect models where the role of the parent is a transformational role—in the case of the surgeon, often a private equity (PE) firm, this is what they do; for the architect, it may be a one-time transformation of an enterprise. The third situation is when any company acquires an asset that is strategically important to the company but requires transformation to fit or perform well.

In the case of the surgeon, the role of M&A is central. The surgeon is looking for companies that are undermanaged or undervalued. Surgeons add value by improving performance. They seek to own a company at least long enough to exact a turnaround or to restructure it, but may also wait for the right market conditions before selling. There is an exit strategy at the outset and typically a practiced process of acquisition, engagement, monitoring, and sale.

In most other respects, the role of M&A is similar to the other holding company models already discussed. However, they often seek quite different companies, often the same ones that others reject, because their value added is in the turnaround.

The architect model is situation specific. The role of M&A for the Thomson example was to reposition the company in, ultimately, an entirely different business and business model. Divestitures were used to exit newspapers and fund acquisitions of subscription-based information services. Acquisitions also brought the necessary competencies and technology platforms critical to the new space. Acquisitions were focused to build leading positions in selected sectors, resulting in shared platforms and dominant positions in niche markets.

While each situation is different, the role of M&A within the transformation is similar—"out with the old; in with the new." The break up of the railway conglomerates similarly involved shedding real estate, hotel, and other assets to invest in the broadening of the freight railway systems through acquisition. The ultimate transformation of the water company Compagnie Général des Eaux into the media company Vivendi also involved the sale of assets to fund investment in the new sector.

In the third case, a company not in the business of turnarounds is acquiring a strategic asset that must be transformed. This needs to be recognized as an M&A role outside of the skill set of the company.

In most cases, these deals fail. The strategic rationale may be compelling, but few operating companies have the competencies and capacity to turn around an acquired asset. The saying "strength buys strength" is derived from these lessons. It is hard enough to integrate two good companies and hard enough to manage a turnaround. An operating company that acquires a poorly performing company has to do both the turnaround and integration at the same time. All too frequently there is contagion, and the combined company gets in trouble. If such deals must be done, the challenge must be recognized for what it is and the right skills hired to make it work.

How is the role of M&A determined for the enterprise-level strategy?

At the enterprise level, including the more "hands-off" forms of holding company models (e.g., the controller role from Chapter 1), assets are typically not under common management. The strategy comprises investment and divestment decisions that may be based on industry focus or company size, management, or performance characteristics.

M&A strategy as pure investment, where there is no value-added strategy of the parent except in the selection, is essentially an investment strategy rather than a business strategy. Investment strategy is beyond the scope of this book.

Endnotes

1. Speech by Geoff Beattie, president of the Woodbridge Corporation, at the Seminar of the Institute of Corporate Directors, Toronto, November 2008.
2. Michael Porter, *Competitive Strategy* (New York: Free Press, 1998). This is the most recent edition of this book, which has gone through more than 60 printings.
3. Walmart company website, http://walmartstores.com/about us/7603.aspx.
4. Douglas Martin, "James J. Ling, Who Built Conglomerates, Dies at 81," *New York Times,* December 26, 2004.
5. Ibid.
6. Ibid.
7. See Carlton Osakwe and Peggy Hedges, "The Diversification Discount: The Case of Canadian Pacific Limited," Working Paper Number 2002-17, Haskayne School of Business, University of Calgary, November 2002.
8. Thomson-Reuters company website, http://thomsonreuters.com/.
9. See Company Histories and Profiles, *Funding Universe*, accessed October 14, 2011, http://www.fundinguniverse.com/company-histories/Olympia-amp;-York-Developments-Ltd-Company-History.html.
10. For a company history from 2001 to present, see http://www.vivendi.com/vivendi/Company-history; for an earlier history from a secondary source, see Company Histories and Profiles, *Funding Universe,* http://www.fundinguniverse.com/company-histories/Vivendi-Universal-SA-Company-History.html.
11. See Company Histories and Profiles, *Funding Universe,* http://www.fundinguniverse.com/company-histories/AnheuserBusch-Companies-Inc-Company-History.html.
12. See GE Organization Chart on GE company website, http://www.ge.com/pdf/company/ge_organization_chart.pdf.
13. The "W" framework was developed by SECOR Consulting of Montreal, www.secorgroup.com.
14. Alon USA Energy Inc. Annual Reports 2006, 2007, 2008.
15. Michael Porter, *Competitive Strategy*.
16. The Bank Holding Company Act of 1956 prohibited bank holding companies headquartered in one state from acquiring a bank in another state. The interstate restrictions of the Bank Holding Company Act were repealed by the Riegle-Neal Interstate Banking and Branching Efficiency Act of 1994. For analysis and discussion see Philip E. Strahan, "The Real Effects of U.S. Banking Deregula-

tion," Boston College, Carroll School of Management and Wharton Financial Institutions Center, September 2002.

17. See, for example, David Stauffer, *Best Practices for Benchmarking* (Boston, MA: Harvard Business School Working Knowledge for Business Leaders, 2003).
18. See Elliott Jaques, *Requisite Organization* (Fleming Island, FL: Cason Hall & Co., 1998).
19. See Michael Hammer and James Champy, *Reengineering the Corporation* (New York: HarperCollins, 1993).
20. See, for example, Emiko Banfield, *Harnessing Value in the Supply Chain: Strategic Sourcing in Action* (New York: John Wiley & Sons, 1999).
21. See, for example, Michael F. Corbett, *The Outsourcing Revolution—Why It Makes Sense and How to Do It Right* (Chicago, IL: Dearborn, 2004).
22. Alexandra R. Lajoux, *The Art of M&A Integration: A Guide to Merging Resources, Processes, and Responsibilities*, 2nd ed. (New York: McGraw-Hill, 2006).
23. Information from company website, http://www.heinekeninternational.com.
24. From Company Histories and Profiles, *Funding Universe,* http://www.funding universe.com/company-histories/Interbrew-SA-Company-History.html.
25. Stanley Foster Reed and Alexandra Reed Lajoux, *The Art of M&A: A Merger Acquisition Buyout Guide,* 4th ed. (New York: McGraw-Hill, 2007).

Chapter 6

Searching, Screening, and Selection

"What are you looking for?" asked a passerby.

"My keys," said the man, scouring the curbside under the streetlight.

"Did you drop them here?"

"No, but the light's good here."

—*Anonymous*

Once a company decides on its strategic goals and determines that M&A can help meet them, the next step is to set criteria for a thorough comparative screening and selection of possible acquisition candidates. Even if one company seems perfect for the strategy—or so good that it inspires a new strategy—it is important to consider the alternatives. At the very least, knowing the alternatives will help determine an appropriate price for the opportunity at hand. However, in most cases there is more than one potential combination that will achieve a strategic objective, even if the other potential partners don't know it yet. If the alternatives are few, then they can all be considered in detail and can even be approached.

Consider the next round of North American railway mergers, for example, if the U.S. Department of Justice ever released its de facto moratorium on railway mergers.[1] With only six major railways remaining in North America and the deal logic compelling for any pairing, then enumerating the alternatives will be easy. Each railway has only five partners from which to choose. In fact, each railway has already considered the benefits of merging with each of the others in previous rounds. They all know each other's assets well because they collaborate in interline freight movements. Also, many of the executives have worked in the other companies, and they spend time with each other on industry and interline freight issues. Moreover, the synergy potential and even the integration challenges between any two railways are known to some degree.

The problem is that one must think not only of one's own merger but also of all the other possible mergers. The value of integration with each potential M&A partner must be understood in the context of the other pairings that may occur because the other mergers will determine the new competitive landscape and the competitive position of each new company.

This is no small task. Thankfully, it is bounded by the number of acquisition partner alternatives for each company and then those remaining for the others (15 possibilities in total). It would likely be further bounded by restrictions the regulator would impose if the de facto moratorium were lifted.

However, it is more often the case that the alternatives are many. Consider, for example, the pharmaceutical companies seeking to capture intellectual property (IP) that may be in development across a multitude of biotech firms, or a company like Microsoft seeking to maintain its competitive position staring at thousands of startups that could be "the next Skype," or the consumer goods companies seeking to enter the developing markets where there are established players in every product category in every country of interest, or the portfolio company seeking to develop a new industry grouping, or the computer software developer or biotech or food science entrepreneur seeking a buyer or merger partner that has needed skills in marketing, distribution, or manufacturing. The fact is that there are many acquirable companies that may advance the strategy, many that will not be known to the buyer or the advisors, and many that may or may not have considered a merger, sale, or acquisition.

So herein lies a dilemma of corporate development. On the one hand, strategy calls for a proactive approach to considering the alternatives. Responding only to the opportunities that walk in the door can hardly be called strategic, and the deals made on the golf course have often put the egos or wallets of the CEOs ahead of the interests of shareholders. Surely a strategic approach is independent, comprehensive, and fact based.

On the other hand, it is simply not practical to analyze all the partner alternatives at the level of detail required to understand value potential. Even the analysis required to choose the right railway partner above, where there are only five alternatives for a given company, would be months of work. In most industries, the work to properly assess all the alternatives would simply create paralysis by analysis.

This chapter resolves this dilemma of corporate development by outlining a practical way to see a larger universe of alternatives and then screen from many to few to one. The approach first widens the scope of the search and then uses analytical sieves from coarse to fine to get to those partners that will be approached or analyzed in detail.

DEFINING THE SEARCH UNIVERSE

How should an acquiring company define the relevant universe of potential partners?

The search begins with review of the strategy: how M&A will be deployed to advance the strategy and how the buyer will add value. This was essentially the subject of the previous chapter—choosing where M&A could be deployed to achieve strategic goals at the functional, SBU, or corporate level.

Considering the strategic objectives, the search should then define the relevant universe. Creative approaches to initially expand the options beyond the obvious can result in new and valuable ideas. This is best illustrated with examples representing some of the generic M&A roles outlined in Part I—*portfolio development*, *consolidation*, *growth*, and the *creation of real options*.

How should portfolio companies define their relevant universe?

It really depends on their role. To borrow again from the paradigm outlined in Chapter 1, we can see these roles as controller, coach, orchestrator, surgeon, or architect.

Portfolio Controller

As outlined in Chapter 1, Berkshire Hathaway as a controller looks for large, well-managed companies that may be undervalued. That may sound like a large universe, but when the markets are efficient, it is in fact quite a small one. Those companies that are large enough to be of interest to Berkshire Hathaway have the attention of analysts and will generally trade at fair value.

However, market disruptions can leave gaps to fair value, at least temporarily. For example, the dramatic fall of the markets during the financial crisis punished virtually all stocks. For those investors able to differentiate between companies with justifiably low valuations and companies that were simply caught in the downdraft, this disruption created opportunities.

Berkshire Hathaway has picked up the pace of its acquisitions since the markets' steep fall in 2008. For example: Berkshire Hathaway acquired Constellation Energy in September 2008 for $26.5 per share versus trading prices over $80 per share the prior October; it invested $5 billion in September 2008 in Goldman Sachs preferred shares that pay 10 percent interest, plus warrants on common shares that earned $437 million within days; and it completed its largest acquisition in history in 2009, acquiring the remainder of Burlington Northern Sante Fe Corporation (BNSF) for $100 per share—this was a premium of over $20 per share but was ~10 percent below pre-crisis trading values.[2]

Not all controllers are structured as holdings companies that make controlling investments. Some are funds that make partial investments that may not be controlling. The large pension plans were also mentioned in Chapter 1 as portfolio companies in the controller role. Many of these funds are growing due to the demographic makeup of their members and hence must seek an increasingly larger universe for investments.

For example, the Canada Pension Plan is conservatively managed by its investment board (CPPIB) and defines its universe partly based on its sector knowledge—it will invest only in sectors that management understands well. Therefore, to expand its universe CPPIB must develop expertise in new sectors. A case in point is CPPIB's growth in commercial real estate. From fiscal 2005 to 2011, CPPIB built a commercial real estate investment team of 24 professionals and has grown the real estate portfolio from $0.8 billion to $10.8 billion, investing in the sector as it gained skills and experience market by market.[3]

While the U.S. commercial real estate market has been soft following the crisis, CPPIB has been in a position to invest. For example, in New York CPPIB acquired with partners a 45 percent interest in 600 Lexington Avenue, and it acquired a 45 percent stake in 1221 Avenue of the Americas (also known as the McGraw-Hill Building) with the balance held by Rockefeller Group International.[4] As an outsider to the market, CPPIB has a capital position very much superior to those investors that were highly invested in the U.S. commercial real estate market before the financial crisis. In addition, the experienced real estate team developed at CPPIB has put it in a strong position to define U.S. commercial real estate as a target market.

So while the search universe for portfolio companies in the controller role may be the least restricted, the successful players invest only in what they can understand well, and they must seek a time or situation in which the assets are not fully valued. Unlike other types of portfolio companies, the controller cannot rely on the value added to earn back a premium.

Portfolio Coach

As an acquirer in the coach role, GE chooses the industries in which it believes it can build a leadership position. It developed GE Capital as an industry leader in financing largely by acquisition. GE Capital completed over 100 acquisitions in the last decade alone.[5]

The universe for GE Capital was made large by its consideration of both competitors in the business and the customers of the business. They acquired the hidden competition of companies with in-house financing services, such as Bombardier Capital. Bombardier, like many others who sell expensive equipment, provided financing to dealers and customers. However, these in-house financing arms can be problematic—it is difficult for them to be objective in assessing the customer's creditworthiness and to be tough on collections. In 2005, GE Capital acquired the inventory financing for Bombardier's recreational products for $2.4 billion. This followed purchases of financing and leasing assets from Boeing Capital in 2004 and ABB's structured finance and equipment leasing in 2002.[6]

GE Capital also acquired noncore commercial financing operations from other financial services companies, such as the commercial finance arm of Merrill Lynch in 2007,[7] and the UK invoice discounting and factoring arm of Crédit Agricole in 2011.[8] Other companies that have grown by acquiring in-house assets include Accenture and EDS in the United States and CGI Group Inc. in Canada.

Note that acquisitions of in-house service assets are private transactions and often uncontested. A comparative analysis conducted by one of the authors of this book found superior returns to the acquirer on private deals over public deals.[9] The study defined "private" versus "public" by the company acquired and included selloffs of company units. The reasons are twofold:

1. Many of the private deals studied were selloffs. When a company decides to divest a noncore asset it is usually highly

motivated to move the asset at any price that would not be embarrassing. This means a low price paid by the acquirer for the sold-off unit. Buying low is a good start to creating value.

2. Competition on private transactions is limited to those invited to bid. In fact, if a buyer approaches a company with a reasonably attractive proposition to take over a nonproductive asset, there may be no competition at all.

Other portfolio companies in the coach role seek businesses in which they can leverage their skills. Traditional media companies have therefore looked across media and then across geographies. For example, what originally took News Corporation from Australia and Thomson Corporation from Canada into the UK and U.S. newspaper markets was simply a large universe of target newspapers. They each had efficient newspaper management models, and the UK and the United States had a lot of newspapers still privately held by their founding families. Restricting their searches to Australia or Canada, respectively, would have imposed an unnecessary constraint for a value creation model that relied on skills, not market knowledge or synergies between assets.

Note that it was their particular basis of adding value that made geographic expansion a much safer bet than, say, retailer Canadian Tire Corporation's acquisition of White Stores in the United States, which ultimately failed. News Corp and Thomson were adding value through a better operating model for each newspaper in a portfolio; each newspaper in turn retained its brand and its knowledge and position in the local market. For retail, market knowledge is key, and a winning formula from one market may utterly fail in another.

These and other successful portfolio companies operating in the coach role have stuck to the skills that they know how to leverage and have expanded the target universe by looking beyond the defined boundaries of their respective industries.

Portfolio Orchestrator

Orchestrators developing a portfolio with synergies between assets are typically looking at one or more of three growth axes: (1) horizontal—to determine which assets can leverage shared skills and corporate infrastructure; (2) vertical—to determine whether ownership of suppliers or customers would provide additional cost or revenue synergies; (3) platform—to determine whether additional infrastructure platforms could be leveraged across assets.

The ImpreMedia story provides an example of an expanded search universe based on redefining the horizontal axis. The New York Spanish-language newspaper *La Prensa* had been part of the Gannett newspaper group, a leading chain of major daily newspapers. El Diario Associates acquired *La Prensa* from Gannett for $20 million in 1989 and initiated a series of mergers and acquisitions to create a pan-American Spanish-language media company. Publications include *La Opinión*, *La Raza*, *Hoy*, *Impre*, and many others. ImpreMedia is now the leading Hispanic news and information company in the United States in print and online. The network is also the nation's largest Hispanic newspaper publisher with newspapers in top U.S. Hispanic markets, reaching 15 markets in total that represent 59 percent of the U.S. Hispanic population.[10]

Whether this could have been done under Gannett's ownership is unclear. However, the point is that in three-dimensional space the horizontal axis defines a plane. Orchestrators can look from the perspective of any asset for acquisitions that leverage the skills and infrastructure of the existing base.

Similar opportunities may exist along the vertical axis. Manufacturers have occasionally integrated downstream into distribution and sales, but some are now looking at Web-services firms. The logic is this: many fashion and hard goods companies are selling direct to consumers on the Internet. For some, their retail partners are servicing the sales as part of a cooperative arrangement. However, others are serviced by independents, and the manufacturers in some cases would rather control the quality of service, capitalize on some transportation and inventory management synergies, and keep the margins.

Finally, on leveraging the platform, which platform? Some companies have multiple physical, computer, or skills-based platforms that could be the source of cost or revenue synergies in acquisitions. A modern media company, for example, is distributing news and advertising through their various titles (physical), they have a shared digital platform for news and advertising content (computer), and they have a news-gathering team and advertising sales force that each could be leveraged by other titles (skills).

Portfolio Surgeon

The universe of the surgeon may run across industries, similar to that of the controller. However, the first screen is reversed. Where the controller is screening for well-managed assets that may be undervalued, the surgeon is looking for companies in which value can be created through major change. For example, while assets like Toys "R" Us and Kodak may very well have been presented to Berkshire Hathaway as well as Kohlberg Kravis Roberts & Company (KKR), Berkshire Hathaway would have declined these opportunities for the same reasons KKR embraced them.

As with the controller, the universe of possibilities is very large. (Unfortunately, there has never been a shortage of underperforming companies.) Controllers expand the universe by gaining an understanding of new industries or geographies in which they can make insightful investment and provide informed oversight. For surgeons, the core skills are the turnaround skills, which can be applied in a wide range of industries.

One newer dimension for these firms is looking for value when a change is required in the industry, not just the company. For example, it is likely that the various private equity firms that participated in the Bell Canada Enterprises (BCE) auction, KKR included, were not solely interested in fixing BCE but were also contemplating the removal of Canadian ownership restrictions and the North–South industry restructuring that would follow.

Portfolio Architect

The universe of the architect is not so much a company that can be transformed as it is a situation within an existing portfolio that offers transformational opportunity. For example, Thomson's acquisitions in information services were driven by a vision for the sector: initially seeing the value potential in owning essential information for professions like law, accounting, health care, and financial services, and later seeing the economies of scale and scope in digitization. Once the direction is set, the definition of the target universe is parallel to the orchestrator, guided by the strategic vision for the transformation.

What kinds of targets should the consolidator consider?

The relevant universe for consolidation would seem obvious—competitors, right? However, many industries have competitors serving different market segments. In addition, globalization has blurred the definition of the relevant geographic markets.

For example, while U.S. banks were consolidating through headlined mergers in the early years of the past decade, the banks' role in the consolidation of the insurance brokerage industry has gone almost unnoticed. As noted in Chapter 3, banks acquired more brokerages than banks during this period. (Albeit the value of the bank acquisitions was much larger.)

This was not consolidation from the banks' perspective—for the banks there were product–market revenue synergies. However, the insurance brokers were looking for the economies of scale needed to compete in a consolidating insurance brokerage industry. They could look in three possible directions: to other brokerages, to insurers, or to banks. While the banks offered less relevant industry skills as merger partners, they had much deeper technology skills—skills becoming vital in the brokerage industry and, in fact, one of the factors driving consolidation.

By looking in unusual places for consolidation partners, you may also derive competitive advantages. In the previous example, the brokerages acquired by banks have access to deeper skills in technology than would be available through mergers with other brokerages and, in addition, the potential for new customers from bank channels. So the brokerages that merged with banks achieved the needed scale plus a sustainable advantage for ongoing customer acquisition.

Consolidation in the financial sector not only crosses industry lines, it also crosses national boundaries. During the extreme downturn in the U.S. financial sector since 2007, the U.S. bank consolidation—which had been very heated for much of the decade—slowed down and may have stopped altogether if it weren't for some partners across national lines. For example, Bank North of Portland, Maine; Commerce One of Cherry-Hill, New Jersey; and the South Financial Group of Greenville, South Carolina, have been able to merge as part of the North American growth of Toronto-Dominion Bank (TD Bank).

U.S. companies have largely lacked the financial resources and the management capacity to advance consolidation while dealing with the fallout of the financial crisis. However, the Canadian banks, as part of a more conservatively regulated industry, were significantly less affected by the crisis and had both capital and management capacity available. In addition, further mergers of the major banks within the Canadian market are prohibited so they have had to look outside of Canada for growth. So again, it is instructive to look at both sides of the strategy story. From the perspective of TD Bank, expansion into the United States was a growth opportunity, but from the perspective of the U.S. banks involved, they have been able to merge into an institution now $189 billion in assets that ranks 14th among U.S. bank holding companies.[11]

In defining the universe for consolidation, acquirers set different thresholds for the size of their potential acquisition partner. Some companies seek only large acquisitions, whereas others seek only small deals. Those who favor large acquisitions point to economies of scale in the deal: it costs about the same in management capacity to successfully close a $100 million deal as it does a $1 billion dollar deal. Those who favor smaller deals point to efficiencies after closing: one can integrate many small companies in the time it takes to integrate one large one.

The size universe should really be defined by the skills of the acquirer; the skills required for large versus small deals are very different. Although a major deal with a company of similar size presents a large cost-savings opportunity, it also presents a major integration challenge. Implementation of the cost saving opportunities requires a great deal of work, which must be done as quickly as possible and with minimal impact on the customers. Such deals take time and energy, and there are usually years between such transactions. Large consolidation transactions fail more often than not, as noted in Chapter 2.[12]

By contrast, companies that execute many small deals can routinize the pre- and postdeal processes so that they consume less management capacity, can be completed quickly, and can be done in rapid succession. The success rates are higher on small deals, and when they fail the consequences are less severe.

However, at some stage of the consolidation of an industry larger deals may be necessary to build a leadership position. Fortunately, experience in integrating smaller deals can prepare the way. Mining company Xstrata of Switzerland, for example, grew rapidly through a series of smaller acquisitions before acquiring nickel giant Falconbridge. Integrating small deals faster than competitors is a competitive advantage in the early stages, but ultimately this skill must be developed to deal with the larger-scale integration projects and the more sensitive culture and ego issues involved in the major deals that will be required at the latter stages of consolidation.

What about competition laws?

Competition laws (also called "antitrust" laws) exist in most countries to ensure that customers and suppliers to an industry are not exploited. Consolidation in the extreme can result in companies becoming effective monopolies with which suppliers and customers have little choice but to do business. Lack of competition in due course often results in inefficiencies and loss of innovation and product development.

All major deals, but especially consolidation deals, are subject to review in most countries. Companies participating in industry consolidation should become familiar with the competition policies in each relevant country or legal jurisdiction.[13]

What is the relevant target company universe for the acquirer focused on growth?

The target universe for acquisitions motivated by revenue growth is defined well by the dimensions of growth set out in Chapter 3: targets operating in current markets and current products; targets in current markets with new products; targets with same products in new markets; and targets with new products in new markets.

Current Products in Current Markets

As observed earlier in Chapter 3, merging with companies operating in current markets with competing products is essentially consolidation. The revenue synergies will likely be negative, so there must be enough cost-savings opportunity to make such deals pay off. This case has been covered in the earlier discussion of consolidation.

However, as noted in Chapter 3, acquisitions can play a role in the improvement of current products to gain new customers or increase usage. Such a search has parallels to acquisitions as part of an R&D strategy. The strategic objective is to continuously develop the product line for competitive advantage. The search begins with a search for the improvements that will make a real difference. This is typically accomplished by surveying customers and studying usage to gain insight into how needs can be better met, while simultaneously scanning the related markets, domestically and internationally, for improvement ideas. Some acquisition candidates may surface from the latter; however, product improvements can more often be made internally, with the benefit of ideas gathered from the market scan.

Note that this should be viewed as a continuous exercise with a multiyear development cycle. If product improvements are to be made internally, it takes time in most businesses to develop, test, and launch improvements. If product improvements are to benefit from acquired innovations, these will seldom come "made to measure" but will rather be additions to capabilities in the development pipeline, as in the Google examples referenced in Chapter 3.

New Products in Current Markets

Defining the target universe for adding new products in current markets is really a search for customer and channel synergies. What else are your target customers or channels buying that would have affinity with your products or brand?

The best way to expand this universe is in concentric circles. (See Exhibit 6.1.) We'll use Teacher's blended Scotch whisky to illustrate the idea. Teacher's is a direct competitor of other blended "bar Scotches" like J&B and Johnny Walker Red Label. These we show here, but such acquisitions would essentially be consolidation.

However, do the customers that buy blended Scotch also buy premium or single malt Scotch for special occasions? What other spirits do they buy? What other alcoholic beverages do they buy? Are there marketing opportunities between these product categories that could benefit sales?

Now consider the channels—retailers, restaurants and bars, and the distributors that supply them. Could you promote Teacher's as the standard "bar Scotch" if you supplied popular single malts at favorable prices? Could you become the supplier of convenience if you carried a popular brand of each spirit—Scotch, bourbon, rye, rum, vodka, and gin? What about other alcoholic beverages, such as beer and wine? Such analysis has led to the formation of major spirits producers, such as Diageo and Pernod Ricard that produce products in each category at multiple price points.

The example of IBM's acquisition of Lotus outlined in Chapter 3 would be in a circle outside of IBM's products at that time. Similarly, the example of UPS's acquisition of Livingston International Inc. customs brokerage would be from an even larger circle of ideas outside of current products, but relevant to certain key target customers in a related context.

Exhibit 6.1. Concentric search illustration.

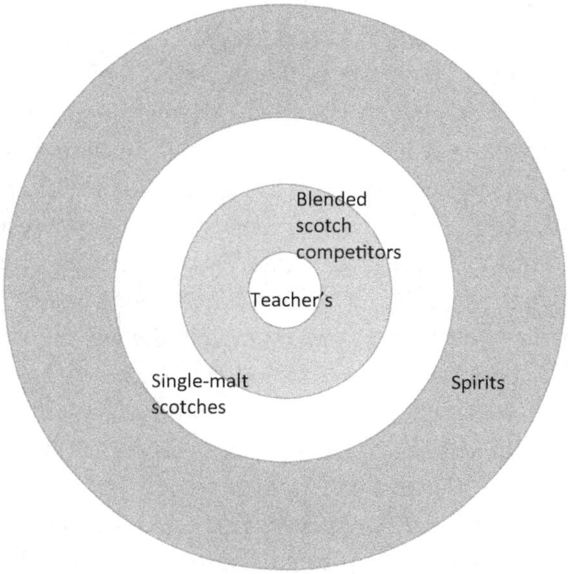

Current Products in New Markets

Targeting current products in new markets involves the acquisition of companies in a similar business in another market segment or geography. In most product categories, acquisitions across market segments within a given geography are difficult because they require the buyer to understand and serve a market segment that has eluded them in the past. For example, it would be difficult for the producer of cheap kitchen knives to appreciate the value the chef places on the characteristics of fine knives, or for the producer of high-quality knives to produce anything at the price point of the mass-market knives.

Nevertheless, there are successful revenue growth acquisitions across market segments. For example, Canada's leading food retailer, Loblaw Companies Limited, acquired the ethnic food retailer T&T Ethnic Mart in 2009 for $225 million[14] and both chains are benefiting from the deal. The search should prioritize markets previously missed over markets with fundamentally different values. For example, the merger of high-end retailers in different U.S. ethnic markets is more likely to yield positive results than the clash of values between high-end and mass market retailers or product manufacturers.

In most industries, acquisitions in new geographies represent a more substantial revenue growth opportunity, especially in today's globalizing markets. Making the target universe large is not difficult. In addition to the markets in the developed countries, the developing countries of Brazil, Russia, India, China, and others now offer real opportunities in most industries. Many industries are well developed in these markets, and their previously protected economies are increasingly open, with interesting acquisition or partnership opportunities and a great interest in investment and acquisitions abroad. For example, North American companies as diverse as Walmart, PepsiCo, John Deere, and Four Seasons Hotels have all made acquisitions or partnerships in India in the last few years.

Which geographic markets should be considered first will depend on the industry. For example, for education, training, and other service industries the large English-speaking markets of India are attractive. Resource and infrastructure industries will want to enter countries early in their economic development, whereas success in many consumer goods industries will depend on the existence of some distribution and retail infrastructure.

Some industries have developed benchmarks that can be applied to assess market potential. For example, life insurers look at ratios of average income to insurance. If incomes are low, there is not much of a market for life insurance. However, looking across markets at these ratios reveals the markets that are "underinsured" relative to others of similar income levels. These become the prime targets for entry (greenfield or by acquisition) and market development.

However, finding and screening the right kind of companies in such a distant and foreign universe is a challenge and will in most cases benefit from a local partner or an advisor. The role of advisors will be discussed at length in Chapter 11.

New Markets and New Products

For acquisitions in new markets and new products the universe can start out very large. However, this should not be an exercise in unrelated diversification. Therefore the universe must be defined by some affinity to current markets, products, or competencies.

One approach to defining this quadrant is to first define the other two growth quadrants—the new products of interest in current markets and the new markets of interest for current products. Then the universe of new markets for new products can be derived from this. For example, Zwilling (discussed in Chapter 3) may have seen France as a market in which to grow its cooking knife sales and may have seen cast iron cookware as a new product category of interest to its knife customers and channels. The acquisition of Staub was essentially a new product and a new market acquisition but related on both dimensions.

Another approach is to root the search in the competencies or unique skills of the corporation. In this case, the universe could be defined based on a broad scan of industries or sectors in which the skills could apply and for which there may be some synergy with the existing business. For example, one of the major global mining companies used the periodic table to define the universe. All elements of the periodic table and all the industries that created value from those elements were considered. Ultimately, the company found a close fit for skills and the potential for substantial revenue and distribution synergies in surprising places, not in the metals it currently mined, but in its processing capabilities and market channels that turned out to be relevant to quite different elements found in the periodic table.

Finally, what is the relevant target company universe for the "real options" acquirer?

An acquirer rarely starts out looking first and foremost for real options. As explained in Chapter 4, when it comes to a deal that offers real options, the specific deal may not create value in and of itself but rather it can position the buyer for future steps that will create value. Thus the search for real options should in most cases be a secondary consideration as part of the screening, valuation, and postdeal planning. The real options should be considered, therefore, to know the value of the target to the buyer and to plan postdeal development in a manner that retains the most valuable options, and exercises those that become feasible in due course.

However, in some cases the search can be about the real options, and the target may ultimately turn out to have been merely a vehicle. As one example, consider a Western food processor that would like to be positioned in the developing markets of Africa. The market for processed food is small in many African countries, with much of the food now being distributed daily from farm to table, in some cases supplemented by foreign aid. Food processors could look at the farms under development in the rich soils of the Nile basin in South Sudan, for example, as potential supply to an export business. However, this could lead to much larger opportunity in the region if the political climate stabilizes and the agribusiness economy develops as hoped. That is, the producers which step in now to develop a narrow array of products for export will hold real options for the development of the local food markets.

As another example, we can turn to China. The many companies that entered that country early also had the real option potential in mind (although they may not have referred to it as such). For example, GE and BMO Capital Markets operated for a long time with low or no profit, but they are now insiders in a rapidly developing economy.

Real options may also be the primary motivation for acquisitions in markets that are expected to change, such as heavily regulated markets poised for deregulation. For example, in the financial services markets of Canada and Australia that continue to prohibit banks from selling insurance products, many banks have acquired a position in insurance. The insurance businesses of these banks are small relative to the banking operations. However, those that have entered the business stand to gain disproportionately from regulatory change if and when they are permitted to market these products through their vast retail and online banking channels. The value of the real options exceeds the "as is" value of many of these insurance operations.

To recap, the target universe for most companies will consider real options only secondarily. However, in markets of strategic importance, farsighted companies will consider all means of entry that could provide options for the future.

TARGET SCREENING

If the potential universe of targets is so large, how can the candidate list be narrowed down?

The best way is to look at candidates in stages, with cuts at each stage. For the first stage, basic information is assembled on the company's products, markets, revenues, profitability, ownership structure, executives, and directors. Then the corporate development team can select 10 to 15 candidates for stage two analyses. The second-stage analysis uses secondary research and analysis of all available data to further prioritize candidates to select, say, five. The third stage then conducts more detailed research (in a preliminary due diligence) and prepares for a possible approach to the target.

In gathering and weighing information, two types of criteria are considered: those that determine target attractiveness and those that determine the likelihood of the deal. Candidates that are not subject to detailed analysis are not rejected, but merely set aside in favor of candidates that appear more attractive or more likely to become interested. If the candidates selected for detailed analysis or approach prove unattractive or impossible, then those candidates that were left behind can be reconsidered in priority order.

The criteria and approach are outlined in Exhibit 6.2. After stage one analysis, the screener can rank candidates using two preliminary grids: one for target attractiveness considering candidate characteristics and value creation potential (bottom right of Exhibit 6.2), and the other for deal probability based on assessed needs of the target and apparent interest (top left of Exhibit 6.2). Ranking on each of these preliminary grids in turn determines the ranking on the corresponding axis of the third grid (top right of Exhibit 6.2), which is then used to prioritize the targets. The candidates that fall the highest on one or both axes are subject to the next level of analysis—more detailed analysis of the same basic criteria. The second level of analysis will then be used to prioritize candidates that merit primary research and direct approach.

Exhibit 6.2. Opportunity prioritization.

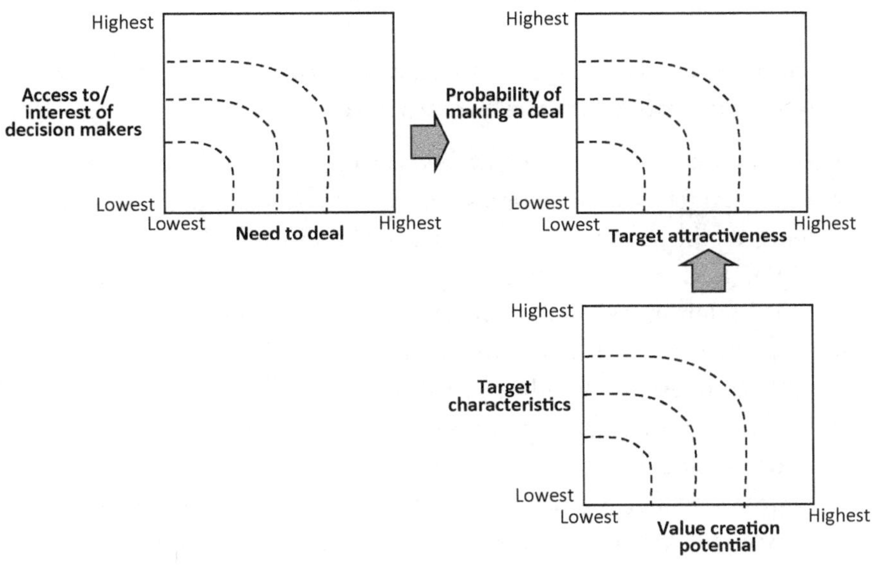

What are some potentially desirable target characteristics and how might they be analyzed?

Obviously different buyers could be looking for companies with quite different characteristics. For example, companies like Berkshire Hathaway may be looking for companies with good management and strong performance based on a sound business plan, whereas a buyer looking for turnaround or raider opportunities may be attracted to companies with weak performance that would respond to new management or a new strategy.

However, in any case the basic analysis of the target includes an understanding of all the business basics, including the company's products and markets, market share and competitive position in each business line, capital structure and financial performance, ownership and governance structure, organizational structure, and management team. At the second level of analysis, these same dimensions would be examined at the more detailed level of a stock analyst's report—including ratios, industry comparisons, assessment of strategies, and potential.

At the third level, the analysis can go deeper as required. For example, executive search firms can be employed to assess management. Customers can be surveyed (blindly) to assess competitive position of products and market share. If the relative cost position is important, suppliers can be interviewed or surveyed, employees or ex-employees can be contacted, and—for brick and mortar firms—cars in the factory parking lots can even be counted to estimate employment.

How can an acquirer assess the potential of a given target company to create future value?

This question is not really about the target as a stand-alone company; it is about the target in combination with the acquiring company, so its answer depends on the acquirer's strategy and capabilities.

For portfolio company acquirers, the question is whether the parent's value creation model will solve the problems or otherwise improve the performance or opportunities of the target. For example, if GE bought the target, one question would be whether or not GE's Six Sigma approach would yield performance improvement. Or, for another example, if a media holding company bought the target, the question would be whether the access to content or the technology platform of the media holding company would improve the success of a target media company.

For consolidation or revenue growth companies, the analysis involves the identification of cost or revenue synergy opportunities and successively more detailed estimates of the value of each opportunity at the three levels. For a proposition to merge two courier companies, for example, the third-level analysis included an extensive disguised survey of customers to determine with whom they would ship under various merger scenarios, including the one under study. The cost synergies in this case could only be determined accurately by designing the new route plan for the combined company—a painstaking analysis that also provided a detailed postmerger operations plan.

For consolidation deals in particular, as an acquirer you should highlight the value-adding opportunities unique to your company versus other buyers/partners. This will make you more attractive to the seller and will make the transaction more interesting to stakeholders such as shareholders. Remember that common opportunities will usually be negotiated into the price, so the real value-creation potential of any transaction relies on unique opportunities or distinctive implementation ability.

What would motivate a company to be acquired?

The answer will vary by company. You need to see the world from the target company's perspective. The best way to do this is to use the information you have or can gather on the company and the industry to develop the target's strategic options. At the first and second level, this may be available in analyst reports. This is usually sufficient on this dimension.

If a more detailed assessment is required, then the same techniques noted earlier to detail the target's cost and market position could be used here to understand problems and opportunities from the target's perspective. Once sufficient data is gathered, competitive simulations or role plays can be used to develop strategy from the perspective of the target and of other relevant market players. Consultants, advisors, and internal resources can be assigned to play the roles of each key competitor in the industry. With sufficient data, the role-play will usually determine the key elements of the strategy. If the target's strategy as developed in the simulation calls for merger, then at the most detailed level of analysis the role-play can even estimate acceptable terms with reasonable accuracy.

Scenario analysis can be very useful in industries undergoing transformation. In the most recent round of North American railway industry restructuring, extensive scenario analysis was used to determine each party's best and next best alternatives. This analysis revealed who should be most interested in whom and how much they would lose if they were forced to go to their next best alternatives.[15] Such analysis not only helps assess what interest the candidate should have in a transaction but it also begins to establish the negotiating range.

SOURCES AND DATA MANAGEMENT

What resources can be used to define the universe of companies and inform screening?

For high-level analysis, there are many possible public sources of information, including publications, websites, and associations that are dedicated to the target industries, especially those that report on M&A activity in those specific industries.[16]

A basic overview of industry trends is often available in security analyst reports. Sources are listed annually in *Nelson's Directory of Investment Managers.* Consulting firms may also have an analysis of an industry that they may share at a cost or for marketing purposes, or they can be engaged to create an industry analysis, but this will only be worthwhile if the screen has taken you to a level where the cost of the assistance is warranted.

Also, the U.S. government (as well as other national governments) has an abundance of free or low-cost data about industries and even about specific companies. Trade magazines and websites are another good source. Consider also M&A publications and databases, such as *Mergers & Acquisitions* and its website and database.[17] There are a number of sites that identify companies that are "for sale," although as mentioned it is not necessary to limit a search to companies that are overtly "selling."

If necessary, a high-level industry analysis can be developed from scratch using a framework like Porter's five forces.[18] An industry analysis should include the following:

- Market size and structure
- Key industry players and market share of each
- Level of market concentration
- Supply chain and key players in the supply chain, both upstream and downstream of the industry

- External forces that may be affecting the industry (e.g., market, technology, or regulatory changes)
- The nature of competition in the industry (e.g., aggressive price-based competition, capital investments, and so forth).

For most industries there are industry gurus—those that write about the industry or sell industry reports. These people can often share a quick understanding of the industry dynamic and may also have data on employees, pricing, market shares, product reputation, and key player contacts.

Once an acquirer finds companies of interest within a particular sector or industry, how should it organize the information?

Company profiles should be assembled as the layers of analysis are completed. Initially they may be sketchy, but for those companies that survive the initial screens, the following detailed profiles can be developed:

- Financial information in annual reports, 10Ks, D&B credit reports
- Company fact books and product catalogs
- Press releases, print advertisements, published articles, and executive speeches
- Director and officer profiles.

Securities disclosure rules require that a lot of information about publically traded companies be made available. In addition to annual reports, look at the companies' Securities and Exchange Commission (SEC) filings (10Ks, 10Qs, prospectuses, and proxy statements at http://www.sec.gov), as well as press releases, product literature, catalogs, company case studies, and executive speeches. The U.S. Treasury also has good data based on tax filings (www.irs.gov/taxstats/index).

Other sources for public companies include the following:

- *Corporate Affiliations*—in eight volumes or on CD-ROM[19] (http://www.lexisnexis.com/dca)
- Frost & Sullivan (http://www.frost.com)
- Moody's publications (http://www.moodys.com)
- Proquest Dialog (http://www.dialog.com/about/)[20]

- Standard and Poor's publications (http://www2.standardandpoors.com)
- *Thomas Register* (http://www.thomasnet.com)
- *Value Line Investment Survey* (http://www.valueline.com)
- Proquest Dialog (originally developed by Lockheed, prior to its merger with Martin Marietta to become Lockheed Martin) (http://www.dialog.com/about/).[21]

How can a buyer find information on private companies?

Private companies rarely give out financial information such as balance sheet and profit and loss numbers. Even when they have done it for credit purposes, many do not keep it up to date. However, some states compile the information through their chambers of commerce or their economic development programs.

A good starting place is Dun & Bradstreet's *Million Dollar Directory*, which lists both public and private companies. Dun & Bradstreet also has online services at http://www.dnb.com/us/. The D&B suite of offerings includes directories from Harris InfoSource (http://www.harrisinfo.com).

Another source is Hoover's (http://hoovers.com), known for its lists. The company offers "list-building tools" with applications in M&A that enable an acquirer to identify and retrieve various kinds of information. Hoover's also has a product called Family Tree (similar to the Corporate Affiliations source listed earlier from LexisNexis) that makes it possible to identify and map corporate connections between parent companies, branches, and subsidiaries. Hoover's also gives access to overviews and profiles from industry experts.

If neither D&B nor Hoover's has financial information on a particular private company, it is extremely difficult to obtain the information without getting it directly from the company itself. However, many states, especially those with extractive activity, require both public and private businesses, whether incorporated or not, to file annually various types of information, including year of establishment, names of principal owners, key personnel, number of employees, annual sales, principal lines of business, plant size, and import/export activity. Sometimes asset, liability, and profit information must also be submitted.

Some data may have to be gathered directly by the acquirer. Hoover's ConnectMail (to cite just one product of this nature) enables an acquirer to "deliver targeted, relevant messages directly to a prospect or potential partner's inbox." Such an approach would not be appropriate for an important and sensitive inquiry, but it could prepare the way through information gathering. An acquirer looking at hundreds of companies in a particular sector who wants to know if they do or do not sell a particular product might send out a personalized e-mail or letter asking about availability. While this can hardly be considered approaching the company, it may turn out to be the key that opens the door, so it should be done in the most professional manner possible.

How long does a search-and-screen program last?

For strategic acquisitions it depends on the scope of the program and how much in-house data is available on the subject. Normally, to produce a few viable candidates, a search-and-screen program takes a minimum of six months. At the end of six months, some target negotiations should be under way.

However, in changing industries the search can and should be continuous. The particular approach outlined earlier is highly suited to a continuous process of assessment and prioritization of candidates in a restructuring industry. After each deal, whether yours or others', the grids change, some attractive targets are removed while others become more interesting and more interested. Once initiated, the analytical framework is relatively easy to maintain as the guidebook of an industry in transition.

Endnotes

1. The Surface Transportation Board held a two-day hearing June 22–23, 2011, on the subject of "Rail Competition." At the current time, railroads are discouraged from merger. See Russell Pittman, "The Economics of Railroad 'Captive Shipper' Legislation," U.S. Department of Justice Antitrust Division Economic Analysis Group, January 2010.
2. Bloomberg, Business Wire, Annual Reports.

3. CPPIB Annual Reports, 2006–2011.
4. CPPIB Annual Report, 2006.
5. Ronald N. Ashkenas, Lawrence J. DeMonaco, Suzanne C. Francis, "Making the Deal Real: How GE Capital Integrates Acquisitions," *Harvard Business Review*, January–February 1998.
6. GE Company website, http://www.ge.com/files/usa/company/investro/downloads/bombardier.pdf.
7. www.thestreet.com.
8. Bloomberg.
9. See Smith, "Creating Shareholder Value in Mergers & Acquisitions," in *Mergers & Acquisitions of Privately-Held Businesses*, ed. Wayne P. Albo, Randal Henderson, and Gabor G. S. Takach (Rotenberg, 1999).
10. From ImpreMedia website, media kit, press releases.
11. Federal Reserve System, National Information Center, Bank Holding Company Rankings by Assets, accessed June 30, 2011, https://www4.harrisbank.com/spopup/0,4535,129778_7009715,00.html.
12. See Appendix to Part I.
13. For U.S. combined issues see Horizontal Merger Guidelines, U.S. Department of Justice and the Federal Trade Commission, issued August 19, 2010.
14. Marina Strauss, "Loblaw Buys Asian Grocery Chain," *Globe & Mail*, July 24, 2009.
15. The analysis was conducted by one of the authors; the details are confidential.
16. See also Appendix to Part II with data-gathering tips excerpted from Stanley Foster Reed and Alexandra Reed Lajoux, *The Art of M&A: A Merger Acquisition Buyout Guide,* 3rd ed. (New York: McGraw-Hill, 1998).
17. *Mergers & Acquisitions: The Dealmaker's Journal*, is the official publication of the Association for Corporate Growth. It was founded in 1966 by Stanley Foster Reed, the father of the coauthor of this book. For more information visit http://www.themiddlemarket.com/madb/.
18. Michael Porter, *Competitive Strategy: Techniques for Analyzing Industries and Competitors* (New York: Free Press, 1998).
19. LexisNexis Corporate Affiliations Plus gives access to all the information found in the eight-volume print directory, in electronic format. Its coding enables 29 search criteria, including parent company, subsidiaries, sales/revenue, earnings, assets liabilities, net worth, SIC codes, and number of employees.
20. This database was originally developed by Lockheed, prior to its merger with Martin Marietta (becoming Lockheed Martin). The Dialog portfolio of products and services, including Dialog and DataStar, offers organizations the ability to precisely retrieve data from more than 1.4 billion unique records of key information, accessible via the Internet or through delivery to enterprise intranets.
21. The Dialog portfolio of products and services, including Dialog and DataStar, offers organizations the ability to precisely retrieve data from more than 1.4 billion unique records of key information, accessible via the Internet or through delivery to enterprise intranets.

CHAPTER 7

To Be a Buyer or a Seller?

You got to know when to hold 'em, know when to fold 'em,
Know when to walk away and know when to run.

—*Kenny Rogers, "The Gambler"*

Most companies have to consider acquisitions and divestitures at different stages of development. Portfolio companies, of course, buy and sell companies as their primary business activity. Most other companies will also consider acquisitions as they grow, and they will sell assets or divisions as they optimize. Ultimately, most companies will also be faced with an opportunity to sell the entire company, and in some cases there will be little choice if shareholders like the premium being offered.

Yet, many companies do not consider acquisitions, divestures or, in particular, the ultimate sale of the company as part of strategy development. The ways in which M&A can create value were discussed in Part I of this book, but who should get the value and how is it maximized? So far in Part II, we have discussed how to determine the role of business combinations in your strategy and have outlined a process to identify and screen potential partners, but on what side of the table should you be sitting? Moreover, how should a company decide to be a buyer or a seller and when?

A case in the business press at the time of writing serves to illustrate the importance and difficulty of these questions. Research In Motion (RIM) is the company that invented the BlackBerry pager. By any measure, the company was hugely successful up to 2010. The very idea of "push" wireless e-mail exchange on handheld devices was new when RIM was founded and launched the BlackBerry in 1999.[1] The product quickly became an essential business communications device and was indeed the sole means of communications for thousands in the financial industry two years later during the tragedy of 9/11.

A tech startup from Waterloo, Canada, RIM passed $1 billion in revenue in less than five years and was operating worldwide. Wall Street was so dependent on and comfortable with the BlackBerry that even as smartphones added e-mail capabilities at the millennium, the money men preferred to carry two devices on their belts rather than give up their Blackberries. Ultimately, RIM added telephony to the BlackBerry, initially with a device that required a headset and then with integrated speaker and microphones in 2003. By 2006, the BlackBerry was second to only Nokia in smartphones globally and dominated the U.S. market.[2]

RIM's success to this point was in part due to its singular focus on serving the business segment. For example, RIM's 2006 annual report stated that it provided "software and services to keep *mobile professionals* globally connected to the people, data and resources that drive their day" (emphasis added).

However, perhaps reluctantly, RIM was drawn in to compete with consumer offerings. In particular, Apple's iPhone bridged the consumer and business markets and surpassed RIM and Nokia in sales.[3] BlackBerry responded with more consumer-friendly smartphones and a tablet to compete with Apple's iPad. In the 2010 annual report, the earlier emphasis on the professional is muted, and RIM speaks more of "customers" and "consumers."[4]

By the middle of 2011, the market was indicating considerable pessimism about RIM's future in this new competitive arena. RIM's valuation fell about 50 percent from a year earlier,[5] and there was speculation that RIM could be a takeover target. This leads to a series of questions about if and when RIM should have sold or found a partner.

Should RIM founders have sold their patents or the company when they had merely proven the success of the idea? Most tech startups sell early, and the inventors and investors make a few million, perhaps to invest in their next venture. They leave the business building and its rewards to others. The founders of RIM went on to create billions in value for shareholders by commercializing their invention, ultimately revolutionizing modern business communications.

Should RIM have sold when telephony became an expected feature of PDAs? While somewhat slow to respond, RIM developed telephony capability and became the leading smartphone in the United States for a time. Whether or not it was the intent, the BlackBerry smartphone also succeeded in penetrating the high-end consumer market.

Should RIM have sold when it became clear that the business and consumer markets would converge? This forced RIM out of its comfort zone and placed it in direct competition with the consumer tech giants.

Or should RIM have bought? Should it have sought business combinations in anticipation of the business-consumer market convergence? And if such foresight is unreasonable to expect, should it have acquired simply because it could, and because with the high valuations of its stock it could have acquired real options covering a range of market outcomes along with building greater scale and R&D capacity?

Moreover, did RIM need an exit strategy and/or an M&A strategy beyond its singular focus on the professional market well before facing these challenges?

Our purpose is not to second-guess RIM's strategy but rather to illustrate that these questions are relevant even for the most successful companies. In this chapter, we make the case that acquisitions and divestures should be considered routinely as part of strategy development. We provide some guidance on when and how to consider acquisitions and divestitures to maximize value creation and how to ensure that your company reaps its share of the deal reward whether as the buyer or as the seller.

AN EXTERNAL PERSPECTIVE

What can be learned from the portfolio companies?

As noted earlier, portfolio companies buy and sell companies as a primary business activity. Their top executives have the advantage of being one step removed from the businesses in the portfolio, which can bring greater objectivity. They also face buy and sell decisions as often in a year as most executives do in a career.

Successful portfolio companies have a clear idea of how they will add value, well matched to the interests and competencies of the parent company. We described earlier the role of M&A in strategy and how M&A strategy is developed in portfolio companies (in Chapters 1 and 5, respectively), referencing various roles of controller, coach, orchestrator, surgeon, and architect.

Portfolio companies also understand the value of growth. The cumulative size of such a company provides it with the means to raise cash and with the financial scale to look at larger deals. For the portfolio companies that are publicly held, a value-creating growth trajectory also supports high stock valuations, which reduces the likelihood of unwanted takeover.

Most successful portfolio companies define exit strategies in advance, with the possible exception of companies that actively develop synergies between or among their holdings. Controller Berkshire Hathaway, for example, has defined when it will sell. It will hold assets "as long as we expect them to generate at least some cash and as long as we feel good about their managers and labor relations."[6] This may seem like a low bar, but the strategy is logical for a company that has an impeccable eye for good businesses, is not interested in managing the companies it holds, and is not constrained by capital.

Coach GE's mantra is to be first or second in each industry or get out. In the past three decades, GE has sold six out of ten acquisitions. From 1981 to 2011, GE bought 780 companies and 255 stakes, and sold 610 companies or stakes.[7] Notable sales under Jeff Immelt (CEO at this time) have included the sale of its plastics division to Saudi Basic Industries Corporation in 2007 for $11.6 billion and the sale of a majority stake in NBCUniversal to Comcast in 2011 for $6.5 billion plus contributions from programming assets.[8]

The media companies in the coach role each buy and sell titles as they grow to build a portfolio that will advance the strategy and leverage parent competencies. For example, News Corp. has grown by acquisition but has also sold a number of companies. From 1981 to 2011, the company bought 177 companies and took stakes in another 116 companies, making a total of 207 divestitures in the same period, most recently selling MySpace to redeploy capital in strategic priorities.[9] Time Inc. sold Time Warner Books, Turner South, the Atlanta Braves, and Time Warner Cable over the past five years as it focused on the magazine titles and related digital media in select market segments.[10]

Architect Thomson's transformation to an information services company (now Thomson Reuters) was in part funded through the sale of its newspaper assets.

In all these examples of portfolio companies, there is a long-term view of shareholder value creation through pursuit of growth by acquisition, including defined sale criteria so that funds can be redeployed to the best use within the defined growth strategy.

How can these lessons be applied in operating companies?

The approach of the successful portfolio companies can be applied in most businesses. Many businesses over time become "accidental holding companies," accumulating or developing assets that could be separable businesses. For fully integrated corporations and even single-business companies, looking at the company as a portfolio of assets can lead to new ideas for value optimization, including acquisitions and asset sales. Such an outside-in, objective view puts management in the role of the parent company of a portfolio of assets; that is, considering what the company is worth (valuation), and what a dispassionate new owner would do to maximize value (value maximization).

Valuation in and of itself is a topic worthy of book-length treatment—and indeed there are several well-regarded tomes on the topic. The gold standard is of course *Security Analysis* by Benjamin Graham and David Dodd (still in print with a sixth edition), but others include books by finance professor Aswath Damodaran of New York University, by investment bankers Joshua Rosenbaum and Joshua Pearl, and one recently written with Robert A. G. Monks by the coauthor of this book. That book, *Corporate Valuation for Portfolio Investment*, may be the broadest as it covers a variety of valuation approaches, including those based on assets, earnings, cash flow, stock price, and combinations of these elements, along with analysis of governance and special situations.

Regarding *value maximization*, in their book *Valuation: Measuring and Managing the Value of Companies,*[11] Tom Copeland, Tim Koller, and Jack Murrin of McKinsey & Company introduced the "Valuation Pentagon"—a five-step process to determine how a company could achieve its optimal value and to estimate the value gap. A sixth step was added in later editions and the framework was given a more action-oriented title of "Restructuring Hexagon." For each step, we outline below how any company can gain new insights from taking this portfolio manager or corporate raider perspective, even though restructuring may not be your intent.

1. Current market value

The process described by the McKinsey team begins with an estimate of market value. For a public company, the market value is the market capitalization: stock price × shares outstanding.[12] For a private company, the market value can be estimated by identifying comparable public companies and calculating the ratios of their market capitalization to accounting-based performance indicators such as revenue and earnings before interest, taxes, depreciation, and amortization (EBITDA) and applying those ratios to the private company. For example, if public companies in a particular industry typically have a market capitalization of X times sales and Y times EBITDA, we can estimate the market value for a private company using the same multiples of sales and EBITDA.

(Note that for these purposes we are not considering market value as what a company would sell for, which would typically include a sale premium.)

2. Value as is

The next step is a straightforward valuation of projected cash flows for your business "as is." This establishes the "perception gap"—the difference between the market value and the intrinsic value of the company. Every company should know this. At the very least, it tells you if the market perceives the company correctly as a going concern. If the market value is much higher than the intrinsic value, then the market may anticipate growth not in the cash flow valuation, perhaps based on industry growth. Why is this not in the cash flow valuation? Is there opportunity being missed? Is the strategy not as aggressive as it could be?

If the market valuation is much lower than the intrinsic value, then the company could be an easy target. If the company's cash flow valuation is reasonably accurate, there is work to be done to communicate the value and get the stock price up.

3. Value with internal improvements

The third step is to estimate the value of the company based on its best internal strategy. This should be based on the best strategy for growth and performance improvement using solely organic growth and internal measures to improve performance. Again, every company should know the value impact of its strategy, but few do. Determining the value impact of the organic strategy is obviously a useful, arguably essential, measure of the strategy. That is, if the company is to invest in the strategy, what's the return?

If so measured, many companies would discover their strategies add little value and so need to be reconsidered, or they add outrageous value and so the assumptions need to be revisited. In addition, this step determines a basis of comparison with external solutions.

4. Value with internal improvements and disposals

This step adds the possibility of asset sales. For portfolio companies, this is routine. For other companies, it is a useful discipline to incorporate asset sales into the strategic thinking. Companies should consider the sale value of defined subsidiaries and business units, for example, not with a view of selling necessarily, but to gain insight on the potential for value creation. For example, if a business unit is valued highly by third parties because of untapped performance potential, then the internal strategy should be revisited. If it is valued highly due to synergies, then perhaps mergers or acquisitions should be considered.

In addition to considering defined subsidiaries and business units, the company should also consider businesses that *could* be separated, or other assets that could be worth more to others, such as real estate or intellectual property (IP). Again, this can reveal undervalued or underleveraged assets —it is useful to know the value whether or not these assets would really be candidates for sale.

5. Value with growth, internal improvements, and disposals

This step adds consideration of growth opportunities beyond the internal improvements in the earlier step, including new products, new markets, acquisitions and partnerships. The M&A strategy determined in Chapter 5 and the representative targets screened in Chapter 6 provide the solutions that can be considered. Put in this context, however, adds the portfolio manager's perspective to the acquisition options. That is, considering the value others may place in some businesses or assets of the company can shed new light on what assets should form the base for future growth versus assets that may ultimately be better developed by others. This can sharpen the M&A strategy as well as the internal growth strategy.

6. Total potential value

The optimal value is obtained by choosing the combination of internal and external solutions that yield the highest total value and optimizing the capital structure, the final step being the financial engineering. The gap between the step 1 and step 6 of McKinsey's Restructuring Hexagon is the full opportunity for value creation.

The application here has been to provide management of the integrated or single-business company the dispassionate perspective of the portfolio manager. You don't have to do what the portfolio manager would do, but knowing can yield valuable insights into strategies and options that you may not have considered otherwise.

Effective acquirers will look at a variety of means to improve performance, including internal means (organic growth, organization change, and business performance improvement) and external means (acquisitions, partnerships, and divestitures of company units or assets). Divestitures are particularly common for raiders—short-term investors without ambitions to operate companies.[13] However, every company should at least examine its divestiture opportunities from time to time because many become holding companies by accident.

Could you elaborate on the concept of the "accidental holding company"?

An accidental holding company is a company that, after a period of growth (whether from internal organic development or through acquisitions) finds itself with some separable businesses, even though the intention had been the development of an integrated business.

The history of railways in North America provides a good example. As the railways first sprawled across North America, it was natural that they would provide freight and passenger transportation, plus lodging at key destinations. Decades later they found themselves in three different and separable businesses—freight transportation, passenger transportation, and hotel management. The passenger businesses needed cross-country integration and public subsidies, so they were restructured into Amtrak in the United States and VIA Rail in Canada. The hotels were eventually sold. For example, the Fairmont Hotels chain, now operating such landmark hotels as the Plaza in New York, the Savoy in London, the Royal York Hotel in Toronto, and, of course, the Fairmont in San Francisco, was spun off from Canadian Pacific Limited (CPR's holding company) in 2001.[14]

How would you define a "separable asset" and how common are they?

A separable asset is a company division or asset (product or service) that can be removed from the company without harming the operations or reputation of the company and that would have value to a buyer. In fact, many companies develop separable businesses as they grow. More often than not, they recognize the need to organize them into separate units. However, they are usually reluctant to consider the option to spin off such assets, as were the railways, and as a result fail to recognize the potential value of these assets and fail to grow and develop them fully.

Another kind of business that sometimes becomes separable is the business defined by a product. For example, a media company that has developed a new magazine can separate the magazine's operations and sell the magazine as a business to another media company.

Less obvious as separable assets are outsourcing opportunities. The transfer of functions to a third-party supplier is, in effect, a divestiture. Outsourcing contracts of IT or back-office functions often include a valuation of the assets, employees, and processes that are transferred.

Everything should be "on the table" when looking at value maximization of the company. Identifying separable assets, even when those assets are not actually for sale, will often yield insights into the potential value that an outsider would see. You may have reasons to hold onto such assets, but this exercise puts those reasons to the test—keeping them must be of greater value than they would be worth in others' hands.

Should every asset be for sale?

In theory, if selling maximizes value then it should be considered. At the asset level, considering all assets as salable can change how they are managed, usually for the better. This was the trend in the early 1990s when an activity known generally as corporate restructuring became widespread as a response to low stock valuations that made many public companies vulnerable to hostile takeovers. Typically, a company that became an acquisition target, or feared that it might, would take a raider's perspective to identify assets that could be sold, either immediately or following some improvement. Immediate sales would give cash to the company and enable it to buy back stock, decreasing its exposure to takeover. When improvements were longer term, the improvement plans could be used to appeal to shareholders to withhold their shares in the event of a tender offer.[15] Notwithstanding the value of the exercise as a defensive strategy, most companies that undertook to restructure in this way became more tightly focused, improved their financial returns, and were better positioned for growth, all to the benefit of shareholders.

So at least *considering* how assets would be valued by an alternate owner is a valuable exercise for every asset. There are many considerations before a sale decision though. In some cases the asset may be vital to the company or its future. Are you sure you understand the long-term value of the asset to the business? Are there synergies with the core business that will be lost? Are there valuable real options that would be lost?

Should every company be open to takeover?

Again, in theory, yes. If the sale value is higher than the value the company *can* achieve by remaining independent, then sale should be considered. However, too many companies are let go for a premium over value as is, without adequate consideration for potential value.

The famous "Revlon doctrine," generally applied to public companies, established the principle that a board must consider an attractive offer. This has been in the Delaware courts since the chief justice of the Delaware Supreme Court pounded the gavel in *Revlon, Inc. v. MacAndrews & Forbes Holdings, Inc.*, 506 A.2d 173 (Del. 1986). But nothing is simple in corporate law, and since the days of Revlon a number of exceptions to the rule have arisen. The Revlon doctrine only comes into place once the company is itself "in play." It is not tantamount to a doctrine that would force a sale in any and all cases to the highest bidder. As Steven Radin points out in his 2,000-page tome on the business judgment rule, there are a number of scenarios in which the board may be justified in refusing to sell to a bidder even though its bid is high.[16]

For privately held companies, the Revlon doctrine is moot. However, owners should be open to sale at values greater than can be achieved on their own. Certainly, most private equity firms understand this. Owners of family-owned or owner-operated firms have the right to refuse any offer for nonfinancial reasons, but they may pay a price in value.

The question really comes down to timing. On the one hand, consider that virtually every company will ultimately be sold in whole or in parts in the long run. Of the *Fortune* 500, only 62 companies have appeared on the list every year since the magazine began publishing it in 1955. Another 1,952 have come and gone—71 of them in past two years alone. In a little more than half a century, 88 percent of what were the largest companies were gone from the original list: acquired, broken up, or shrunken. So in one sense it is not a question of if but when. For many leaders *when* is after they themselves are gone; for others it is how they intend to cash out—not necessarily in the best interests of the company in either case.

Taking a cue from the portfolio companies, the exit strategy should be considered even if there is no intention to sell in the short term. Considering the exit strategy can lead to good questions about how to maximize value. Every company that considers exit can then consider the optimal time and circumstances, and how to get to the optimal position and performance. In most cases, consideration of exit will result in more aggressive growth plans. Once a company determines that a strategic partner (i.e., a merger or sale) is necessary, ultimately, it might accelerate growth and performance improvement programs so that the company could be positioned well for a desirable partner.

On the other hand, most companies sell too early or cede industry leadership to a more ambitious competitor. More often than not, there is more value created in corporate growth than in invention and early-stage development. For example, when it comes to intellectual property, patents are valuable, but it is what a company does about its patents that determines long-term success. Part of the power of Thomas A. Edison was that he was not only in the laboratory inventing things, but he was also in the boardroom leveraging them.[17] So his legacy is not only the light bulb but also in General Electric.

For mature companies in restructuring industries, there is yet more value created by industry leaders. Companies like Xstrata in mining, InBev in brewing, Kraft in consumer goods, Manulife in financial services, and Thomson Reuters in information services have all created more value than all the companies that sold to them combined.

Not every company can come out on top—there must be buyers and sellers—but every company should evaluate the buyer/consolidator option as well as the exit option and then weigh the returns against their competencies; the ambition of the company, its board, and its shareholders; the risks of trying and failing; the risk of selling too late; and the opportunity cost of selling too early.

WEIGHING THE OPTIONS

How can a company determine its minimum sale price?

This is a good question because one of the reasons companies sell too early is that they don't know what they're worth. They look for a premium over market value or intrinsic value, typically. Sometimes they also account for internal improvements and disclose improvement plans, expecting something for the value in the plans.

The minimum sale value should be the optimal value adjusted for risk, incorporating internal and external improvements, and including the value of real options, but all suitably discounted given that none of this is guaranteed. Selling for less fails the shareholders of the seller.

One might argue that buyers are unlikely to pay for all that. In fact, the buyers should not pay for all that and should likely not consider an acquisition unless they bring some additional value as buyers. Additional value could come in the form of better skills to execute on the internal improvements, new external solutions, revenue or cost synergies between the businesses, needed capital, or new real options. If the buyer brings no additional value then a deal is unlikely to create new value. In this case, it is a zero-sum negotiating game, and the buyer can only win at the expense of the seller and vice versa. The would-be seller should be realistic about the value of its growth strategy. If it is only a dream, it is not worth much to the seller or to the buyer.

Capitalizing on the potential value of a realistic growth strategy requires resisting the temptation to sell along the way for what can appear to be an attractive premium over market value. For example, BMO Financial of Montreal held onto Harris Bank of Chicago from its acquisition in 1984 through the most heated years of U.S. bank consolidation. BMO would have been approached many times by U.S. consolidators. However, by holding the asset BMO held a valuable real option to grow its position in the United States off the base of Harris Bank. Eventually, it acquired the Diner's Club International franchise in North America from Citibank in 2009 when credit markets were still spooked by the financial crisis of the previous two years. In 2010, BMO acquired Marshall & Ilsley Corporation and merged it with Harris Bank, creating a Midwest leader ranking 22nd in the United States with over $120 billion in combined assets.[18] The value potential of BMO's U.S. strategy far exceeds the premiums that would have been offered for Harris alone.

How should the value of the acquirer's stock be assessed when the acquirer uses it to pay for the deal?

Acquisitions are often paid for with a combination of cash and stock. The ultimate test that there is truly value in the deal is for the seller to consider the value of the acquirer's stock as a currency in the transaction. Considering that about half of all deals depress the acquirer's stock relative to industry indexes, sellers should be very wary of the acquirer's stock as currency.

The only way the acquirer's stock is worth its current market value (or more) is if the deal logic creates value in excess of the price of the deal and if the deal logic is implemented well and in a timely fashion. However, as noted earlier, about half of major deals result in the relative decline of the acquirer's stock in the two to three years following the deal.[19] In many cases it has declined by as much as the former value of the acquired company, so sellers who thought they had sold at a premium actually sold at a discount when the merger was properly assessed by the market in the fullness of time. (Of course, some short-term investors can get out before the postdeal management reveals the true value, but that's not the point.) Such results explain why transactions financed by cash, including borrowed cash, tend to do better than those financed by stock.[20] Stock-based transactions fail everyone unless the stock appreciates in value, which usually means that the deal helped create value for the buyer as well as the seller.

Is it only the price that matters?

To shareholders with an extremely short-term perspective (such as day traders), price is all that matters. However, for other shareholders (such as company employees or pension funds), and for the long-term interests of the corporation, the most important factor is whether or not the deal will ultimately create value. The deal logic and the ability of the combined companies to implement the deal logic are more important than the price.

While the price of the deal sets the bar, the implementation of a value-creating strategy determines whether the deal will fall short or exceed the potential paid for in the price.

In an all cash deal, it is easier to argue that the directors of the seller can "wash their hands" of it. However, in many jurisdictions boards can be taken to task for lining the pockets of directors and shareholders while failing to act in the interests of the corporation. For example, in one case last decade (the parties are confidential as part of the terms of an out-of-court settlement), directors of the selling company were held partially liable for including a strategy in the prospectus that ultimately did not succeed in the hands of the buyer. A more recent example is when NewAlliance Bancshares, Inc. (NYSE:NAL) and First Niagara Financial Group, Inc. (Nasdaq:FNFG) announced a merger agreement in August 2010. The proposed deal drew criticism from John DeStefano, mayor of New Haven, Connecticut, concerned about losing a major employer in the city. Ten lawsuits were filed, including one that alleged, "CEO Patterson stands to gain over $33.8 million from the transaction," and asserting, "the proposed acquisition is . . . the product of a flawed sales process not designed to maximize the value of the Company's shares to stockholders, and does not appear to represent the best strategic alternative going forward for the Company."[21] The lawsuits did not succeed in stopping the merger, which closed in April 2011. However, the plaintiffs did succeed in obtaining an out-of-court settlement to repay their legal expenses, indicating that these lawsuits were not considered frivolous.

The sale of a company can affect many stakeholders in addition to stockholders—employees, bondholders, communities, and even the general public. Other stakeholders can and should be considered. Indeed, in the United States, many states have laws referred to as other constituency statutes that protect the right of a board of directors to consider nonshareholder constituencies when responding to a merger offer. (See Chapter 8 on the role of the board in M&A.)

But even aside from the interests of these other constituencies, one reason to consider the broader impacts of a transaction is to preserve the value promised to shareholders in the deal. Most fundamentally, ignoring the interests of any stakeholder group can backfire on shareholders, as all stakeholders contribute value to the enterprise. In addition, there may be legal reasons to consider other stakeholders. For example, companies that have acquired in France intending to implement cost synergies through downsizing the workforce have discovered that French labor laws make this very difficult. Acquirers in that country would be well advised to create a postmerger employment plan that can withstand regulatory scrutiny.

Yet another reason to consider all stakeholders is the growing power of social media. Brands and stock value can be quickly damaged when rumors fly. Social media can accelerate and broaden the rumor mill exponentially. The comment function on news stories is used increasingly, for example, but more powerful are the individuals or groups who create websites and social media campaigns opposing the merger and encouraging others to comment.[22]

Consideration of stakeholders can extend to an entire industry. In 2011, the shareholders of the Toronto Stock Exchange (TSE) were ultimately turned against a financially attractive acquisition offer from the London Stock Exchange (LSE), at least in part over concerns of long-term impact on Canadian capital markets. The TSE owner, TMX Group, said it would pay a $10.3 million termination fee to the LSE, and a further $29.8 million if the acquisition with Maple (a more stakeholder-friendly rival offer) goes through within 12 months.[23] So the cost of accepting a deal proposal without appropriate consideration of stakeholder interests can be high.

How does the company find/attract the best buyer and the maximum value for an asset?

Chapter 6 defines a process the acquirers can use for M&A search, screening, and selection. That process applies equally to sellers in search of a buyer. For example, such a process was used for the disposition of assets during the restructuring of one of the major pulp and paper companies. A strategic assessment of the asset portfolio determined that various downstream manufacturing and distribution businesses were not core and could be worth more in others' hands. There were several separable businesses worth well over $1 billion in total. An auction of these businesses would have been quick and easy but would have resulted in significant discounting.

Instead, for each business the company undertook a search for the best buyer. Financial buyers were considered, but the search also identified many buyers that were in similar or adjacent businesses to the businesses for sale. Applying the analyses of attractiveness of the target and probability of a deal (as outlined in Chapter 6), the field was narrowed to the best partners. Before the potential buyers were approached, the company outlined the deal logic from the buyer's perspective and was able to estimate the value of revenue and cost synergies.

Ultimately, these businesses were all sold to buyers with whom there were synergies, some of whom were not looking and would not have considered such an acquisition had they not been approached. In all cases, the deals closed at prices in excess of market or intrinsic value.

In a restructuring industry, should you be a buyer or a seller?

As noted earlier, the market rewards growth, and successful acquirers in a restructuring industry will usually create more value than the sellers. However, not all that choose to be the leaders are successful. For example, it was noted in Chapter 2 that, on average, the buyers in the U.S. bank consolidation have destroyed value. The choice to be a buyer or a seller and the timing of a purchase or sale should all be determined to maximize value. The wise buyer retains the option to become a seller, and vice versa.

For some companies, the appropriate role is to drive the consolidation or industry restructuring, in which case they become a serial acquirer. To step into the role of consolidator/industry restructurer, a company must have both skill and will. You must take a realistic look at the competencies required to undertake multiple acquisitions—search, company analysis, relationship development, negotiations, regulator management, public relations, deal structuring, due diligence, and postmerger integration, to name a few. In a restructuring industry it is not merely a question of competence, but a question of competitiveness. Are your skills in these areas superior to those of others with whom you will be competing in this new arena—not only in the arena of your products, markets, and manufacturing in which you have been competing successfully, but also in the arena of M&A? (See Chapter 12 for a full discussion of the core competencies of the serial acquirer.)

The wills of management, the board, and shareholders are also major factors. No successful M&A program occurs without an ambitious management team. The board must be willing to accept the risks and to put in the extraordinary time required to do major deals—the board is pushed to the front line on major deals, as we'll discuss more fully in the next chapter. Finally, you need the support of the major shareholders and the capital markets more generally. The ability to raise capital quickly is an important advantage in these situations, so the capital markets must also share your ambition.

To assess the skill and will, compare with competitors internationally. Anyone considering a role in the global restructuring of the brewing industry, for example, faces InBev Brewing, SABMiller, Heineken, and other very experienced acquirers that can likely achieve cost and revenue synergies with many of the same remaining targets. While these may or may not be important competitors in the local beer market or segment of interest, they will be competitors in the market for corporate control.

Selling well also requires skill and can create significant incremental value. For example, the major shareholders of Falconbridge, Hees International Bancorp, chose to sell Falconbridge from the start, not to pursue a role as consolidator. Their timing was superb. Years of effort had paid off in the improved efficiency of the company, nickel prices were high, and the industry was ripe for consolidation. And Falconbridge worked with at least two attractive and ambitious potential buyers: INCO and Xstrata.

In its bid for Falconbridge, INCO was up against a much more experienced acquirer in Xstrata. Xstrata had the experience and competence to bid aggressively, even though INCO had a wealth of physical synergies with Falconbridge. INCO was delayed by French regulators that dragged on the assessment of competition issues related to a relatively small part of the business, while Xstrata, a Swiss company, negotiated fast track approval with Canadian regulators. Finally, Brazil's Vale launched a hostile bid that ultimately took out INCO. So while the synergies of such an INCO–Falconbridge merger would likely have far exceeded the premiums paid by Xstrata for Falconbridge, Xstrata won in the market for corporate control. (And with the subsequent rise in nickel prices, earned back the deal premium quickly.)

Do you have to choose? What about "mergers of equals"?

Merger of equals is a somewhat misunderstood and misused term. Technically, the shareholders of one company must surrender their stock for the deal to take place, so they are the sellers. The premium over book value is accounted for as "good will" on the books of the surviving company and amortized over time.

Until 2000, many acquirers in the United States were permitted to merge by pooling their accounts rather than treating the transaction as a straightforward purchase. However, the widespread use of pooling in large deals was a contributing factor in the poor performance of U.S. acquisitions.[24] The omission of amortization of good will from earnings under pooling made it easier to get deals approved by the boards and shareholders and removed a blatant reminder of the responsibility of management to achieve performance improvements greater than the premium paid. Pooling was "the Diet Coke of business-combination accounting. It tastes good and reminds you of the original without the unpleasant calories."[25] Changes in accounting guidelines in 2000 effectively eliminated pooling accounting.[26]

What are left are "mergers of equals" in name only. There is a well-intended desire on the part of management that the acquired company's management and employees feel a part of the new company and not the victims, partly to lower retention risks. However, this often has unintended consequences, slowing down the implementation of the deal logic. For example, some of the mergers of equals have been burdened with a "Noah's Ark" approach to the new organization—two of each, from co-CEOs on down. Such an approach slows down the process, and it often makes the management look foolish to employees and the market.

The proof is in the pudding. Hostile takeovers, where there can be no doubt of who is the buyer and who is the seller, tend to perform better for shareholders.[27] Rather than dressing up a deal as a merger of equals, with co-CEOs and slow implementation, it is far better to get on with the job of postdeal implementation, assessing everyone on their own merits and treating everyone with respect. Ultimately, you need to build a new organization and a new culture for the new firm—make it the best it can be, and retention of the best people will not be an issue.

STAYING IN CONTROL

If you choose to be a buyer in a restructuring industry, how do you stay on the buy side?

The best defense is a good offense; maximizing value, including being a buyer. However, integration is a key—sloppy or slow integration makes a buyer a target by lowering performance and stock price and leaving easy performance improvement opportunities on the table.

In addition, anti-takeover defenses can be used to discourage unwanted takeovers. Anti-takeover defenses are mechanisms or structures that allow a company to slow down, block, or increase the cost of hostile takeover attempts. There are three types of anti-takeover defenses:

- Pre-bid defenses are designed to discourage unwanted approaches.
- Postbid defenses are designed to help the would-be target deal with a potentially undesirable bid.
- Regulatory defenses are government policies that restrict unwanted acquisitions.

How do pre-bid defenses work?

The most common and efficient pre-bid defenses[28] disconnect ownership and control or prevent access to a significant share of capital. For example, dual-class shares are allowed in some markets, such as Canada. Typically, the voting shares are tightly held, and the common shares available on the market have limited voting rights. Variations are multiple voting shares and subordinate voting shares. In each case, for those that control the vote, even though they might not hold the majority of the company's shares, they have the ability to reject unwanted offers.

Other options include staggered boards and share transfer restrictions. Staggered boards for which, say, only one third of the board is up for election each year can also act as a defense. Such a structure prevents shareholders, even majority shareholders, from replacing the board with friendly directors. This can make the takeover process slow and unattractive. A slight majority of US public company boards have staggered elections.[29] Share transfer restrictions in the company's articles can restrict shareholder responses to bids or require shareholders to hold other shares (known as cross-holdings). Securities laws in some jurisdictions prevent some of these structures. Some companies choose to incorporate and market their shares in jurisdictions that are unfavorable to unwanted takeovers. A majority of US states today have anti-takeover laws.

What if an unwanted offer is nevertheless made to shareholders?

Postbid defenses are exercised once a company is subject to an offer. At this point the board of directors has the responsibility to respond, and they may have some tools to block unwanted advances. For example, many companies have put in place shareholder rights plans, commonly known as poison pills, that give the board the ability to multiply the shares outstanding. In the event of an undesirable offer, the board can invoke the rights plan to issue shares to existing shareholders, effectively making the cost of the deal prohibitive. Such plans must be approved in advance by shareholders, who usually agree because such plans result in higher prices paid in the event of a deal. In the United States, about 35 percent of S&P 500 companies have such plans.[30] Some securities regulators have placed restrictions on rights plans.

Another postbid defense available in some jurisdictions is the "just say no" defense. In the United States, for example, there is legal precedent in support of the board's right to say no to an offer without going to shareholders. For example, when the aluminum industry was consolidating in the last decade, America's Alcoa said no. This right was further protected by State of Delaware legislation by which the state must approve takeovers. Bidders instead surrounded Alcan—Alcan being in Canada where takeover legislation is weak and where at that point the just say no defense had no precedent. Note that even in jurisdictions with legal precedent, directors may be subject to civil action by shareholders so they must have a sound reason for rejecting an offer. Such reason may be that they know a better plan, as noted earlier—again, the best defense is a good offense.

Boards may also act to find a better transaction than the one offered. For example, they may bring a more desirable partner into the bidding, a "white knight." JPMorgan Chase was considered a white knight for Bear Stearns when the latter was vulnerable to hostile takeover (or insolvency) in the early days of the credit crisis. Another defense is to acquire the buyer, known as the Pac-Man defense. For example, when Bendix Corporation attempted to acquire Martin Marietta in 1982, Martin Marietta defended itself by purchasing Bendix stock and sought a white knight in Allied Corporation.[31]

Again, such actions require an advanced understanding of the strategy, its value, and potential partners. Such takeover defenses are not always thought to be in the best interest of shareholders and can be challenged, so even with such defenses available, it is important to know that Plan A, without the uninvited guest, maximizes value in the long run.

What is the role of the regulator in defense?

It pays to know the regulations and to make the regulator your friend. As noted earlier, securities law and takeover legislation can significantly affect the vulnerability of public companies to unwanted offers. Some jurisdictions have opted to remove or reduce the effectiveness of the foregoing defenses, whereas others have acted to protect local companies from takeover. The differences in the approach reflect different views on the respective roles of the board versus the shareholders and on the role of the state in change of control transactions.

In addition, governments and regulators review large transactions that may affect the public good. For example, most jurisdictions review how potential deals may affect the level of competition within an industry (e.g., whether the deal will reduce competition to the detriment of suppliers or customers). Some jurisdictions also act to maintain headquarters locally (e.g., Australia with respect to the BHP–Billiton deal) or to keep selected strategic assets under local control (e.g., the U.S. rebuff of foreign interest in select sea ports). See Chapter 9 for further discussion of takeover legislation in key international jurisdictions.

While state and national policy can restrict takeovers, this "crutch" can also overprotect companies that should be participating in the restructuring of their respective industries. For example, state banking law kept the U.S. banks small and inefficient for many years and was a contributing cause of the high rate of bank failures. More recently, Canada has been struggling with how to open up the telecommunications industry[32]—protecting the industry for decades resulted in small companies uncompetitive on a global scale, but lifting the protection now would make them easy takeover targets.

Moreover, defensive measures by the corporation, regulators, or government can be constructive short-term measures. However, companies should be taking a long view of the industry and their role in it and should be building sustainable scale, scope, and skills or planning their exit, irrespective of available defenses.

Endnotes

1. BlackBerry's launch date was May 4, 1999. See "RIM Announces New Inter@ctive Pager for American Mobile's eLink Wireless Email Service," May 4, 1999, Waterloo, Ontario. http://us.BlackBerry.com/newsroom/news/press/release.jsp?id=702.
2. Research in Motion, 2006 Annual Report; share as reported by Gartner Group.
3. Matt Hartley, "Apple Tops Global Smartphone Rankings, RIM Slides to No. 4," *Financial Post*, August 5, 2011.
4. Research in Motion, 2010 Annual Report.
5. Research in Motion report in the *Global and Mail* website, http://www.theglobeandmail.com/globe-investor/markets/stocks/chart/?q=rim-T.
6. "Letter to Shareholders," Berkshire Hathaway Inc., 2009 Annual Report.
7. "General Electric Company Mergers & Acquisitions." Accessed July 2, 2011, http://www.alacrastore.com/mergers-acquisitions/General_Electric_Company-1006912.
8. NBCUniversal was created when GE under CEO Jeff Immelt combined the legacy NBC (from the 1930 acquisition of RCA) with the more recent 2004 acquisition of Universal. For more history, see "Grading Jeff Immelt," http://management.fortune.cnn.com/2011/02/10/grading-jeff-immelt/stteci.
9. "News Corporation Mergers & Acquisitions." Accessed July 2, 2011, http://www.alacrastore.com/mergers-acquisitions/News_Corporation-1012065.
10. In March 2009, Time Warner Cable was divested from the company in a spin-out. Time Warner Inc. (2009, March 20). "Time Warner Inc. Announces Final Distribution Ratio for Spin-off of Time Warner Cable Inc." Press Releases. March 20, 2009, http://www.timewarner.com/newsroom/press-releases/2009/03/Time_Warner_Inc_Announces_Final_Distribution_Ratio_03-20-2009.php. On February 23, 2006, Turner South, a regional sports and entertainment network in the South, was sold to News Corp's Fox Cable Networks group. The network later became SportSouth. Joe Flint, "News Corp. Buys Turner South For $375 Million," *Wall Street Journal*, February 24, 2006, http://online.wsj.com/article/SB114074230282382000.html?mod=todays_us_marketplace. In the fall of 2006, the Atlanta Braves were sold to Liberty Media in a deal that returned vast amounts of Liberty-owned Time Warner stock back into the company's folds. This sale was made official on May 17, 2007. Matt Woolsey, "Time Warner Divests Atlanta Braves," *Forbes*, February 13, 2007, http://www.forbes.com/2007/02/13/timewarner-braves-update-markets-equity-cx_mw_0213markets08.html. On March 31, 2006, Time Warner sold the Time Warner Book Group to French publisher Hachette Livre, of the Lagardere group. Hachette Book Group USA, Company History, 2010, accessed August 16, 2011, http://www.hachettebookgroupusa.com/about_company-history.aspx.
11. Tom Copeland, Tim Koller, and Jack Murrin, *Valuation: Measuring and Managing the Value of Companies* (New York: John Wiley & Sons, 1990). This book is now in its fifth edition, with the McKinsey firm as its main author. The

Restructuring Hexagon can be found in later editions or see "Pre-empting Hostile Takeovers," by Jenny Askfelt Ruud, Johan Näs, and Vincenzo Tortorici in *McKinsey on Finance,* accessed October 16, 2011, http://corporatefinance.mckinsey.com/_downloads/knowledge/mckinsey_on_finance/MoF_Issue_24.pdf.

12. Use of current stock price includes a future valuation because the price that investors pay includes their own view of the company's future. See Alfred Rappaport and Michael J. Mauboussin, *Expectations Investing: Reading Stock Prices for Bettter Returns* (Boston, MA: Harvard Business School Press, 2001). For a current guide to stock price behavior, see "Valuation Based on Stock Price," in Robert A. G. Monks and Alexandra R. Lajoux, *Corporate Valuation for Portfolio Investment: Analyzing Assets, Earnings, Cash Flow, Stock Price, Governance, and Special Situati*ons (Hoboken, NJ: John Wiley & Sons, 2011), chap. 5.
13. The valuation approach described in this chapter is sometimes called, for dramatic effect, the raider's perspective. However, in real life, raiders rarely make long-term improvements to an operating company. For these investors, also called vulture investors, patience is short and nothing is sacred, and full or near liquidation of assets may result (hence the term *raid*).
14. *CBC News*, August 20, 2001, www.cbc.ca/news/business/story/2001/08/20/cp200801.html. (Note that, while CPR may have started as an accidental holding company, CP Limited went on to make many acquisitions in a range of industries. The point here is simply to illustrate how single-business companies can find themselves with separable, saleable assets.)
15. The authors both have experience in this regard. Ken Smith was an advisor to companies during this period, and Alexandra Lajoux conducted extensive research for *Corporate Restructuring* newsletter (no longer published by MLR Holdings LLC of Philadelphia).
16. Steven Radin, *The Business Judgment Rule: Fiduciary Duties of Corporate Officers*, 6th ed. (New York: Walter Kluwer Law and Business, 2009).
17. Julie L. Davis and Suzanne Harrison, *Edison in the Boardroom: How Leading Companies Realize Value from Their Intellectual Assets* (New York: John Wiley, 2001); Suzanne Harrison and Patrick Sullivan, *Edison in the Boardroom Again* (Hoboken, NJ: John Wiley, 2012).
18. Federal Reserve Board, National Information Center, "Bank Holding Company Ranking by Assets," June 30, 2011, https://www4.harrisbank.com/spopup/0,4535,129778_7009715,00.html.
19. See Appendix to Part I.
20. The superiority of debt-financed acquisitions was established in a classic article by T. Loughran and A. M. Vijh, "Do Long-Term Shareholders Benefit from Corporate Acquisitions?" *Journal of Finance* 52, 1765(1790), 1997. For a discussion of this article in a broader context, see Ching Chieh Chang, "An Investment-based Explanation for the Post-merger Underperformance Puzzle," January 22, 2011.

http://www.efmaefm.org/0EFMAMEETINGS/EFMA%20ANNUAL%20 MEETINGS/2011-Braga/papers/0028.pdf. Foster School of Business, PACCAR Hall, Box 353226, 4295 E. Stevens Way NE, Room 431, Seattle, WA 98195. E-mail: ccchang@uw.edu.

21. New Alliance Bancshares, Inc, "Investor Files Lawsuit against Buyout," http://shareholdersfoundation.com/case/newalliance-bancshares-inc-investor-files-lawsuit-against-buyout. The investor was the Port Authority of Allegheny County Retirement and Disability Allowance Plan for Employees Represented by Local 85 of the Amalgamated Transit Union, accessed July 4, 2011, http://www.barrack.com/brb-files-lawsuit-for-newalliance-bancshares-stockholders.html.
22. See, for example, the Web site for Stop the T-Mobile/AT&T Merger, accessed July 4, 2011, http://www.stopthismerger.com/opinion/201103220307/why-do-you-oppose-the-merger/#comment-112.
23. Associated Press, June 29, 2011.
24. In *White Squalls in 'Pools of Interest'*, Yang Liu and Ken Smith (one of the authors of this book) analyze the impact of pooling on deal success. It turns out that in the decade leading up to the review, 26 percent of $1 billion transactions in the United States were using pooling accounting. Among these, only 24 percent of transactions resulted in shareholder value creation above industry, while 52 percent of all other large deals were successful in generating superior returns. See Yang Liu and Kenneth W. Smith, *White Squals in Pools of Interest* (Montreal/Toronto: Federated Press, 1999).
25. Ibid.
26. The Financial Accounting Standards Board (FASB) confirmed ruling to eliminate pooling-of-interest accounting in a statement January 24, 2001, www.fasb.org/news/nr012401.shtml.
27. See Appendix to Part I.
28. "Winning in the Market for Corporate Control." SECOR Consulting submission to the 2007 federal panel on Canadian Competitiveness.
29. According to the *2011 NACD Public Company Governance Sur*vey (Washington, DC: 2011), 51 percent of boards have staggered elections and 49 percent have annual elections.
30. Ibid.
31. See, for example, "Corporate Takeover Defense: A Shareholder's Perspective," http://www.investopedia.com/articles/stocks/08/corporate-takeover-defense.asp#axzz1VEVtZjk7.
32. Consultation launched by Industry Canada in 2010 as outlined in "Opening Canada's Doors to Foreign Investment in Telecommunications: Options for Reform," accessed October 16, 2011, http://www.ic.gc.ca/eic/site/smt-gst.nsf/vwapj/TelecomInvestment-eng.pdf/$file/TelecomInvestment-eng.pdf.

CHAPTER 8

The Director's Role in M&A

I hear and I forget. I see and I remember. I do and I understand.

—*Confucius*

While boards are responsible for reviewing and approving strategic plans and for making strategic decisions, in most cases the formulation of plans and strategies is the role of management. However, major deals put directors on the front line. In the case of a takeover offer, in particular, it is the board that must consider and respond to the offer, engaging shareholders, management, and other stakeholders as appropriate. Even when on the buy side, major M&A decisions require board and sometimes shareholder approval. The stakes and risks involved put these decisions at the top of the agenda and require careful consideration.[1]

Notwithstanding the requirements for direct board involvement in major deals, the failure rates are high, and many boards aren't helping. On the buy side, few deals proposed by management are turned down. Turning down a major deal proposal of the CEO is regarded as a vote of nonconfidence and is often followed by the departure of the CEO.

On the sell side, unless boards are supported in their company's state of incorporation by anti-takeover legislation or a clear judicial pattern respecting board decision making, the response to takeover offers involving a good premium on the market value is typically a negotiation or an auction. That gets the best result in the moment, but it is hardly strategic.

It seems that directors all too often have a merely neutral impact on M&A decisions. At worst, the directors who view their role principally as risk managers may be inclined to dampen the ambition required of leading companies in a restructuring industry. And many lack the courage to say no to a good offer and are inclined to sell too early in the company's development, sometimes justifiably concerned about shareholder lawsuits in the absence of a clear plan of superior value to the offer on the table.

A CHALLENGING ROLE FOR DIRECTORS

Why are directors not more effective in M&A decisions?

Board members, just like the CEOs and managers involved, are generally doing their best to serve the interests of the corporation, at times under difficult circumstances. However, large deals present extraordinary decision challenges, just when the stakes are the highest.

Loss of Objectivity

The CEO, senior management, and directors can lose some objectivity as they progress through various stages of the deal. While they may be objective initially, as a deal moves closer to being a real possibility it is natural for them to get excited—about running a much larger business, about the admiration of their peers, about their legacy, and even about the likelihood of increased compensation. Few deal proponents will admit publicly that personal compensation is a driving force; after all, as fiduciaries directors and officers must put the firm's interest ahead of their own. But the strong correlation between company size and compensation is hard to ignore. Ultimately, management and directors can "fall in love" with a deal and see only its beauty and none of its weaknesses. And the closer it gets, the more difficult it becomes to contemplate the loss of face and the effort that will have been wasted if the decision is ultimately "no-go."

To make matters worse, outside advisors have their own motivations, which may come into play to varying degrees. Investment bankers may have invested heavily in the creation of the opportunity, the valuation, the structure of the deal, or the negotiation, and they may be driven to keep the deal alive to continue receiving compensation; those who are paid in part or in whole on contingency may want to close the deal in order to recover fees for all the work they have done. Accountants and lawyers stand to gain substantial work for their firms if the deal proceeds, or they may simply wish to please their client and will defer the business decision to management.

Insufficient Knowledge

Most boards have a wide representation of valuable skills and backgrounds. However, due in part to the push for board independence,[2] as well as antitrust laws in some highly regulated industries, there are generally only a few directors who deeply understand the industry sectors of the companies they serve, leaving most directors dependent on management for the interpretation of the business environment. While directors can and do use independent advisors, there are natural barriers to this arrangement.[3]

While many boards today engage in developing the company strategy, discussions may not be in depth and some directors may have only a superficial understanding of it. On some boards, the strategy gets presented in a lengthy PowerPoint document, and directors ask only a few questions.

By the time the board is faced with making a decision on a possible acquisition, the management team has typically rallied behind the CEO in recommending the deal. Board members usually do not get the benefit of listening to dissenting views, and unless they request an independent study (which is rare), they are dependent on management's analysis of the opportunity.[4] Management, with the best of intentions, may have an incorrect view of the situation or may have lost perspective along the way.

Lack of Time

Unless the company is in crisis, most boards meet at predetermined dates chosen a long time in advance to ensure full board participation. Adding an additional board meeting at the last minute, given heavy director schedules, is difficult at best. For issues that arise between meetings, boards more often than not resort to conference calls, usually in the evenings. Clearly, this is not the best venue for an important decision, but on occasion an opportunity arises that requires a decision between meetings.

Even when acquisitions are discussed face to face at a regular board meeting, time and process are often lacking. The agenda of a normal board meeting has a number of predetermined items to cover, such as reviews of the financials and the operations, reports of the various committees of the board, and unavoidable consent agenda items, all of this reducing the amount of time available for nonroutine items. If the chair has committed to end on time or there are flights to catch, discussion of the pros and cons will be rushed, and a decision may be taken under time pressure.

Group Dynamics

Group dynamics can play a role in any board decision, but in the case of mergers, the role can be difficult to detect due to the relentless progress of the deal. If management has done its job properly, it will already have alerted the board to the possibility of this acquisition earlier in the year, and it will have sent advanced reading material outlining why this acquisition makes sense, presenting some of the risks, commenting on the alternatives, quantifying the impact on earnings per share, and outlining other relevant factors. At the meeting itself, the CEO will articulate once again why he or she believes this is right for the company, senior managers will come in to present their supporting views, and outside advisors will voice their support, putting directors in most cases in a reactive, questioning frame of mind.

It is not easy to object in these circumstances. As questions are answered and concerns are dealt with, some respected directors may start to voice their increasing comfort with the proposal. At that point, discussion will subtly shift from the "if" to the "when" and "how." As an implicit consensus is reached, it can feel inappropriate to raise direct objections. The remaining concerns are often expressed in the form of consenting cautions, such as: "If you proceed with this, you'd better make sure that . . . "

Surprises

All of the foregoing are exacerbated if the deal opportunity is a surprise. Generally, management will have alerted the board to possible acquisitions. However, at any given point, management may present opportunities that were not given serious consideration before. For example, an attractive but previously unattainable target may be forced into play by a hostile offer, or a controlling shareholder of a competitor may unexpectedly decide to sell. Conversely, an unexpected offer may come to acquire the company. Such deals must be considered, even if they were not in the plans and the time lines are not convenient. Good opportunities should not be ignored simply because they were not in the plan!

Are directors legally responsible for mergers?

Corporate directors have duties of care and loyalty under state law, and these duties apply to the merger context. (The overarching duty of good faith—basically meaning integrity—need not be discussed here.) The duty of care requires that directors be informed and exercise appropriate diligence and good faith as they make business decisions and otherwise fulfill their general oversight responsibilities. The duty of loyalty requires that directors act in the best interests of the corporation rather than in their own interests.

When reviewing plans to buy another company, sell a company unit, or merge with another company, the board needs to exercise proper oversight of management. The duty of care especially applies in issues of strategy, pricing, and compliance with various legal obligations such as disclosure obligations. The board also needs to exercise independence (duty of loyalty). It can do this by appointing a standing committee of the board composed entirely of independent directors to review a particular transaction.

In evaluating a particular transaction, directors should seek specific information about the price, timing, and certainty of the transaction and should be proactive in overseeing negotiations. Directors should understand how the transaction will be financed and the projected financial impact on the company under reasonably likely scenarios. Where the size of the transaction warrants it, directors should consider independent financial advice from outside experts together with management's financial assessment.

Directors should also obtain a high-level analysis of the merger documentation, including an understanding of the most important representations, covenants, and indemnities contained therein and their application to the company and the transaction. In addition, directors should receive input from market and investor relations experts about the best manner in which to position the transaction and the likely reception from investors and creditors. As with any other matter before them, directors should independently evaluate all the information they have obtained and arrive at an independent assessment instead of relying exclusively on management's views.

Directors should also be alert to the ways that the interests of management may differ from those of stockholders in negotiating a particular transaction—for example, who will continue to work for the merged company and with what responsibilities—while stockholders generally are not significantly concerned about such issues.[5]

Do boards have to sell to the highest bidder to meet their responsibility to shareholders?

Not necessarily. It is true, as noted in Chapter 7, that once the company is for sale, if the sale value is higher than the value the company can achieve by remaining independent, then sale must be considered, per *Revlon, Inc. v. MacAndrews & Forbes Holdings, Inc.*, 506 A.2d 173 (Del. 1986), which also emphasized getting the highest price for stockholders.

In July 1989, however, in the case of *Time Inc. v. Paramount Communications*, the Delaware Chancery Court ruled that Time should be allowed to proceed with its $14 billion acquisition of Warner despite a protest from would-be Time acquirer Paramount. Chancellor William T. Allen wrote the following:

> Clearly not every offer or transaction affecting the corporate structure invokes the Revlon duties [to sell to the highest bidder]. A refusal to entertain offers may comport with a valid exercise of business judgment. . . . Circumstances may dictate that an offer be rebuffed, given the nature and timing of the offer; its legality, feasibility and effect on the corporation and the stockholders; the alternatives available and their effect on the various constituencies, particularly the stockholders; *the company's long-term strategic plans*; and any special factors bearing on stockholder and public interests.[6] (Emphasis added.)

In defense of the Time board, Chancellor Allen wrote that the Time-approved transaction, "even though 'reactive' in important respects, has its origin and central purpose in *bona fide strategic business planning*, and not in questions of corporate control."[7] (Emphasis added.)

Later, Time Warner would go on to merge with AOL in a transaction that is still undergoing legal challenge.[8] Still, the Time Warner case from the Allen court clearly establishes the legal importance of having a sound strategic plan.

WHAT DIRECTORS NEED TO KNOW

How can boards be better prepared for their role in high-stakes M&A decisions?[9]

M&A decisions should be made in the context of the strategy, so having an effective role in M&A decisions must begin with an understanding of the industry context of the company, the strategic vision, the competitive strategy, and the role of M&A.

Responsible M&A decisions require more than just a superficial acquaintance with the industry context and strategy. Remember that the board in these circumstances is often directly responsible for the decision to be made. While directors can seek advice from management and external advisors, they may not have the time to learn enough to make an informed decision unless they have made a substantial investment in education in advance.

The board that is current on industry developments, understands the company's growth strategy, and has assessed the upside potential of both the growth and sale options will be in a better position to take control of a situation and assess the best value creation strategy, adjusted for risk.

What do boards need to know about a company's strategy? Are there implications for the skills needed on the board?

There are several levels of strategy that can be relevant to board decisions. Typically, boards focus on the overall corporate vision and long-term strategy. However, there can be more immediate strategic issues at each level right down to strategies for functions. As noted in Chapter 5, M&A can play a role at each level. Not only should directors understand the strategy at each level, but also, if they have suitable experience and are engaged in the process, they can bring valuable external perspectives to management's thinking.

What exactly do directors need to know about the strategic vision?

As noted in Chapter 5, the most useful strategic visions are not simply aspirational statements, but are based on the following:

- *A perspective on the future context for the industry and the company*: for example, how may the context be affected by changes in technology, regulation, globalization, industry (e.g., restructuring), or the actions of competitors?
- *Choice of the markets or arenas in which to compete*: that is, given the view of the future, where will the company compete; for example, in what geographies or market segments, or in what parts of the industry value chain?

- *The basis of the company's competitive advantage*: for example, what assets, market position, or competencies will provide the company with the ability to succeed in the chosen markets in the future?

These elements are clearly relevant to the key strategic choices of the company, including M&A decisions, so the board needs to understand them in order to have a constructive role in supporting the strategy. More than that, with their external perspective, directors can help ensure that the company's strategic vision is truly forward thinking yet realistic. If directors understand these elements, they will be in a much better position to understand deal proposals, to recognize good opportunities, and to support strategic imperatives.

What do directors need to know to oversee corporate strategy?

Some of the most important decisions and risks will be associated with how the company's industries may be restructuring and what role the company should play in the restructuring.

There are a variety of ways that industries can restructure as outlined in Part I of this book. The most familiar is consolidation, when like companies within a market merge, such as in the U.S. banking industry. Industries may also restructure along the value chain, either vertically integrating as the oil industry has from oil exploration to gasoline retailing, or disaggregating as the natural gas industry has into producers, pipelines, utilities, and retailers.

Finally, relevant to many industries today is restructuring related to globalization. Industries that were once defined by country borders are becoming global, and competitors have to either defend geographic niches or develop the scale and scope to compete internationally. Included among the players driving restructuring are the major sovereign wealth funds seeking to secure access to resources or to markets.

When an industry is restructuring, this is a major change in the future context for competitors. The required scale, scope, and skills to compete may change. The board needs to understand why and how the industry may restructure in order to assess the company's strategy in the right future context.

In such industries, the companies that do not acquire will often become targets. While sale premiums can be attractive, boards should also consider the value created by those that lead such restructurings. So, in the long-term interests of the corporation, directors need to be in front of such developments or they may eventually be faced with a sale and few options.

This requires an informed view on the industry and the company's development. The companies that lead industry restructurings start early, build skills and financial capacity, and establish a track record of deal success. Those that wait may be presented with an offer to purchase, including a premium for the stock that would be attractive to shareholders. In the absence of a compelling growth plan of its own, the board presented with such an offer has little option but to auction the company.

A plan to sell the company to consolidators can also be a legitimate and even the optimal choice in a restructuring industry. Again, understanding why and how an industry may restructure can lead to strategies that will position the company as an attractive sale candidate to the most desirable partners and will optimize the timing and value of the sale. When the board is faced with an offer, it is too late to better position the company or have much influence on partner selection or timing.

What should directors know about the strategy of portfolio companies?

The director of a company who owns multiple separate businesses needs to understand how the company, as the parent company, is to add value. The competencies of the parent and the corporate strategy should align with this role. As outlined in Chapter 1, the company may hold a diversified portfolio of businesses that has little potential for integration. In such cases, the parent company (in the controller role) may play an investor role only, such as Berkshire Hathaway, and choose not to intervene in the individual business other than through the exercise of fiduciary duties on any boards of its holdings. The parent company's role is essentially to grow and allocate shareholder capital through buying and selling of companies or shares of companies, and monitoring performance. In turn, the board needs to understand the investment criteria and the investment environment. Ideally, such a board includes seasoned investment professionals as well as senior experience from a range of industries.

A diversified portfolio may also be held by a parent company that directly adds value to the portfolio in the coach or orchestrator role. The board needs to understand the basis of that value added and where it applies. Drawing on the examples referenced in Chapter 1, a GE director should understand Six Sigma and other key principles and practices relevant to how GE's corporate center adds value. A director of a traditional media holding company would need to understand digital media and its implications and related opportunities. And a director of AREVA would have to understand the global power industry.

That does not mean these boards need to recruit experts in these areas. On the contrary, some of the world's best experts in each of these respective areas are already in the companies these boards oversee. To add value, the board needs to bring an alternate perspective and independence. However, to be effective directors they do need to learn the elements of the business that are fundamental to the parent company's strategy and value added.

Perhaps in contrast, the directors of portfolio companies in a surgeon role need to understand how to recognize when a company is heading for distress and have the "stomach" for the tough decisions. Experience in turnarounds, bankruptcies, and workouts would be an asset in this case.

The role of the parent as an architect embarking on a company or industry transformation is situational. Directors would need to understand the nature of the business(es) to which they are headed and would be helped in most cases by some additions from the targeted industries or sectors.

Do directors of portfolio companies need to understand the underlying businesses?

This depends on the size and governance structure of the portfolio. When financial companies control mutual funds, they may have separate boards for the parent and the manager of the funds—which can insulate parent company directors from liability for fund losses.[10] In health care organizations, it is also common to have multiple boards.[11]

However, any issues fundamental to the strategy and strategic risks of the larger enterprise need to be understood, regardless. For example, directors of the parent company need to understand the governance structure below to ensure it is sound. They also need to ensure that the right processes and communications structures are in place so that issues and decisions are brought to the right level.

In all but the largest companies, the board of the parent company will play a direct role in decisions related to the corporate strategy of the underlying businesses—mergers, acquisitions, and divestitures—and this has implications for what directors need to know about the underlying businesses.

What do directors need to know to oversee strategy of a single-business company?

For a single-business company (or for each business in a portfolio or diversified company), the competitive strategy is the integrated set of actions that will advance the company in its selected markets (i.e., *how* the company will compete). Directors need to understand the competitive strategy, the choices required, the options left open or closed by those choices, and the risks introduced.

This does not mean they need to understand all the ins and outs of the strategy and all of the underlying analysis. In short, they need to understand the context, the goals, and how the proposed strategy will advance the company toward those goals. They also need to understand what circumstances or strategic choices could result in decisions for the board, such as M&A decisions, because for these decisions the board may need to develop a deeper understanding of the relevant context and options.

What do directors need to know about the functional and geographic strategies?

Boards often tend to stay at a high level and review strategic vision, corporate strategy, and overall business strategies. However, "the devil is in the details." For example, many of the banks caught holding large portfolios of mortgages and real estate derivatives had in the years leading up to the financial crisis committed significant resources to the development of these portfolios (including acquisitions) and they had generated large profits. Understanding where the money was coming from and the risks that were coming with it would have required directors to have an understanding of the associated product strategies.

While it is a lot to ask of the board to understand all of the functional strategy detail, directors can and should go deep where it counts. In some industries, there are select functions that will always be key to the strategy. For example, the R&D strategy of a pharmaceutical company, the brand strategy of a consumer goods company, or the supply chain strategy of a retailer may be key to the organization's success or a major source of strategic risk.

These same critical functions may drive M&A decisions as outlined in Chapter 5. Boards should discuss which functions are key to a particular industry context or proposed strategy. For example, it may be important to review the sourcing strategy in anticipation of a new free-trade lane (should they acquire abroad?); the sales strategy for a company entering a new market (should they acquire a distributor?); or the manufacturing strategy in the context of rising foreign currency (should they sell some foreign operations?).

The question of how deep a board should go should not be about planning level (corporate strategy versus business unit strategy versus functional strategies), nor should it be about level of detail (goals versus overall strategic direction versus strategic actions). Rather, it should be about level of importance. The board has the right and responsibility to understand the elements of strategy that are important to the future of the company or material to the risks or could lead to decisions on the board agenda, such as M&A.

ENGAGING THE BOARD EFFECTIVELY IN M&A

How is the board supposed to understand all this!?! What about management?

Process is key. It is neither necessary nor appropriate to duplicate management's role. The board can be engaged in ways that add value, while at the same time providing the level of engagement for directors that is essential to responsible understanding and effective decisions on critical issues, including mergers, acquisitions, and divestitures.

How can the board gain an understanding of the strategic context?

Many companies try to provide all the relevant information in one strategic planning document or in the annual board strategy retreat. Unfortunately, most people don't learn much that way. It is too much at once and too passive.

A better approach is to include time for independent outside experts to occasionally address the board on relevant market, technology and competitive trends, and potential outcomes. This provides a third-party perspective and alternate views to be considered. Best practices include independent competitor briefings from industry analysts or consultants. Such analysis risks the perception that the board will be "second guessing" management's analysis, so it should be clearly defined as a director education initiative, and the analysis should be fact-checked (though not filtered) by management.

Ideally, such education sessions are forward looking. Directors typically have enough data on the company's and the industry's pasts. Informed discussions of alternative future scenarios considering industry, market, or competitor dynamics can prepare directors for strategy decisions.

When management has developed the strategic vision as a basis for planning, this too can simply be presented to the board. However, in a changing environment, it may be important for the board not just to read it but to understand it more deeply, especially if it could lead to merger, acquisition, or divestiture decisions that the board will have to make.

A best practice is to engage the board directly in a scenario planning session. In most industries, management must develop the strategic vision in the face of an uncertain future. Alternate scenarios are increasingly used in strategic planning to develop more dynamic strategies that are not dependent on one fixed set of assumptions.

If management has developed the scenarios and the strategic vision, the board can be engaged in a retreat setting in "war games" in which directors and managers work together in teams, role-playing competitors in the prepared future scenarios. The result is typically a board that truly understands the future context and the strategic vision and some new ideas for the strategy or risks to be considered. The board has not second-guessed management, but *the process* often delivers new insights.

What role should the board play in the development of the strategic plan?

Even if strategic planning is delegated to management, given the importance of the strategy, the board should understand the process. Just as an understanding of the company's risk management process is part of good risk oversight, so is an understanding of the strategic planning process integral to the board's confidence in the strategic plan.

Again, to understand the process and the plan it is better for the board to be engaged along the way. The trick is to be sufficiently and productively engaged with limited time and without crossing the line into management's responsibilities.

There are many strategic planning processes in use. The best processes incorporate the following:

- *Future oriented*: The future context and goals should be considered early. The board has an important role to play in setting an appropriately long time horizon, as management is increasingly pressured by the markets to focus on short-term financial performance.
- *Internal as well as external considerations*: Ultimately, the external considerations could lead to M&A decisions. It is important to know the direction of industry and competitors to know what will be the future competitive scale, scope, and skill requirements.
- *Appropriate level and focus of analysis*: There is a tendency to analyze what is available, rather than what is important. For example, competitive analysis is often light because it is hard to get, but it can be critically important and highly relevant to M&A considerations. However, exhaustive analysis of unimportant issues can be a distraction from the quality thinking required of management and the board.
- *Action plans*: Many strategies merely define the strategic orientation. Strategy should define what actions will be taken, including internal and external measures, and include metrics and milestones that can be incorporated in board reporting.
- *Financial models*: Well thought out action plans can be used to develop financial models of the outcomes of the strategy. Such models are far more valuable than the more typical extrapolations of past performance, and they also make it relatively easy to test a range of input assumptions, including M&A assumptions, and to quantify risks.

- *Risk analysis*: Even with extensive analysis, uncertainty remains. Uncertainty can be your friend. Consider downside risks, upside opportunities, and the presence of real options in the current business or that could be acquired.
- *Appropriate level of involvement*: The collective knowledge and thinking of management and the board can be of value in strategy development, and involvement also builds "buy-in." However, more is not always better. Exhaustive company-wide planning exercises can consume valuable resources, and too much board involvement can result in interference and the undermining of management accountability.

One such process outlined in Chapter 5 is SECOR's "W" process. It is designed to engage the board at the three peaks of the "W": first to launch the process, set the time horizon, and identify issues important from the board's perspective; second to review and comment on the proposed direction and options before the dye is cast; third to review and approve the final plan.

Achieving the right kind of engagement is a subtle task. If the strategy is presented as a complete "for approval" agenda item, then the engagement will be insufficient for the directors to gain real insight and understand the implications for their decisions that may come later, M&A decisions in particular. However, too much engagement may cross the line, taking responsibility away from management and therefore undermining management accountability.

A best practice for board engagement in strategy review is to deploy the board specifically in risk assessment and to facilitate a sufficiently engaging exercise that they can understand the strategy well and identify additional risks and opportunities. This leverages well the role and talents of directors without subjecting the entire strategy to hands-on revision.

With reference to "uncertainty is your friend," isn't a key role of the board to reduce risk?

No. Many directors believe that their role in risk oversight is to minimize risk, modulate executive exuberance, and prevent disasters. However, risk only exists in the presence of uncertainty. Reducing uncertainty by reverting to more conservative strategies can truncate the potential upside for the corporation as well as the downside. In a restructuring industry, such conservative risk management could relegate the company to a seller position or worse.

The role of the board with respect to risk is to establish the level of risk tolerance suitable for the industry and the shareholders, and then to ensure that the company is operating within that defined tolerance. The risks associated with the context and decisions of M&A strategy are among the most significant risks of the company. Therefore, directors should discuss the nature of the uncertainties in the industry and the strategic risks appropriate for the company in the given circumstances.

Furthermore, the risk of inaction is often ignored. In the ever-changing business environment (e.g., globalization, public policy/regulatory change, industry restructuring, and new technology, products, and competitors), the safest course is seldom the status quo. So even if the board is inclined to minimize risk, minimizing change is not the means. The board must, therefore, understand the strategic context and ensure sound M&A strategies within the company's tolerance for risk, rather than its tolerance for change.

What about flexibility?

Strategy is sometimes regarded as making choices. However, while choices do have to be made eventually, in a dynamic and uncertain industry environment the best strategies keep as many doors open as long as possible. As outlined in Chapter 4, flexibility has value.

A new strategy may close some doors and open others. For example, IBM pretty much closed the door on PC manufacturing when these functions were all outsourced and the capabilities spun off. However, the acquisition of Lotus opened many new possibilities for other software development and distribution through IBM's channels.

Therefore, to properly assess upside and downside risk, the board should look not just at the choices made but also at the alternatives or options that may be lost or gained in the pursuit of the proposed M&A strategy.

How should the review of a specific deal be managed?

Assuming that the board is already aware that a large deal may be part of the strategy, the proposed deal should be brought forward on a preliminary basis early to "set the table" and agree on process and roles toward review and approval. The CEO or the chair should arrange for a briefing to cover the basics of the transaction, highlighting the deal logic, the stakes (financial and competitive), and the risks. Limited discussion, but no approval or rejection of the deal, should take place at this first session.

Terms of reference for the review of the deal should be agreed to at the initial meeting or by correspondence shortly after, highlighting the particular aspects of the deal that warrant attention by the board.

While it would be preferred to include the full board in a detailed review of a major deal, this might not be practical in some cases and, if forced, could create inappropriate constraints on the review process. In such cases, the chair should assign an ad hoc deal review committee, including an independent chair and, if needed, an independent consultant to assist in the facilitation of the review process. The committee should be an extension of the strategy committee (if one exists) to include representatives of the audit committee and the human resources (HR) committee, at least, because there are issues in each of these areas that could make or break the deal.

The board or the deal review committee (as determined earlier) should examine critical aspects of the deal, as identified in the terms of reference. For a large, complex transaction, there may be a need to meet several times to review:

- The deal logic versus the company strategy
- The key sources of value creation potential
- The risks and the means of mitigating those risks
- The organization architecture and key assignments
- The integration plan, metrics, and key milestones.

The board or deal review committee should have access, if needed, to supporting studies and the experts outside the company to analyze specific issues to ensure a careful and unfiltered interpretation of the facts and analyses.

To gain the true support of the board for such an important deal, the last step is a full board review of the foregoing details, consideration of alternative scenarios that will "stress test" the deal and implementation plan, and reflection on all directors' M&A experience to assess the benefits and risks of the transaction from the perspectives of shareholders and other key stakeholders. This would ideally take place in a workshop setting—the deal should be the only item on the agenda, and the premeeting material and the process should be designed to ensure a thorough review of the key issues as well as the engagement of all directors in questions and discussion. Before a final decision on the deal, independent directors should meet in executive session with the CEO (and also separately) to raise and resolve any lingering questions.

Does the board have a role in postdeal implementation?

As part of its risk oversight role, the board must monitor the postdeal implementation process. It is well established that most deal failures are failures in implementation[12]—sound deal logic either not implemented well or undermined by organizational issues. Again, this is not to say the board should be directly involved in implementation. However, they have put a lot of shareholder money at risk, and they have a right and obligation to follow the progress.

Of course, this implies that there is a robust postdeal plan to follow. The board should review the postdeal implementation plans and, in particular, ensure that there are meaningful milestones and metrics that will be reported regularly to the board. This attention alone will improve the odds of deal success. Most postdeal plans lack specificity, they are implemented too slowly, and the organization issues are wished away by forming integrated organizational structures. Asking for more specific plans with milestones and metrics will in many cases cause the dramatic improvement in these plans.[13]

Directors meet only several times a year, and between meetings, conditions can change; how can directors make sure that the company's M&A strategy keeps pace?

Every important board decision, including M&A, should be made in the context of the strategy. However, one should not assume that, in dynamic market conditions, the strategy as blessed is fixed and can simply be deployed without further consideration.

To ensure that the board assesses risk and makes decisions in the context of strategy, directors should make strategy a part of every meeting and every important decision. This need not be extensive or time consuming if the board has previously been educated on the industry context and engaged in the strategic planning process as already outlined.

When an M&A opportunity seems right but is not aligned with strategy, there are three possibilities:

1. *This decision would take the company down one of the alternative paths considered in the plan as a contingency plan or strategic option.* In this case, the board should confirm that the change in circumstances for which the alternate plan was developed has indeed occurred. It remains to fine tune the strategy to the new circumstances.
2. *This decision changes the strategy.* In this case, choosing this path is an acknowledgment that the strategy was wrong. That may be the case, but it should be acknowledged as such. It is important for the company to then develop a new strategy; otherwise, the organization will be taking other actions or decisions based on the old (abandoned) strategy or based on no strategy at all.
3. *The strategy was right, and this decision should not be taken.* This, frankly, is the most common case but is often not recognized as such. For example, when an attractive acquisition opportunity is presented the strategy is often ignored. Or when a takeover offer is presented with a large premium, the long-term value of the strategy is dismissed. Management and the board should be resisting the lure of the deal in favor of longer-term strategic interests.

The board needs to be in a position to identify off-strategy propositions and to provide an informed and independent perspective on the choices and consequences.

Is all this doable?

The board is ultimately responsible for the strategic direction of the company. However, management typically formulates the strategic plan, including M&A strategy. In most respects this is positive—management has the resources to execute a rigorous process and can more easily implement and be held accountable for a plan managers developed themselves.

As a result, however, many directors are not close enough to the issues or the process to make informed decisions when they are thrust to the front line, such as in major mergers, acquisitions, or divestitures. The dynamic environments of most companies make this even more challenging, as boards are faced with takeover offers and acquisition opportunities that were not contemplated in the strategic plans.

So, ideally, the board is engaged sufficiently to exercise its role without duplicating the work of management. As outlined earlier, the board should be constructively engaged in the strategy process, including the general plans for growth through acquisition, the review of all major transactions for their strategic impact, and the tracking of postdeal implementation. This need not be an overwhelming burden if the board is educated on an ongoing basis and engaged early on the important issues and opportunities, and if the right processes are used to achieve appropriate involvement consistent with board responsibilities.

Moreover, in restructuring industries where some of the company-defining decisions will involve major mergers or acquisitions, the board is likely to be thrust into the frontline at some point. If directors have been sufficiently engaged to truly understand the context and have confidence in the strategy, then they will serve the company well when the stakes are the highest.

Endnotes

1. This chapter draws on ideas also used in the development of Ken Smith, *20 Questions Directors Should Ask about Strategy*—a prepublication draft prepared for the Canadian Institute of Chartered Accountants (CICA). This chapter and the CICA document also draw on Jean-René Halde and Ken Smith, "What's the Big Deal?: The Role of the Board in Major Deal Decisions," *Director,* October 2004.
2. The New York Stock Exchange-Euronext and Nasdaq both require that boards have a majority of independent directors and that the audit, compensation, and nominating/governance committee be independent (with some exceptions in the case of Nasdaq).
3. See the chapter on "Information" in *Bridging Board Gaps: Report of the Study Group on Corporate Boards* (New York/Newark, DE: Columbia Business School and the Weinberg Center for Corporate Governance, sponsored by the Rockefeller Foundation, April 2011).
4. See the chapters on "Dissent" and "Advice" in *Bridging Board Gaps*, note 3.

5. For more on director duties in M&A, see "The M&A Litmus Test," a five-part blog published August 9, 2010, http://blog.nacdonline.org/author/alexlajoux/.
6. See http://de.findacase.com/research/wfrmDocViewer.aspx/xq/fac.%5CSAC%5CDE%5C1989%5C19890714_0002.DE.htm/qx.
7. Ibid.
8. The U.S. Supreme Court recently (2011) declined to revive a shareholder lawsuit accusing accounting firm Ernst & Young of approving misleading financial statements in the 2001 merger of AOL and Time Warner. "Supreme Court Won't Review Suit Over AOL-Time Warner Merger, *Amorosa v. Ernst & Young*, 24 No. 9 Westlaw Journal Software law 6, July 13, 2011.
9. NACD guidelines on board responsibilities for strategy and M&A can be found in the appendix for Part II.
10. For example, Janus Capital Group Inc. has a parent company board, described in its governance guidelines, but it also maintains separate boards for its two subsidiaries, as noted in a recent U.S. Supreme Court case. "JCM and Janus Investment Fund remain legally separate entities, and Janus Investment Fund's board of trustees was more independent than the statute requires." The court found that investment advisors to a mutual fund cannot be sued under federal securities law for false statements made by the fund (even though the fund and the adviser were overseen by the same parent company). *Janus Capital Group, Inc., et al. v. First Derivative Traders*, No. 09-525, U.S. Supreme Court, 2011, http://www.supremecourt.gov/opinions/10pdf/09-525.pdf.
11. "The vast majority of health systems have multiple boards engaging in hierarchical governance. That is, a system or parent board oversees and coordinates the functions and activities of subordinate or subsidiary boards, which perform discrete governance functions for their individual entities and report back to the system board." Source: Orlikoff, J.E. and Totten, M.K., "The Challenges of System Governance," Trustee Workbook, *Trustee*, April 2006, http://www.americangovernance.com/americangovernance/BRP/files/J-Tool.pdf, accessed July 17, 2011.
12. See, for example, research in Albert Banal-Estañol and Jo Seldeslachts, "Merger Failures," *Journal of Economics and Management Strategy*, Vol. 20, No. 2 (Summer 2011), pp. 587–624, http://onlinelibrary.wiley.com/doi/10.1111/j.1530-9134.2011.00298.x/full. This paper proposes an explanation as to why some mergers fail, based on the interaction between the pre- and post-merger processes. See also Alexandra R. Lajoux, *The Art of M&A Integration: A Guide to Merging Resources, Processes, and Responsibilities* (New York: McGraw-Hill, 2007), citing research by Ken Smith and others.
13. For a full discussion of postmerger planning, see Alexandra R. Lajoux, *The Art of M&A Integration: A Guide to Merging Resources, Processes, and Responsiblities*, 2nd ed. (New York: McGraw-Hill, 2007).

PART III

When the M&A Program Is Central to Strategy

This book has used both positive and negative examples throughout to illustrate key concepts in M&A strategy. Part I outlined the principal roles of M&A in strategy and used examples to illustrate the role in different types of portfolio companies, in consolidation strategies, in revenue growth, and in creating options for future development. Part II provided a guide to M&A strategy development and execution, using examples to illustrate the importance of choosing the right role for M&A in the business strategy, how to search and screen candidates, how and when to consider being the buyer versus the seller, and how the board should be engaged in the process.

It is no accident that most of the positive examples came from serial acquirers, companies for which M&A is a core business activity, such as GE and Thomson Reuters, or companies for which it became a core activity because of changes in the industry that created the necessity or opportunity to win by acquisition, companies like Manulife, Xstrata, and InBev Brewing. These serial acquirers have demonstrated best practices in M&A because when M&A is central to strategy, superior skills in M&A are central to success.

Companies that leaped into M&A programs without experience and competitive M&A skills have provided lessons of the other kind. Some have been able to make a graceful exit, such as INCO ultimately selling to Vale Mining for a handsome premium. Others fell apart, like Federated Stores, and the pieces are in others' hands.

However, some—like IBM—were bruised but not beaten by early experiences and have developed into successful serial acquirers. The IBM story and others like it show that the perspective, ambition, and skills required to be successful in a sustained M&A program *can be developed.* This concluding portion of the book, therefore, takes a deeper look at the critical aspects of M&A strategy and capabilities for companies that will do multiple acquisitions and for whom M&A will play a central role in strategy.

In particular, for most industries a successful growth strategy will be international in scope. Globalization of markets and the development of new economies are driving restructuring of most industries across borders and oceans, and public policy and regulation are critical aspects of international M&A strategies. Chapter 9 examines the international market of M&A and the role of policy and regulation.

Chapter 10 explores postmerger integration. This is a large topic, much of which is beyond the scope of this book on M&A strategy. However, there are aspects of postmerger integration that are integral to the M&A strategy. Chapter 10 looks at how strategic value is captured after the deal and how to merge organizations so as to align cultures with the longer-term strategic vision. Moreover, this chapter demonstrates how excellence in the management of integration can influence the understanding and valuation of subsequent deals.

Throughout the deal cycle there are advisors available to assist in strategic analysis, candidate search, valuation, negotiation, deal structuring, due diligence, and postmerger integration. The stakes are high in major deals, so getting help can make sense. Chapter 11 looks at the different types of advisors for each stage of the deal cycle, how to decide if an advisor is needed, and how to choose the right advisors.

With or without help from advisors, a successful sustaining M&A program requires that M&A itself become a core competency of the corporation. Just as a pharmaceutical company must have superior skills in research and development, as a service company has to define and manage its service culture, and as a food company must have impeccable food safety processes, so a company for which M&A is central to its strategy must have superior M&A skills to create value in a competitive market for corporate control. Chapter 12 outlines and benchmarks these core competencies.

CHAPTER 9

Global Industry Restructuring

We are going to wake up one day and discover that we are no longer in control of our affairs.

—*Dominic D'Alessandro,*
CEO of Manulife Financial, 2008[1]

Global industry restructuring is a significant business trend, driving a dramatic increase in cross-border acquisitions. While such restructuring is a natural outcome of the globalizing economy, it changes the game in two ways. First, the playing field for many industries is global. This means that the markets are much larger. It also means there are more competitors, and many of those competitors are unfamiliar. The implications for M&A strategy are a greater need to consider international business combinations in order to maintain competitive scale and scope, and a larger and, in many cases, unfamiliar set of potential buyers and sellers.

Second, the rules of the game include regulation, public policy, and practices in foreign jurisdictions. Of course, large domestic deals have always faced policy issues regarding industry concentration and, in some countries and states, takeover restrictions. However, when taken to the global stage, increasingly including developing economies, such policies can be murky and are not always practiced as written, and they are changing. The implications for M&A strategy are a larger set of both the written and the unwritten rules that need to be understood, a greater interest on the part of many governments in M&A activity, and an imperative to incorporate public policy considerations in M&A strategy.

This chapter examines the trends in international M&A and some of the underlying drivers, including public policy. It also looks at the implications for government and corporate planning with respect to international

M&A. This chapter draws on studies of international M&A conducted by SECOR Consulting under the leadership of one of the authors.[2]

INTERNATIONAL TRENDS AND IMPLICATIONS

International M&A is not new—has it increased significantly?

While the financial crisis slowed down the volume of M&A of all types, the proportion of deals that are cross-border has been steadily rising (see Exhibit 9.1). From 15 percent of deals in 2000, cross-border deals have risen to 50 percent of the total global M&A activity. International deals are predicted to dominate the global M&A market going forward.[3]

This is a predictable outcome of the globalization of markets, freer trade, and the development of international economies.

Exhibit 9.1. Cross-border deal volume 2000–2010,[4] % of total M&A (black) and US$billions.

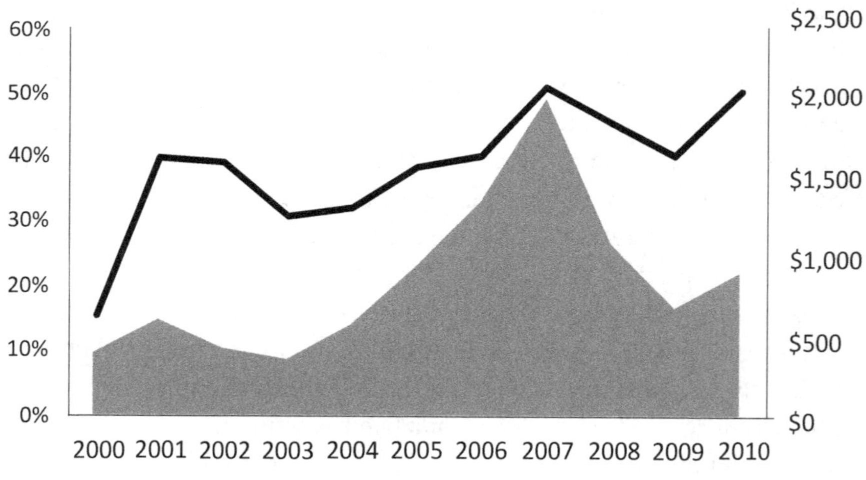

Who is buying whom?

In the 10 years leading up to the crisis, most of the large international acquisitions ($1 billion plus) were between continental Europe, the United States, the United Kingdom, and Canada. (See Exhibit 9.2.) While China was very active, most of its investments were minority positions, not involving a change in control. Similarly, the large investments of Western companies in Asia have in general not been acquisitions but, rather, minority positions or joint ventures.

Continental Europe dominates on the buy side. The Netherlands slid into negative territory with the single sale of ABN AMRO for $100 billion and was otherwise a net buyer. Denmark is close to neutral. By country of origin, the largest net buyers (value of acquisitions less value of divestitures) were France, Spain, Switzerland, Belgium, and Germany.

The United States, the United Kingdom, and Canada were the largest net sellers. For the United States and the United Kingdom, this is a change from earlier periods during which the large consumer goods companies, automakers, energy companies, and pharmaceutical firms were building their international operations.

In the United States almost every major sector has been in a net sale position. The largest deficit has been in the consumer noncyclical segment (pharmaceuticals, food, and beverages) with foreign firms like Teva Pharmaceuticals from Israel, Takeda Pharmaceutical from Japan, Novartis from Switzerland, the Fresenius Group from Germany, Roche Holding AG-Genusschein from Switzerland, Shire PLC from Britain, and GlaxoSmithKline from Britain buying the assets. The communications, industrial, and basic materials segments have also had large acquisition deficits. The only major sector that has been in a net buyer position (only slightly) is consumer cyclical.

UK sales have been led by utilities, although in many of these cases the United Kingdom has retained "golden shares," shares with special voting rights that retain domestic control for some decisions. (Such control tools will be further discussed later in the chapter.) Sales in Canada have been led by the basic materials sector—a controversial trend with Canada seeing a growing proportion of its prized natural resources under foreign control.

The only time during the 10-year period when the United States was a net buyer was the period 2003 to 2004. However, the acquisition market was at its lowest point in those years so the United States acquired a large share of not much. Those years were swamped by the activity over the rest of the period in which the sale of U.S. companies to foreign companies overwhelmed the purchases by U.S. companies abroad. The pattern is similar for Canada. The only active M&A year in the period in which the United Kingdom was a net buyer was 2007, solely because of the RFS Holland Holding BV acquisition of ABN AMRO Holding NV from the Netherlands for $100 billion.

(Note that deals in which the acquiring companies are from more than one country are noted in Exhibit 9.2 as multinational.)

Why does this imbalance matter to corporations?

As industries restructure on a global basis, there have to be both buyers and sellers, and, as discussed in Chapter 7, for many companies the optimal strategy is to sell. However, the potential for value creation is much greater for those companies that are able to succeed as leaders in industry restructurings than the value of any one-time sale premium.

It was also noted in Chapter 3 that international deals are generally more about revenue growth than cost consolidation. Whereas in-market consolidation deals typically transfer most of the value to the seller, cross-market transactions can create new product–market opportunities. In addition, those companies that are entering new markets through acquisitions are also acquiring real options, essentially acquiring a base for growing in these markets as conditions and opportunities allow—particularly valuable in developing countries.

The value creation opportunity in global industry restructuring is borne out by the success rates of European buyers. International acquisitions

Exhibit 9.2. Change of ownership control in international acquisitions by country.

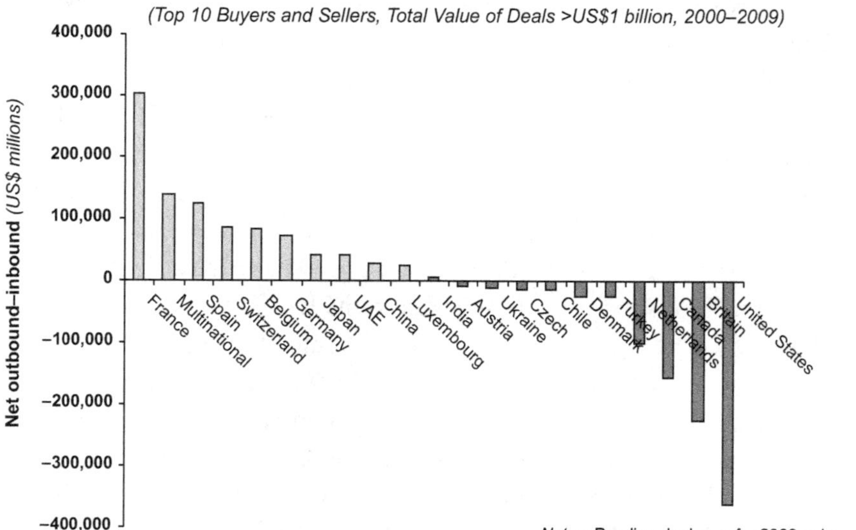

Source: Bloomberg, SECOR analysis.

Notes: Pending deals are for 2009 only, Multinational includes deals with multiple acquirers from different countries.

by European companies have historically yielded success rates of ~60 percent, significantly higher than their own domestic deals. Canadian companies have also been more successful with international deals than with domestic transactions.

However, the U.S. performance on international deals is poor, with success rates of only ~40 percent, even worse than U.S. domestic deals. Having been burned before could be one of the reasons U.S. companies have not been as aggressive internationally. A more constructive response would be to develop better acquisition skills, especially for international transactions, and participate more fully in the value that is being created by global industry restructuring.[5]

Are governments concerned?

There is concern in countries that have seen significant loss of corporate control. For example, Australia had been a net seller until 2000 and made changes to foreign takeover policies. In particular, they have since been more protective of corporate headquarters. For example, the approval of the BHP-Billiton merger, which formed the second-largest mining company in the world,[6] was approved under strict conditions regarding the maintenance of a real head office in Australia, including makeup of the board, trading of shares, location of board meetings, residences of key executives, and so forth.[7] Australia reversed the net seller trend and has been a net buyer since the millennium.

Canada undertook a major review of policy in 2008. Modest changes were made to stated policy, which continues to strongly encourage foreign investment. Significantly, however, a proposed $38 billion takeover of Potash Corporation by BHP Billiton was turned down by the government of Canada for offering "no net benefit to Canada."[8]

The United Kingdom has a standing review committee. The Panel on Takeovers and Mergers (the Panel) is an independent body, established in 1968, whose main functions are to issue and administer the City Code on Takeovers and Mergers (the Code) and to supervise and regulate takeovers and other matters to which the Code applies. Its central objective is to ensure fair treatment for all shareholders in takeover bids.[9] Under pressure from the public, the Panel undertook a consultation on policies in 2010, resulting in policy amendments that became effective September 19, 2011.[10]

Following the financial crisis, there was talk of more protectionist policies in the United States, but no formal policy changes have resulted. Nevertheless, a number of deals have been discouraged as "not in the national interest." For example, the bid by the China National Offshore Oil Corporation to buy Unocal in 2005 was turned down.[11] In addition, some states have strong antitakeover legislation. Delaware, for example, kept Alcoa out of reach during the consolidation of the basic materials segment, while competitor Alcan of Quebec was sold to Rio Tinto in 2007[12] with no comparable resistance from the Canadian or the Quebec governments.

In continental Europe there is a range of formal and informal barriers to foreign acquisitions (discussed more fully later), and in the largest developing countries, China and India, there are significant barriers to foreign acquisitions. This is allowing their companies to build strength and expand internationally. While all this may seem in conflict with the development of a global economy, there are some legitimate arguments both for and against more open M&A policies.

What are the arguments for more open M&A policies?

The more open the global economy, the more efficiently it will operate as a global economy. The theory of efficient markets would suggest that free and open trade provides the competitive forces to maximize efficiency and ensure the greatest access to goods and services at the lowest possible prices. Similarly, applying the same notion to the capital markets suggests that, subject to effective concentration limits, unrestricted capital markets will yield the most efficient and highest-value corporate structures. In other words, if we let the market prevail in both trade and business combinations, the most efficient new industry structures will result along with the greatest access to goods and services at the lowest possible prices.

From the perspective of an individual nation, the foreign investment that would accompany such open markets should also be positive. To the extent that foreign direct investment results in resource development, increased R&D, improved operations efficiency, or new product markets, the investment creates wealth in that nation and improves the competitiveness of its economy.

From the perspective of corporations, more open markets provide for larger customer markets, more choices among suppliers, and more possibilities for business combinations. For companies that may acquire, it means more growth options. For companies that could be sellers, open markets usually result in higher ongoing stock price valuations because the markets tend to reflect comparable sale multiples (discounted, of course).

What are the arguments against more open M&A policies?

While foreign direct investment that results in resource development, increased R&D, improved operations efficiency, or new product markets creates wealth, an acquisition in and of itself does none of this. An acquisition simply changes ownership control. Only if that change in control results in needed new capital to invest or smarter management or competitive advantages derived from synergies, does the acquisition, like other foreign investment, create wealth in the economy.

Whether foreign investment creates value or simply changes ownership control is a distinction worth making.[13] As a country's corporations are sold off, especially large ones, there are typically losses to the local economy. Some or all head-office functions move to the buyer's headquarters. The consolidation of head-office functions is inevitably followed by a migration of their supporting professional and business infrastructures; that is, the lawyers, accountants, bankers, and consultants that supported the old head office are no longer needed there. The ripple effects can be severe. After all, the headquarters of large corporations and their associated capital markets and services are core to major cities. What they spend and what their well-paid employees and service providers spend can represent a large portion of a city's economy. For example, what would New York be without its many headquarters and the supporting capital markets and services?

In addition to the direct economic benefits to an economy from being the home to many corporations, especially large ones, corporate ownership also enhances a country's domestic control and international influence. The directors and senior management may consider the national interests in their decisions. This is especially true in developing countries but also in some developed countries such as France where business and political communities are tightly interwoven. Moreover, the benefits of open economies may accrue mostly to the strongest economies and to where the buyers reside. Some degree of protectionism may be needed in developing countries if they are to develop strong, stable local industries.[14]

So there are differences in views and in policies–what are the implications for M&A strategy?

While one might argue for or against more open M&A markets, the stark reality is that the global market for corporate control is not played on a level playing field. Sovereign governments have the right to determine the regulations and policies that govern corporate takeovers and there is no global court of appeal. As a result, corporations domiciled in the most open jurisdictions operate at a disadvantage as industries restructure on a global basis. More closed policies abroad make it more difficult for them to acquire, and more open policies at home make them more vulnerable to takeover. Therefore, at the very least, M&A strategy must be developed with an understanding of international regulations and practices that may facilitate or frustrate international growth. However, in light of the current imbalances, there is also a need for more ambitious business and public policy with respect to international growth through M&A.

INTERNATIONAL POLICIES AND PRACTICES

What are the key international policies and practices affecting international M&A? Are changes expected?[15]

United States

In the United States, corporate law is state law. Although the federal government also seeks to intervene in hostile takeovers or acquisitions deemed to be a threat to national security, it is state law that regulates the vast majority of defensive tactics. One of the most significant state law evolutions over the last decades was the development of state anti-takeover laws aimed at providing protection to the local incumbent board. More than 40 states have implemented such laws since 1968, when this trend was initiated in Virginia, to regulate tender offers more thoroughly than the federal Williams Act did previously.

In the vast majority of states (including Delaware, the reference jurisdiction in the United States for corporate law), this evolution translates into a situation where the board of directors is the primary decision-making authority regarding the business of the corporation. The key presumption here is that the directors are better equipped to make informed business decisions, and that they act in good faith. By default, courts tend to respect this presumption. In the event of a hostile bid, this means that U.S. boards of directors should be in a position to decide whether the deal should go through or not.

The logical consequence is that U.S. boards have powerful defensive tools at hand. Poison pills, for instance, can act as a showstopper in situations involving a hostile bid. U.S. boards can use poison pills without shareholder approval provided they demonstrate both of the following:

1. That they have reasonable grounds for believing that a danger to corporate policy exists because of another person's stock ownership
2. That any defensive measure adopted is reasonable with the threat posed.

This scrutiny test (also known as the Unocal test following *Unocal Corp. vs. Mesa Petroleum* (Del. 1985) creates a case-by-case approach. If the board of directors meets these two requirements, its decision will be protected from judicial intervention. Over time, this rule has given U.S. boards a significant (though not absolute) power to decide whether a deal should go through or not. Beyond poison pills, there are other tools used strategically by U.S. boards to prevent hostile bids:

- *Staggered boards*: more than 30 U.S. state corporate law statutes allow for staggered boards, which can discourage hostile bids and proxy contests.
- *Advance-notice bylaws*: frequently used in the United States, advance-notice bylaws require shareholder proposals and director nominations to be presented to the company well in advance of the date of the meeting where they are to be put to a vote, therefore delaying the potential replacement of target board members.

As a consequence, defensive tactics are more effective in the United States than in some other jurisdictions, such as Canada for example, where securities policy favors shareholders over boards. The relative power of the U.S. board is illustrated by the availability of the "just say no" defense in the United States: the common law legal precedent was established in *Moore Corp. Ltd. v. Wallace Computer Services Inc.*, 907

F.Supp. 1545 (D. Del. 1995) to block a bid because the target's recently adopted capital expenditure plan was beginning to show better than expected results.

However, the balance of power favoring boards over shareholders in the United States has been shifting in favor of shareholders. Corporate scandals at Enron, WorldCom, and other major U.S. firms at the turn of the century have been perceived as demonstrations that powerful boards and management teams can act against the interest of the shareholders. This has led to stronger shareholder activism over the last few years, driven in particular by increasing influence of hedge funds. (There are almost 10,000 hedge funds in the United States, collectively controlling more than $2 trillion in assets.) Recently, hedge funds have become adept at gaining support from institutional investors, which results in the formation of large groups of shareholders that give less deference to recommendations of boards than ordinary investors. This trend has been reinforced by the financial crisis. For example, in the aftermath of the crisis and the ensuing public attention on executive compensation, boards have largely relented on shareholder "say on pay."

This increased shareholder activism means an increased pressure on the boards to maximize shareholder value creation, for instance, through special dividends, share buybacks, asset sales, and lower defenses against hostile bids. For example, although U.S. boards have the legal right to institute "shareholder rights" (poison pill) plans,[16] the number of U.S. companies with such plans has declined. Boards are also declassifying, although a significant share of S&P companies still have classified (staggered) boards.

However, it remains for the boards to argue for long-term value creation strategies over short-term value "hits." U.S. boards that understand the longer-term strategy and its potential to create value remain powerful in the event of a hostile bid.

Europe

In the vast majority of European Union (EU) member countries, company-specific barriers protected by national laws can be used to frustrate hostile bids. Examples include the following:

- *The Netherlands*: companies can issue protective preference shares to a friendly entity.

- *Spain*: caps are placed on voting rights regardless of the size of a shareholder's equity ownership.
- *Sweden*: dual-class share systems are common, with one class conferring 10 voting rights per share.
- *Belgium*: companies can issue shares or buy them back for a three-year period when they are "in grave and imminent danger."
- *Germany*: shareholder agreements bind shareholders to maintain cross-shareholdings or otherwise govern their responses to hostile bids.
- *France*: double-voting rights are provided to long-term shareholders (typically more than two years); shareholder agreements are in place in a number of companies, and legislation allowing poison pills has been adopted.

Golden shares also continue to be used in several European countries. These shares give the government or another holder the right to veto certain actions or prevent certain companies or individuals from acquiring shares. Despite a ruling by the European Commission making the existence of such shares illegal in 2002, more than 140 major EU companies still had them in place at the end of 2005. These included companies in "sensitive sectors" such as telecommunications, energy, transport, and defense (e.g., Rolls-Royce PLC, a British maker of aircraft engines; KPN NV, the Dutch telecommunications company; ENI SpA, an Italian energy concern; Telefonica SA, the Spanish telecom giant; BAA, the UK Airport; Elf Aquitaine, the French oil company). Among the largest companies still controlled with golden shares are Germany's Volkswagen AG and Portugal's Energias de Portugal.[17]

As a consequence, the market for corporate control in the European Union is relatively small (if we exclude the UK), especially when it comes to cross-border deals. For instance, over the last 10 years, cross-border M&A activity in Germany has been comparable to Canada's, even though Germany's gross domestic product is 2.3 times bigger than Canada's.

In this context of national protectionism, the European Union approved in late 2003 a takeover directive aimed at harmonizing practices across member countries and supporting the emergence of a more dynamic market for corporate control (Directive 2004/25/EC). This directive was the result of more than 10 years of debate and failed attempts, indicating how sensitive the issue of takeover is in the European Union. The guiding principles behind the directive push for a neutral board and shareholder choice to accept a tender offer or use defensive tactics. They translate into two key provisions:

- *Board neutrality*: companies must gain shareholder approval before taking any action to frustrate a bid.
- *Breakthrough rule*: during a takeover period, disproportionate control rights do not apply any more; as a consequence, defensive tactics based on separating ownership from control (e.g., multiple voting rights) are made ineffective.

These provisions would clearly give the final say to shareholders (as opposed to boards) in the event of a hostile takeover attempt, which is in line with the Canadian approach and differs from the U.S. approach where the board often has the power to accept or reject a hostile takeover.

However, to get political support in the European Parliament and Council and to avoid another vote rejecting the directive (as was the case in 2001), compromises had to be made. Member countries have the choice to impose or not to impose the two key provisions (Board Neutrality and Breakthrough Rule). A reciprocity rule was added which specifies that under certain circumstances companies can ignore the two provisions even if their country decided to impose them. In effect, the reciprocity rule gives the target company a right to use the same anti-takeover defenses as the ones available to the bidding company. In other words, application of the directive was optional, so its effectiveness depends on the good will of member countries.

Today, key conclusions regarding its implementation are as follows:

- *Board Neutrality*: 18 countries have adopted the rule, but, with one exception, all of them already had some version of this principle in place.
- *Breakthrough Rule*: only the three Baltic states have imposed it, thus mandating it for just 1 percent of listed companies in the EU in terms of market capitalization.
- *Reciprocity Rule*: the majority of member states have allowed companies to reciprocate against a bidder not subject to the Board Neutrality Rule or Breakthrough Rule. This includes all

major economies in the European Union except the United Kingdom (e.g., France, Germany, Italy, Spain, the Netherlands).

In the longer term the directive might lead to a more open market but, based on reports from the European Union itself, so far the way the directive has been implemented is likely to reinforce rather than remove defensive tactics available to European companies.[18] As of late 2011, member states continue to maintain effective sovereignty over foreign investment rules.[19]

Finally, it is fair to say that the directive has been implemented in a fairly protectionist way. Member states have shown a strong reluctance to adopt the fundamental rules of the directive, illustrating a continued preference for the prevention of unwanted takeovers over more open markets and the free flow of capital.

Japan

Despite its role as a global economy, Japan is a small player in the market for corporate control. The economy (and culture for that matter) is somewhat isolated. Corporate Japan has been dominated by conglomerates with strong connections to banks and one another. Seven such *zaibatsus* (literally *plutocrats* or *financial cliques*) currently dominate Japanese industry: Sharp, Sanyo–Panasonic, Mitsubishi, Toshiba, Mitsui, Honda, and Kyocera.

However, major shifts have been taking place in Japanese corporate ownership over the last decade. Traditional management-friendly shareholders, such as banks and business partners, have been dwindling, and in their place have come domestic and foreign institutional investors, many of whom are willing to tender their shares to a hostile acquirer. Managers are coming to recognize that excessive expansion into low-profit, noncore businesses, coupled with conservative capital strategy, has left them vulnerable to an acquirer who can easily turn a profit by restructuring the company.

This evolution has made the case for poison pills. Poison pills did not exist in Japan before 2005, but now many Japanese companies have put them in place, sparking concern about management entrenchment.[20] Other protectionist initiatives are also being implemented to prevent foreign hostile deals. These include a partial return to cross-shareholdings (e.g., three steel firms agreed in 2007 to a hold 2 percent to 5 percent of each other's outstanding equity) and a dividend defense (several target companies have increased their dividend payouts 10 to 15 times, thus boosting the share price and making the hostile bid more expensive). As a consequence, Japan remains today a marginal player in the market for corporate control, and Japanese targets are still very difficult to acquire for foreign investors.

Canada

Equity instruments traded in Canada have a high degree of diversity and transparency. The Toronto Stock Exchange identifies five types (see Table 9.1). Many Canadian companies have a controlling shareholder, often exercising control through a dual-class share structure. About 30 percent to 40 percent of the companies listed on the Toronto Stock Exchange (TSX) have a controlling shareholder or use some form of dual-class share structure. These dual-class share structures can take different forms, but the primary purpose remains the same: to confer a disproportionate amount of control on one group of shareholders relative to their equity participation in the company.

Table 9.1 Share Identification on the Toronto Stock Exchange

Type	Description
Nonvoting shares	Shares that have no right to vote, or a right to vote only in certain limited circumstances.
Multiple-voting shares	Shares that have more votes than the issuer's standard voting shares.
Subordinate-voting shares	Shares that carry a right to vote, where there is another class or classes of shares outstanding that carry a greater voting right on a per-share basis.
Limited-voting shares	Shares that have the right to vote only in certain limited circumstances.
Restricted-voting shares	Shares that carry a right to vote, subject to some restriction on the number or percentage of shares that may be voted by the owner.

Source: Toronto Stock Exchange.

Companies so controlled include major international companies such as Bombardier Inc., Magna International Inc., Rogers Communications Inc., and Onex Corporation. Such companies are sheltered from hostile takeovers.

Remaining firms, which represent the majority of TSX-listed companies, are generally vulnerable to acquisition. Other capital characteristics that may prevent takeovers in other jurisdictions (e.g., golden shares, share transfer restrictions, staggered boards, which are common practices in European countries) are not used in Canada largely due to more shareholder-friendly securities law. For example, staggered boards are rendered ineffective because under provincial and federal business corporation statutes, directors can be removed at any time without cause by a simple majority vote of shareholders. Corporate governance practices have also led to director independence. More than 75 percent of directors in the United States and Canada are independent, in contrast with closely tied director communities in the EU.[21]

Historically, the "just say no" defense had not been used in Canada. However, recent cases have provided some legal precedent with restrictions. Canadian boards can use poison pills, and many Canadian corporations have poison pills in place. However, securities policy makes poison pills effective in slowing down a deal but not in blocking it.[22]

The Investment Canada Act provides the government of Canada the ability to turn down foreign acquisitions if it determines there is no "net benefit to Canada." (The Act was recently amended to add a national security clause.) However, since its adoption in 1986, over 1,600 projects have been reviewed under the Investment Canada Act, and only 3 have been turned down, the most recent one being the BHP Billiton offer to acquire Potash Corporation. (There are no data available on firms that withdrew themselves from the process; the available data are for deals that went through the full review process.)

Finally, special sector-related rules have placed effective limitations on foreign acquisitions in a series of protected industries, including financial services, telecommunications, and transport. The orderly withdrawal of restrictions in telecommunications is currently being planned. For example, the government of Canada conducted a public consultation in 2010 seeking input on how (not if) to withdraw foreign ownership restrictions in telecommunications.[23]

However, Canada is unlikely to relax foreign ownership rules for the financial services sector. Canada was largely shielded from the financial crisis by a conservatively regulated and operated banking sector. Any calls for relaxation of foreign ownership restrictions were silenced after the crisis.

Developing Countries

Regulation governing international M&A in developing economies is, in general, more protective in both the centrally managed economies and the democratic states. In China, for example, it is difficult for a foreign enterprise to own a Chinese company. Most companies that have set up operations in China have done so by forming joint ventures with Chinese companies. As a central economy, Chinese acquisitions abroad have been regarded differently than corporate acquisitions. For example, many regarded the interest of China Minmetals in Noranda in 2004/05 as a potential sale of Canadian natural resources to a foreign government.[24] The deal was discouraged, and, ultimately, the offer was withdrawn. And, as mentioned earlier, the bid for Unocal by the China National Offshore Oil Corporation was turned down by the U.S. government. China has instead secured access to needed resources though minority investments tied to supply contracts.

It is unclear how companies that are owned or controlled by foreign governments will participate in global industry restructuring. Such companies are not for sale, so will they be allowed to acquire? China Minmetals and China National Offshore Oil Corp were rebuffed in Canada and the United States, respectively. Yet state-owned enterprises from democratic states do not meet the same resistance. For example, Vale Mining, a Brazilian state-controlled company, acquired Canadian resources company INCO. AREVA, a state-controlled French company, has acquired uranium mining and nuclear power operations that span North America and Europe.[25]

India, a democratic jurisdiction, has restrictions on foreign ownership for many industries. In addition, many Indian companies have a controlling shareholder, and many others are part of intricate multi-industry conglomerates. As a consequence, joint ventures with Indian companies are popular entry vehicles. John Deere, Fairfax Insurance, PepsiCo, and Walmart all operate in India through joint ventures. Indian companies have, however, been active in acquisitions abroad, notably Tata Group with acquisitions across North America, Europe, and Asia in strategic sectors.[26]

As India increasingly opens itself to the world, discussions of foreign ownership restrictions are ongoing. India is engaged in free trade discussions and sees its future as a trading nation. There is no doubt that India will have to be more open to foreign acquisitions—the only question is how and when the rules will change.

Policies and practices that discourage takeovers are being challenged; how quickly will the more protective M&A markets open up?

This question is interwoven with many other issues being exposed as we march toward more global markets. Cultural differences, differences in the role of the state in services such as health care and in providing job security, the resulting differences in corporate and personal tax levels, differences in regulation and in the role of the state in business are all deeply rooted and of broader importance than merely international M&A policy.

Even between the Western business cultures of continental Europe and the Anglo-American economies there are fundamental differences, differences that are in part responsible for the great acquisition surpluses of continental Europe at the expense of the United States, the United Kingdom, and Canada. At the management level, some of the incentives that encourage sales in the United States are muted in Europe. For example, "golden parachutes," common in executive packages in America, are much less prevalent in continental Europe. In Germany, the notion of a large payout in the event of a takeover is considered culturally repugnant.[27] Similarly, executive compensation mix in continental Europe favors base salary over stock-based incentives, while it is the reverse in the United States, making a sale premium much more attractive to the management of a buyout target in the United States.

At the governance level, there are double-voting rights of long-term shareholders in France showing preference to the committed shareholder over the speculator or hedge fund. Unions are represented on boards in Germany giving employees a greater voice in all matters and, in particular, making it difficult to pitch an acquisition designed to reduce employment. In Spain, caps are placed on voting rights, creating an egalitarian shareholder structure somewhat independent of equity held.

These differences are all rooted in cultural norms and different expectations of business. The result is that it is a lot harder for an outsider to acquire in continental Europe. If a company is a target, a domestic "solution" will in most cases be easier to execute.

One can argue that such practices hamper market efficiency, will protect bloated corporate structures, and will slow global industry restructuring. However, these practices are consistent with the local norms and expectations of business in the broader sense, and so they are unlikely to change quickly. They foster a longer-term perspective in the event of a takeover—wise in this sense perhaps, but certainly tilting the market for corporate control against the more open M&A markets of the Anglo-American economies.

IMPLICATIONS FOR ACTION

So should the more open M&A markets move to close the gap?

Protectionism would be an unfortunate reaction as this would slow down global industry restructuring, and the benefits to all players would be lost. However, waiting for foreign regulation to create equally open markets abroad is high risk. In light of the deeply rooted cultural differences behind the resistance to foreign takeovers in continental Europe and the need in developing countries to build domestic industries, change will be slow. With the current imbalance in the meantime, the United States, the United Kingdom, and Canada are falling substantially behind in the market for corporate control. A number of actions can be taken in public and business policy to redress this imbalance.

What changes in public policy will level the playing field?

At state and national level, securities statutes can adapt to the global economy; they should not be set in isolation. To the extent that a jurisdiction's securities policy is out of step with competing jurisdictions, its companies are operating at a disadvantage in international M&A markets.

The trends in securities policy favoring shareholders over directors, while well intended, will increasingly pressure companies to respond to the short-term interests of short-term shareholders. Boards have the responsibility, and should have the latitude, to act in the long-term interests of the company. The pressure to sell for the best premium offered, irrespective of the long-term potential of the company, is but one way these trends will in the end fail the company and the economy if left unabated. Further developments in securities policy should consider the long-term interests of the corporation over the short-term interests of speculators and hedge funds.

Governments should maintain or strengthen legislation that gives them power to review foreign takeovers. It should be used very sparingly so as not to retard global development. However, it can be a tool to exact reciprocity when buyers from closed markets arrive to shop. It could also be used to block acquisitions by foreign crown corporations or sovereign wealth funds if their ownership and capitalization are providing them with unfair advantages over commercial entities.

Governments have the right to keep selected strategic assets under domestic ownership. However, the means for doing so should not isolate these industries or restrict foreign competition. Protection of the state banks in the United States and, more recently, the telecommunications industry in Canada retarded the development of these industries. Alternatives, such as the procurement policies in U.S. defense or the "widely held rule" for Canadian financial institutions, can prevent outright acquisition without preventing foreign competition.

Moreover, governments need to take an international perspective in policy development. Many policies and practices were originally designed for the management of the domestic economy in isolation of international practices. Governments now need to take a global view and design policies in an internationally competitive context—policies that are aligned with international norms or that differ with intention and with consideration of the consequences.

In light of persisting policy differences, what can corporations do to win in the global market for corporate control?

While the playing field is not level, this cannot be used as an excuse to stay home or to sell early to the highest bidder. Many companies are succeeding internationally in spite of the challenges, and most companies have the potential to create substantial value in M&A as industries restructure.

Considering the potential for value creation in international deals, highlighted in Chapters 3 and 4 in particular, the M&A strategy and execution should look abroad, but with the following additional considerations.

Directors need to better understand their responsibilities and degrees of freedom with respect to takeover offers. If a growth plan exists for a company and has superior value to an offer presented (adjusted for risk), then the board has the fiduciary responsibility to say no to the offer, not to auction the company to the highest bidder. Of course, in restructuring industries, the board has a responsibility to ensure that the company has a strategic plan to create maximum value as the industry restructures. However, it is too late to be developing the plan when an offer is presented. When a company's existing strategic plan can create value that is comparable or superior to what acquirers can realistically promise, directors are justified in blocking deals.

The resolve to say no must be accompanied by the resolve to say yes to the development of globally competitive companies. There must be corporate ambition to win in the market for corporate control, and the capabilities must be developed to be successful in international M&A, including the knowledge, patience, cultural respect, and flexibility to make deals in less open economies.

International ambition should be promoted, encouraged, and demanded from business leaders. Incentives that promote short-term thinking and disproportionately reward the sale of the enterprise run counter to the interests of the corporation. Management selection, development, expectations, and incentives need to be aligned with the international opportunities.

Business and government should work more effectively together to achieve international success for business, including the development and support of national champions. In particular, global leaders such as BHP–Billiton, Boeing, CEMEX, Deutsche Telekom, and Banco Santander[28] all benefited from a strong position in their domestic markets and from the support of government and government policy to compete on the international stage.

Moreover, business leaders and government need to work more effectively together on international competitiveness. Competing jurisdictions have better aligned international business and public policy, and they have clear and shared international ambitions. The economic benefits of globalization are significant in any event, but they are multiplied if companies are positioned to compete internationally, to be the buyers more often, and to emerge as global leaders in important industries. It should, therefore, be a shared ambition of business and government to win in the global market for corporate control.

Endnotes

1. Conference Board of Canada speech as CEO of Manulife Financial, 2008.
2. See especially Ken Smith, "Losing (Ownership) Control," *Harvard Business Review*, June 2009, Ken Smith and Frank Daufenbach, "Nachhaltig akquirieren," *Business Manager Germany*, September 2009; and SECOR Consulting, *The Global Market for Corporate Control*, submission to the Federal Panel on Canadian Competitiveness, 2008.
3. Seventy-five percent of buyers report that cross-border transactions will be more attractive according to Bloomberg 2011 M&A Outlook, available at http://www.bloomberg.com/apps/news?pid=conewsstory&tkr=BNP:TQ&sid=amUabqSU7rzU.
4. Bloomberg 2011 M&A Outlook, available at http://www.bloomberg.com/apps/news?pid=conewsstory&tkr=BNP:TQ&sid=amUabqSU7rzU.
5. See Appendix to Part I for explanation of the success and failure data.
6. *ABC News* interview transcript March 19, 2001, "BHP–Billiton merger confirmed," http://www.abc.net.au/7.30/stories/s262552.htm.
7. Gordon Pitts, "Australia's BHP Deal a Blueprint for Ottawa," *Globe & Mail*, November 1, 2010.
8. Associated Press, "Canada blocks Potash Corp. bid by BHP Billiton," November 4, 2010, Toronto.
9. See "The Panel on Takeovers and Mergers." The Panel has been designated as the supervisory authority to carry out certain regulatory functions in relation to takeovers under the EC Directive on Takeover Bids, (2004/25/EC) (the Directive). Its statutory functions are set out in and under Chapter 1 of Part 28 of the Companies Act 2006, http://www.thetakeoverpanel.org.uk/.
10. See "Forthcoming Changes to the Takeover Code and the Disclosure Table," Panel Statement 2011/22, http://www.thetakeoverpanel.org.uk/wp-content/uploads/2010/12/2011-25.pdf; and "Amendments to Practice Statements," Panel Statement 2011/25. http://www.thetakeoverpanel.org.uk/wp-content/uploads/2010/12/2011-22.pdf.
11. Paritosh Bansal, Soyoung Kim, Benjamin Lim, "Special Report: The U.S. and China start an M&A Cold War," http://www.reuters.com/article/2011/04/12/us-specialreport-china-merger-idUSTRE73B47V20110412.
12. Rio Tinto press release, http://www.riotinto.com/media/18435_media_releases_6881.asp.
13. Ken Smith, "Losing (Ownership) Control," *Harvard Business Review*, June 2009, http://hbr.org/product/losing-ownership-control/an/F0906F-PDF-ENG.
14. See Ha-Joon Chang, *Bad Samaritans: The Myth of Free Trade and the Secret History of Capitalism* (New York: Bloomsbury Press, 2008), and Daniel W. Drezner, *U.S. Trade Strategy: Free versus Fair* (New York: Council on Foreign Relations, sponsored by the Maurice R. Greenberg Center for Geoeconomic Studies, 2006).

15. This section borrows heavily from "Positioning Canadian Firms in the Global Market for Corporate Control," with permission from SECOR Consulting; work led by Ken Smith, one of the authors of this book.
16. For a summary of major court cases involving poison pills, see Bill Kucera et al (Mayer Brown LLP), "Delaware Supreme Court Upholds Net Operating Loss Poison Pill," *Deal Lawyers*, November-December 2010, describing *Versata Enterprises Inc. v. Selectica Inc.*, No. 193, 2010 (Del. 10/4/10).
17. "Portugal's Holding of Golden Shares in Energias de Portugal is Contrary to European Union Law," press release of the Court of Justice of the European Union, November 11, 2010, http://curia.europa.eu/jcms/upload/docs/application/pdf/2010-11/cp100112en.pdf.
18. "There is a risk that the Board neutrality rule, as implemented in Member States will hold back the emergence of a European market for corporate control, rather than facilitate it. It is unlikely that the breakthrough rule, as implemented in Member States would bring any significant benefits in the short term." Report on the Implementation of the Directive on Takeover Bids (Brussels: Europan Commission, 2007), p. 10.
19. Because of this sovereignity, European Union negotiators have not been able to offer a unified perspective on foreign investment rules during ongoing Canada–EU free trade negotiations.
20. See *Japan Proxy Voting Guidelines* (Rockville MD: Institutional Shareholder Services, January 2011). Also see Yasuhiro Arikawa and Yosuke Mitsusada, "The Adoption of Poison Pills and Managerial Entrenchment: Evidence from Japan," *Japan and the World Economy*, January 2011, pp. 63–77.
21. A 2005 study from the University of Montréal comparing Canadian (TSX 300) and U.S. (S&P 500) boards concludes that Canadian boards have 74 percent independent directors, versus 76 percent in the United States.
22. NP 62-202 on Takeover Bids and Defensive Tactics from the Ontario Securities Commission. Typically, the regulators will cease-trade the poison pill after 45 to 75 days, which is considered a reasonable period of time for the target to search for or develop a value-maximizing alternative such as a "White Night." In addition, in the case that the regulators do not cease-trade the pill within 45 to 75 days (which is rare), TSX rules require shareholder approval within six months of any shareholder rights plan adopted by a Canadian publicly listed firm.
23. Ottawa launched a public consultation on Canada's $40 billion telecommunications industry to seek advice on how it should create more competition, including increased the foreign ownership. Julian Beltrame, "Ottawa Gets Canadians' Advice on Foreign Ownership of Telecom Companies," *Star*, July 11, 2010, http://www.thestar.com/business/companies/rogers/article/822600–ottawa-gets-canadians-advice-on-foreign-ownership-of-telecom-companies. The report, November 30, 2010, *Spectrum Management and Telecommunications Consultation on a Policy and Technical Framework for the 700 MHz Band and Aspects Related to Commercial Mobile Spectrum*, can be viewed at http://www.ic.gc.ca/eic/site/smt-gst.nsf/eng/sf09949.html.

24. *New York Times*, March 10, 2005, http://query.nytimes.com/gst/fullpage.html?res=9F02E0DA163CF933A25750C0A9639C8B63.
25. AREVA annual reports.
26. Tata Group company website, http://www.tata.com/htm/Group_MnA_CompanyWise.htm.
27. Charges laid against Deutsche Bank CEO Josef Ackermann for approving a $15 million bonus to Mannesmann CEO following the sale of Mannesmann to Vodafone.
28. See case studies in the Appendix to Part III.

CHAPTER 10

The Role of Postmerger Integration in M&A Strategy

Without strategy, execution is aimless. Without execution, strategy is useless.

—*Morris Chang, CEO TSMC*

Notwithstanding the importance of M&A strategy, its real value does not lie in the strategy per se, but rather in its successful execution. A deal in and of itself puts two entities together with *potential* for value creation. While some of that potential may be recognized by the market and reflected early in the stock price, no new value can be created until the deal closes and the postdeal execution begins. The toast at the closing party should be with Gatorade, not champagne.

Postdeal execution is particularly important for companies that have centered their strategy around M&A and plan to make a series of acquisitions—whether because they are in a restructuring industry or because their business strategy is to grow by acquisition. While every deal is different, the company that is to successfully execute a series of deals must have an effective and repeatable approach to postdeal management—not only to succeed in each deal but also to ensure sustainable competitive advantage in the market for corporate control.

Deal logic, target selection, negotiation of price and terms, and effective postdeal execution together create a virtuous circle. Companies that implement well have better insight into how they can *really* create value in the next deal. As a result they will often be able to pay what is necessary to win a prized asset, gaining the support of their boards with a precise plan for value creation and a proven track record from previous deals. Indeed, although some of the most successful acquirers are criticized for "overpaying," they usually manage to "overimplement" enough to create value in almost every deal.

Conversely, the company that implements poorly after the deal not only messes up that deal but also arrives at the next one ill equipped to assess it properly, and without the support of the market or its board to pay what it takes to acquire the desirable targets. That becomes a vicious cycle, impeding merger success.

Clearly, postdeal implementation can make or break a strategy. Yet, at the same time, each postdeal implementation is but part of the overall M&A strategy implementation. The overall strategy should influence individual deal implementation decisions, and individual deal decisions can have a bearing on the competitive position of the company for subsequent acquisitions.

Postdeal implementation (we will also use the more common phrase *postmerger integration*, or PMI, although integration per se is not always the objective), is a large subject and indeed the subject of many books, including a book in this series—*The Art of M&A Integration*[1] by one of the authors of this book. The purpose here is to focus on the aspects of PMI that form part of the M&A strategy, specifically that help determine how the company is competing to win in a restructuring industry or as a portfolio company adding value to acquired assets.

What are the aspects of PMI most critical to M&A strategy?

There are three related aspects of PMI integral to the M&A strategy. First is the alignment of the deal logic—the buyer's bases for value creation—with the postdeal project focus. For example, if the company is playing a role in consolidating an industry, then the focus will be on functional integration and elimination of redundancies, but if the company is acquiring for product–market revenue synergies it may choose not to waste time and resources on finding savings opportunities, at least not initially.

Second, PMI itself must be strategic. It needs to be not only aligned with the deal logic but also deliberate and repeatable. The resulting organization will be a new competitive force in the industry ready to execute the next deal. In the best cases, the acquirer develops a reputation as an attractive buyer, which becomes an additional competitive advantage in the M&A market.

Third, the project management of PMI, especially the transition, is key. Implementation of all the postdeal actions can take years, but the companies that can arrive quickly at a stable new state are ready sooner for the next deal.

DEAL LOGIC

The components of value in the deal logic can be categorized into four areas: financial engineering, cost synergies, revenue synergies, and strategic options, corresponding roughly to the four ways M&A can create value outlined in Part I of this book.

What is financial engineering and how is it relevant beyond an individual transaction?

Financial engineering is the use of financial measures (as distinct from strategic or operational measures) to preserve or create economic value. Although some types of financial engineering have backfired in recent years (e.g., the use of complex financial instruments to enable a business plan[2]), this path to value has also had many successes. Indeed, speaking in the broadest terms, one can say that financial engineering is an intrinsic component of all deals.

Financially based strategies, however, do not drive all transactions. They are most critical in deals when there will be little or no integration or when the acquired company is unstable, or when leverage is high. In the first two cases, such deals are typically in the realm of investors or private equity acquirers acting in a controller or surgeon role, such as Berkshire Hathaway, KKR, or Onex. While the associated benefits can be of substantial value (e.g., unused tax losses, pension fund surplus, or capital restructuring), such actions do not usually drive the deals of other types of companies.

However, the third case—a high degree of leverage—can be relevant to any M&A strategy. The financial structure of the company is highly relevant to its ability to acquire. The ability to borrow, the value of the stock, and the cash reserves determine the capacity for the next acquisition.

The financing strategy of serial acquirers always considers the target debt-to-equity ratio, the ongoing value of its stock as currency, and cash reserves. These are not independent of each other. Too much debt or cash can depress the stock value. Rich dividends will raise the stock value but drain the cash reserves. Therefore, the financing and postdeal financial engineering of each transaction are done with a view to an optimal balance of debt, share price, and cash reserves.

Usually, share price dominates. A strong share price can be used to raise capital by issuing stock, although this can take time, and the market cycles may not be in sync with the deal opportunities. A healthy company with a strong share price can also raise debt more easily and cheaply. And obviously, a strong share price raises the value of the stock as currency.

The importance of share price has a virtuous impact on how an acquirer must regard the value creation potential of each deal. Successful deals that create shareholder value will enhance share price in the long run. In fact, the shares of companies that acquire well will outperform their industries, resulting in a further competitive advantage with each successive, successful transaction.

However, it may take time for the market to see the value of any particular deal. Typically, the success or failure of a deal is reflected in the shareholder return after two years, by which time the market has seen the progress in postdeal implementation and its impact on performance. The market may see a deal differently at the outset. Indeed, markets almost always react quickly and strongly to announced transactions. Valuations at close and at the one-year mark are often significantly different than the eventual value delivered by the deal—sometimes much higher based on the sizzle of the announcement and an overestimation of the true value; sometimes much lower based on concern over the value of the asset or the PMI challenge.[3]

The tendency of markets to react with speed to deal announcements—with a strong buy or sell signal—can cause companies to focus on transactions that will have an immediate positive impact on the stock. However, this tendency to go for short-term results can rob the company of two important sources of long-term value: opportunities that may be harder to implement, or real options that cannot be exercised quickly.[4]

Therefore the strategic acquirer needs to build trust in the market. The long-term performance of the company over many deals will affect the market's perception of each individual deal. The promotion of each deal to the market is not just an ego trip for the CEO but is critical to the market's early appreciation of the deal and therefore the value of the stock. The early valuation of the stock will affect the selling shareholders' inclination to accept the offer and will affect the speed with which the company can get its debt-equity ratio and cash reserves back to fighting form.

What aspects of cost synergy implementation are most critical to strategy?

As discussed in Chapter 2, cost synergies are cost reductions that come from eliminating or reducing redundancies between two or more firms with similar operations after they merge. For example, when two banks in the same market merge there will typically be branch and back-office redundancies.

For consolidation strategies, achievement of cost synergies to gain economies of scale is often fundamental to the strategy. However, every company must operate efficiently, so capitalizing on available cost synergies will be part of most postdeal implementation programs. In fact, postdeal cost-reduction strategies are often continuations of cost-reduction strategies in the prior operations of the merger partners, especially the buyer. Postdeal cost-reduction strategies are generally focused on the costs of physical assets, people, systems, and purchased goods and services. These are interrelated.

In consolidations, there is often redundant operations infrastructure. Opportunities to rationalize manufacturing or distribution operations will have been considered in the deal proposal. In the foregoing bank merger example, bank branches would likely be closed. If two manufacturing firms merge, they may or may not need all their plant capacity, but they can likely consolidate sales, marketing, or back-office functions.

Rationalizing operations should be regarded as part of the overall M&A strategy, as these rationalized assets are a significant component of the new firm's competitive position in the market and will be part of the value taken into the next deal. Operations rationalization also takes time and can require substantial investment. For example, if two merging manufacturers each with five plants find that nine plants will be enough, it is likely that investment will be required to equip one or more of the nine plants to manufacture the products or varieties that were made in the plant that will close. For a retail network, it is quite possible that to get down to fewer outlets will require that some of the outlets be in different places. Even in the consolidation of office functions, there are typically renovations required.

Staff reduction usually makes up a large part of the benefit of operations consolidation. However, there are typically other staff reduction opportunities in a merger. Strategic staff reduction looks at eliminating redundant work, not simply some arbitrary percentage of the work force, so it is typically focused on three things: which activities could be eliminated, which activities could be outsourced to a lower-cost provider, and which activities can be reengineered to be operated at lower cost. The postmerger environment is a special case for a review of these same strategic cost-reduction programs.

First, redundant activities and functions between the merging companies can be consolidated. In the preceding example, bank branches may close. If two manufacturing firms merge, they might need all their plant capacity, but they might consolidate sales, marketing, or back-office functions.

Second, the newly combined entity can take a close look at the effective use of internal functions versus outsourcing. Clearly, activities or functions already effectively outsourced by the buyer or the seller can be considered for outsourcing for the combined entity. In addition, the deal is a good time to question the outsourcing potential for any noncore functions, as the integration challenge can then be handed off to the outsource provider (i.e., there is no point integrating functions that will be outsourced later and then integrated again with the service provider's operations.) Conversely, if one merger partner insources and the other outsources, and the insourcing is more effective, the cost reduction may affect the vendor, who could be told that the newly combined entity will not need its services.

Finally, the adoption of the best-engineered processes and systems from either merger partner can be a quick way to improve process quality or lower the costs of activities or functions.[5] It is important to note that some costs may be incurred in the process, such as severance costs, employee and customer retention costs, and systems and brand investments. A thorough calculation of deal "synergies" will include not only postmerger cost-savings but also postmerger costs.

How far is too far for cost reductions; are there strategic assets that should be protected?

As in any cost-reduction program, postmerger cost reductions can go too far and harm the organization by effecting product quality, causing customer service problems, or creating unsustainable workloads for employees, for example.

In the context of a merger program (i.e., an M&A strategy involving multiple deals), there is an additional reason to cut cautiously: some of the acquired assets and resources that appear redundant in the context of the postmerger integration at hand could be valuable in the context of the M&A strategy down the road. For example, fully optimizing distribution and sales channels might not be wise if future acquisitions are contemplated that would add new products or additional manufacturing capacity.

M&A strategy therefore calls for the identification of strategic assets acquired in each deal that could be valuable in the future. This is not to say that rationalization of such assets should not be considered, but it should be considered in the context of the larger strategy, not just the individual deal. For example, when TD Bank acquired Canada Trust in 2000, the two companies had very different approaches to the branch network. TD had a reasonably well rationalized network with hours competitive with the other major banks, while Canada Trust had focused on accessibility and had what others would have considered an overbuilt network for the size of the bank and had extended banking hours as well. Had the new company rationalized the network there would likely have been significant customer attrition. Instead, the accessibility model was studied, improved, and adopted as a TD strategy. Having proven it successful, TD has since taken the model into its U.S. acquisitions, rebranding Bank North, Commerce Bank, and the subsidiaries The South Financial Group, Inc. (Carolina First Bank in North and South Carolina and Mercantile Bank in Florida) as TD Bank, "America's most convenient bank."[6]

Third-party channels deployed to reach lower value customers or to provide superior services to customers can also have strategic value. The reach of such partners can be relevant in target search and assessment as well as in postmerger integration. Nurturing such partnerships can be of strategic value in future competitive M&A situations.

Management of organization and culture integration is also of strategic importance beyond the individual deal. In particular, each deal provides an opportunity to select and develop the talent of the organization and to align the organizational culture with the strategic vision. (There is a full discussion of culture integration later in this chapter.)

What about systems integration: strategic assets or redundancies? How should they be rationalized?

Systems integration strategy is of increasing importance in today's companies. Virtually all industries have critical systems supporting operations and marketing strategies. In some industries the systems *are* the product (e.g., banking); in others they are critical to customer service (e.g., airlines). Clearly it is important to keep systems going efficiently after a merger; it may indeed be the single most important postmerger goal.

Speed is of the essence in PMI, especially for the serial acquirer, so the most effective systems strategies usually leverage the combined suite of systems of the merging parties, choosing the best system for each function and integrating both companies' data. This leverages the assets *and* eliminates redundancies. Some integration failures can be tracked to well-intended but hopelessly slow attempts to build the best new system. For the serial acquirer, this is simply impractical in most cases.

Typically, purchased goods and services also represent a substantial portion of the expense base, often half or more. While sometimes ignored in PMI, a consolidator has a significant opportunity to improve scale economies of the entire supply chain and to leverage ever-increasing buying power. Supply chain cost reduction, or *strategic sourcing* as it is sometimes called, is another postdeal strategy that can enhance the company's insight into the value of the next deal because often the same suppliers are supplying the entire industry.

What aspects of revenue development affect overall M&A strategy?

Recall the postdeal strategies for revenue capture described in Chapter 3 under the 5 Ps of marketing—promotion, place, price, product, and (the forgotten one) people. The postdeal strategies need to be consistent with the desired long-term market positioning of the acquirer as well as with the logic of each deal.

For example, customer segmentation and related product integration and pricing decisions need to be made in each postmerger situation, but these decisions need to be made in the context of the larger strategy. By doing so, the considerable time, energy, and investment required to manage postmerger customer retention and development can be focused on the customers that matter most to the strategy.

Customer segmentation can have strategic value throughout the deal cycle. An acquirer that understands the value and needs of customers in select segments can leverage the information in M&A strategy development and throughout the deal cycle for each transaction—target search, deal pricing, due diligence, and postmerger integration.

Marketing and brand development similarly transcend any individual deal. A company leading a restructuring will have a clear brand positioning that will be considered in target selection and will be implemented postdeal. The brand positioning will evolve, of course, as each acquisition adds new capabilities and new customers. Of particular note for companies acquiring for revenue growth is the common failure of acquirers to retain the entrepreneurial talent of the acquired company, the talent that made the target attractive in the first place.

Again, *thinking beyond the deal* is key. The key people who drove the growth of the acquired company are strategic assets for the new company. Deploying them in a manner that inspires them as well as leverages their talent will often mean identifying a development path outside the acquired asset. Their value to the individual deal versus their potential value to the company needs to be weighed carefully—most entrepreneurial leaders leave.

How should acquired strategic options be integrated into the M&A strategy?

Strategic options, or "real options" as defined in Chapter 4, that are acquired have to be considered and developed as part of the strategy of the larger enterprise, almost by definition. Almost every deal has some real options embedded, and they are not all likely to be exercised during the postmerger integration period. These valuable options need to become incorporated into the strategic planning of the larger company and not squandered for the sake of postmerger integration synergies, or forgotten.

For example, in the postdeal period companies often feel pressed to sell off assets that came with the deal but are not needed. In many cases they sell these assets cheaply—these are private sales by a motivated seller and so frequently become a bargain to the new owner.[7] *Real option considerations can change this thinking.* At the very least, by holding on to such assets, the company holds a divestiture option—the option to sell the asset later may be worth more than the rushed sale during the PMI process. In addition, there may be growth options associated with the asset that were not considered—some time to think beyond the heat of the deal may change perspectives.

Options acquired can also be material considerations in subsequent transactions. For example, a mine acquired as part of an acquisition of a gold company may have greater value when considered in the context of a subsequent acquisition of a company with applicable skills for the development of this type of mineral deposit or with processing and distribution capabilities for some of the co-located minerals.

Similar flexibility or growth options may also lie in the real estate acquired as part of a retail acquisition—some of the real estate may not be suitable for development of the old or the acquired business but could be suitable for the growth of the next business to be acquired.

Moreover, for the company that is being built by acquisition, the long-term strategy must provide the context for the PMI decisions in each successive deal. In each deal, the manner in which the customers, suppliers, capital assets, people, and strategies are integrated, developed, or disposed of is part of the M&A strategy and pertinent not just to the success of one postmerger integration but also to the success of the strategy overall.

INTEGRATION OF ORGANIZATIONS AND CORPORATE CULTURES

It is well recognized that culture integration is often the biggest yet least well understood challenge in the postmerger environment. How should organizations go about integrating and changing something as vague and amorphous as corporate culture? The typical response involves assimilation of people through joint task forces and a "Noah's Ark" approach to populating the organization charts. This is a very accidental approach to something so critical to the organization's future. In addition, such an approach has no bearing on the longer-term strategy of the serial acquirer or the desired culture of the company being created by the M&A strategy.

Organizational issues dominate most postdeal agendas, but not necessarily in productive ways. Organizational solutions need to be designed not to integrate whatever can be integrated, but rather to realize the vision of the deal and to develop the organization of the enterprise. In particular, issues of culture must be dealt with carefully and deliberately. Leaving culture to chance or "splitting the difference" on important decisions, rather than managing toward specific objectives, jeopardizes the value inherent in the transaction and the M&A strategy overall.

When competing or conflicting policies, procedures, traditions, and practices linger, they can paralyze an organization and make employees feel vanquished. Failure to deal with such cultural clashes has not only led to workplace misery, it has been the undoing of many mergers. In fact, failure to deal with corporate culture integration is the most frequently sited reason for merger failure.[8] In contrast, careful attention to matters of culture is credited as an important success factor in deals such as IBM's acquisition of Lotus and the formation of Novartis.

Can corporate culture be "managed"?

Developing an organizational strategy to support an M&A strategy requires the company's refusal to accept the common belief that corporate culture is simply a mysterious art requiring the influence of extraordinary leaders over several years. Most drivers of corporate culture are concrete, manageable, organizational elements. Describing corporate culture in such terms creates a solvable problem. In this way most of what makes up corporate culture can be defined, goals can be set, and all the "levers" of change can be coordinated to affect the desired outcome.

Culture is a force that influences what people believe, think, and do. In an organization, it can shape the following:

- *Attitudes/mental processes*: how people feel and think
- *Behavior*: what actions get performed and rewarded
- *Functions*: how people do things
- *Norms*: what rules get enforced and standards matter
- *Structures*: who does what and the nature of the hierarchy
- *Symbols*: what images and phrases have special meaning
- *History*: what stories and traditions get passed on to future generations.[9]

As a result, it can affect the organization's ability to innovate, relationships with customers, operational effectiveness and efficiency, the effectiveness of teams, and the well-being of employees. Moreover, culture can have a material impact on the implementation of strategy, particularly M&A strategy.

At its core, corporate culture is an interconnected composite of *values*, *work rituals*, and *leadership*. (See Exhibit 10.1.) Each of these is largely composed of more concrete elements that can be identified and influenced—and ultimately designed and managed. This does not

Exhibit 10.1. Corporate culture.

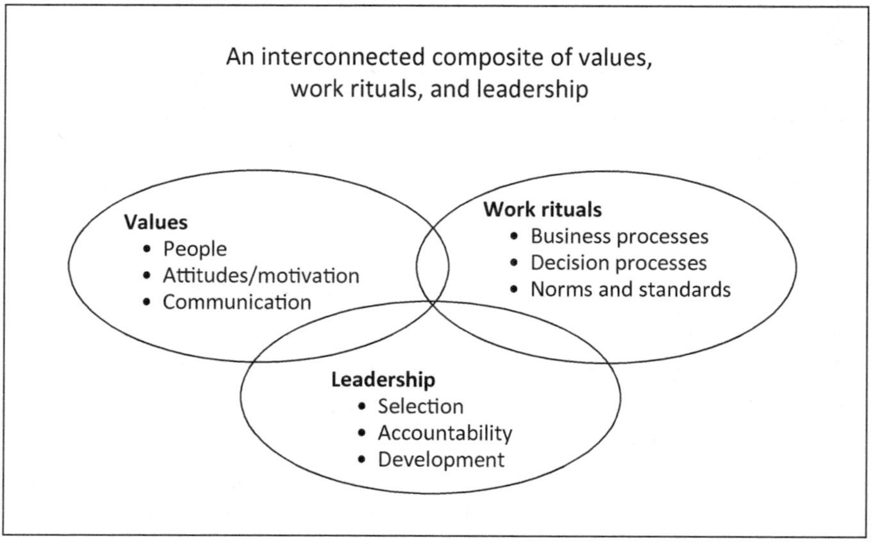

claim the existence of an "artificial intelligence" for corporate culture any more than that exists to create original artworks. Ultimately, real people in a given context make each corporate culture unique to some degree. However, most of what influences corporate culture can be directly managed. Well-designed culture management offers a pragmatic left-brain solution to the right-brain problem of culture change. This is not a formula for original masterpieces but a means to engineer desirable and predictable outcomes.

What is the role of values in achieving postmerger cultural change?

Collective values are largely determined by the values of the people who make up an organization, by what is understood about corporate values, and by what is reinforced or motivated. While individual values are said to be determined very early in life and are difficult to change, the collective values of an organization can be managed by managing people selection, communications, and rewards.

A national or local culture can influence individual values as well. For example, Americans may on average be more competitive, Indians more tolerant, Canadians more polite, Chinese more ambitious, and Australians more "one of the mates." However, even these stereotypes are representative; there is a greater range in values within a given culture than between two cultural stereotypes.

If an organization defines its desired collective values, it can select people with consistent individual values in the recruiting process. For example, if our corporate environment requires more entrepreneurial collective values, we can select for higher individual tolerance of risk. If the environment calls for a rapid pace, we can select for people more likely to act than to analyze. The most brilliant organization comprises not simply brilliant people, but rather a combination of intelligence and other intrinsic characteristics that can be managed for ideas, innovation, and action.[10]

Given the right collection of people, then communications and rewards (financial and nonfinancial) define and motivate the desired collective values. For example, in the integration of Temple, Barker & Sloane with Strategic Planning Associates outlined in Chapter 1, there was a desire for greater collaboration between the predecessor firms in client development. The organizations were largely made up of collaborative people, but integration required acceptance of risk and additional effort to work with unfamiliar people from the offices of the "other" company. Money spoke louder than words in this case. Saying that collaboration was highly valued had only a minor impact, but a new reward system with shared revenue credit rapidly created a more collaborative culture, and the previous boundaries soon blurred.

This cuts both ways. Three years later, senior management shifted its emphasis, directing more attention to "leadership credit" and divisional results. The shared revenue credit reward system remained in place but now included measurement and communication of individual and divisional results. The old collaboration gave way to competition. So collective values are not merely the sum or average of individual values. They are defined by people, communications, and motivation.

When put in these terms, it is clear that leaders have many ways to manage collective values: hiring and severance practices; performance evaluations and rewards; training and career development; statements of mission, vision, and values; communications through company events, publications, as well as other venues and media; and the way the leadership communicates and behaves.

Companies are using these levers all the time but not necessarily with the clear goal of building a corporate culture and attendant values. While collective values cannot be changed overnight, leaders can bring about more rapid and dramatic change by defining their intentions and coordinating the levers of change at their disposal.

What are work rituals and why are they important to postmerger change?

Work rituals represent "the way things get done around here," i.e., the formal and informal work practices. This is the second important determinant of corporate culture. Work rituals are largely determined by business processes, decision processes, and less formal but definable norms and standards.

Michael Hammer and the business process reengineering (BPR) movement have produced volumes on the relationship of business processes to corporate culture.[11] It suffices to acknowledge here that, properly implemented, process (re-)engineering will have a direct impact on many aspects of how work gets done—the steps in a given process, the roles people play in the process, the interfaces among these roles, and so forth. Decision processes are particularly relevant to culture changes in mergers. In merger environments, decisions need to be made faster than before, and they need to be made in a new way—to make the right decisions faster, often closer to the front line.

Norms and standards play a significant role in business and decision processes, complementing the equally important role of individual discretion. The credit union loan officer, for example, has scope for discretion on a good customer's temporary credit line extension, but the officer must also consider standard criteria as well as norms for the frequency with which such a benefit would be extended to any one customer. More subtle are the norms and standards that define the internal work environment. What time do people arrive and leave? Do people typically take time for the cafeteria or do they lunch at their desks? How casual is casual dress? Do professionals type their own letters, get their own coffees, and wash their own cups? Are executive doors open or closed? The answers to questions like these define the work ethic and the nature of the hierarchy and internal relationships. Changes in these norms and standards can be designed to achieve deliberate cultural outcomes.

Therefore, leaders have several direct and indirect levers with which to change work processes, decision making, and accepted norms and standards. These include process redesign, authority levels and approval processes, decision bodies and committees, policies and procedures, and the work ethic, hierarchy, and collaboration exemplified by the leaders. Deliberate and directed action on these levers, ideally in combination, will determine work rituals after the merger.

What is the role of leadership in cultural change?

Leadership is both a major component of corporate culture and a prime agent of change. Corporate leadership is more than the people who lead. It also encompasses the criteria for selecting leaders, as well as leaders' accountability within a structure and their development as leaders.

Criteria for leaders vary by company. It is well recognized that different leadership qualities are required at different times. The command and control skills required in a major project or turnaround may be unnecessary or even detrimental in a phase of development or a function requiring creativity and innovation. These are choices of both required skill set and desired culture.

Structure and accountability of leadership are also familiar instruments of culture. Flattening of organizations has been used to create cultures of greater freedom, whereas narrowing spans of control in sales organizations, has been used to create organizations more responsive to changes in direction or opportunity.

Leadership development is too often overlooked during postmerger integration as a way to manage culture. Most organizations assume that their chosen leaders will know what to do and how to behave during integration. But this ignores an important fact: for the most part, leaders are made, not born. While it is true that truly exceptional leaders seem to know how to lead in any situation, a merger involves many "ordinary" leaders. Ordinary leaders can be developed into better leaders, and through well-designed leadership development their actions can be aligned with the strategy and defined intentions for corporate culture.

Of the three elements—values, work rituals, and leadership—which is the most important to postmerger integration?

Leadership is arguably the most important of the three components of corporate culture because of its effects on the other two. However, it is not a panacea. Individual leaders can be rejected or rendered ineffective by their own organization if their actions seem incongruent with the perceived intended or required direction of the corporation overall. Companies must get the leadership model right—through leadership selection, organizational structure and accountability, and development—while at the same time managing the change levers of collective values and work rituals.

In summary, this vague, amorphous notion of corporate culture can be managed by directed actions on nine elements: collective values are determined by people, communications, and motivation; work rituals are established through business processes, decision processes, and informal norms and standards; and leadership is defined by leader selection, structure and accountability, and leadership development. Each of these yields to comparative analysis, design, managed integration, and alignment with strategy. Operated together, they represent the power to significantly affect corporate culture at surprising speed.

How can the levers of culture change be applied in postmerger integration?

There is no single answer because every deal is different. Requirements for success are highly dependent on the deal logic and the broader strategy of the enterprise, as shown in Table 10.1. Consider the following three general cases for the intended cultural outcome:

- *Case A. Newco takes on the culture of one of the merging companies.* This is often desirable when complete integration is required, as in same market bank mergers, or when one culture is clearly dominant. It may be necessary to go to the market as one entity, and processes and structures are to be completely integrated.
- *Case B. Cultures remain independent of one another.* This may be the case when the synergies are "end to end," such as selling investment banking services to corporate banking clients, or growth oriented international deals. As the banks have acquired investment banks, many processes and structures have remained independent. In most cases, each continues to go to market as a separate entity.

- *Case C. A new culture is formed that is different from both previous cultures.* This is the most difficult to achieve, but it is often a stated objective of acquisitions in changing industries. Frankly, it is usually a hollow promise. However, it can be a genuine goal in a changing industry, for example, as former

Table 10.1 Integration Options—Values

Culture Elements	**A. Newco Takes on Culture of Acquiring Company**	**B. Cultures Remain Independent of One Another**	**C. New Culture Is Formed**
People	– Severance packages are offered to acquired organization employees who do not fit the model – Training and development are used to facilitate changes in others	– Hiring practices and career development of both organizations are kept independent – Career management process remains independent	– Alter hiring and exit practices to develop the desired employee profile – Utilize training to influence/change attitudes and behaviors of remaining employees – A new career management process is created that fits the cultural strategy
Communications	– Adopt the communication mechanisms of the acquiring company by implementing matching information technology and providing appropriate publications to the acquired company's personnel	– Communication mechanisms continue under status quo	– A new communication program is launched to build awareness of the new expectations and its relevance to employees – Publications changes are initiated
Motivation	– Adopt the acquiring company's vision, performance review, and pay philosophy	– Performance review and pay structure remain independent	– Hold new company events, mission statements, reviews, rewards

telecommunications utilities around the world merge to compete in a more open global market.

Values

The value levers to achieve each outcome—culture of acquiring company, cultures remain independent, new culture formed—must be managed differently. For example, an acquirer can impose a culture of accountability quite quickly by holding people accountable—making sure the expectations are clear, rewarding performance, and removing those individuals unable or unwilling to get the job done (Case A). By contrast, IBM pointedly avoided the imposition of its culture on Lotus for fear of stifling the entrepreneurialism. This too had to be managed with internal rules about communications practices between divisions (Case B).

Novartis pushed both Ciba-Geigy and Sandoz to change to create a new company with a unified mission and image (Case C). In CEO Daniel Vassela's words: "Creating a merged company is like having a child, each parent looks for resemblance in the eyes and face. But it has its own identity. Both sides will need to step back a bit and not impose their own culture on it." They set tough goals to motivate a performance culture and overcome integration turf wars (See Table 10.1).

Work Rituals

Like values, work rituals require different approaches post-merger, depending on plans, as shown in Table 10.2. To illustrate, when IBM purchased the phone technology company ROLM Communications, it may have intended to keep the cultures separate (Case B), but it failed to protect ROLM from the IBM business and decision processes. "Keep your culture, but please follow our tried and proven capital appropriation procedures." Hence, IBM's culture dominated, and the ROLM deal became an unintended Case A failure.

Creating a new culture through business process redesign is often too big a task to take on in the process of PMI. When Exxon's Canadian division, Imperial Oil Limited, merged with Texaco Canada it got bogged down for months reinventing everything. If a new culture is required, early impact will more likely come from changing decision processes and

Table 10.2 Integration Options—Work Rituals

	A. Newco Takes on Culture of Acquiring Company	B. Cultures Remain Independent of One Another	C. New Culture is Formed
Business processes	– Redesign processes and structure to harmonize the organization under the work practices of the acquiring company	– Process design and restructuring not used to integrate organizations	– Process redesign is used to build new processes that represent best practices – New organizational structure is developed to drive and support the new processes
Decision processes	– Adopt the acquiring company's decision-making process by changing approval mechanisms, policies, and procedures in the acquired company's operations	– Decision-making processes and policies remain independent	– The decision-making process is modified to adopt new ways of approving initiatives that are consistent with the intended culture
Norms and standards	– Update handbooks – Fit new business into old procedures and social calendar	– Policy manuals, procedures, and social calendars remain independent	– Change to work style/social calendar based on competitor or a defined intent

informal norms and standards. Selected process redesign can come later as part of the broader organization development strategy.

Leadership

Leadership, too, is a domain that requires varying postmerger approaches, as shown in Table 10.3. It is well understood that leadership appointments send clear messages to the organization about the intended culture. Going into the deal, both leadership teams want to survive intact and are reluctant to give up power.

Table 10.3 Integration Options—Leadership

	A. Newco Takes on Culture of Acquiring Company	B. Cultures Remain Independent of One Another	C. New Culture Is Formed
Selection	– More leaders are chosen from the ranks of the acquiring company	– No changes in leadership	– New leadership is brought into the organization, or carefully selected leaders from both sides facilitate new culture
Structure and accountability	– The acquired company's corporate center is incorporated into the acquiring company's structure and reporting mechanisms	– Key elements of structure of leadership in both organizations remain intact	– Corporate centers are merged and redesigned to drive new roles and responsibilities of leadership
Development	– The acquired company's style of leadership is adopted by training and grooming specific employees in key positions of the acquired company	– Leadership development programs determined by each	– Comprehensive new leadership development program defined for all – Leadership communication promotes model of desired work culture

The popularity of the co-CEO solution, such as in the AMB Property Corporation's merger into ProLogis (NYSE: PLD) is an indication of the sensitivity to this issue. So too do the many mergers in which one CEO-chair becomes CEO, and one CEO-chair becomes chair. However, although such power sharing may signal that one company is not to dominate the other, it rarely prevents this from happening. The postdeal roles and styles of the leaders can quickly signal who has acquired whom and what culture will dominate. Rather than leaving this to chance (and to the personalities of the leaders) it is best to plan this. After all, giving leaders titles does not get at the deepest issues—the choice between independent cultures or a new culture and, if the latter, what the intentions of that new culture are.

Again, the solution is to be deliberate. This basically requires two steps. First, define which culture and leadership capabilities are required to be successful in the restructuring industry. Second, select and develop leaders to arrive ultimately at the intended culture. Preparing management for their roles in restructuring industries is a major task. Some acquirers have begun to use leadership development programs to prepare management for the mergers ahead.

These three cases illustrate definitive culture design choices and implementation mechanisms. There are many other effective levers of change available to leaders once they have defined their intentions in the practical terms of the nine elements of corporate culture.

How can newly merged firms manage their cultures in a way consistent with the merger and with the strategy moreover?

There are a number of approaches to analyzing and managing culture.[12] The following steps are ideally included in some form:

1. *Complete an objective, fact-based cultural audit.* In an acquisition, this would take the form of a cultural due diligence. For an issue as important as this, there should be an open assessment of the current values, work rituals, and leadership, identifying both advantages and potential incongruences of the current culture with the imperatives of success defined by the industry environment or the chosen strategy.
2. *Define the new culture required for success.* The new culture can be defined in terms of the nine elements—*values* defined in terms of people, communications, and motivation; *work rituals* prescribed by business processes, decision processes, and informal norms and standards; *leadership* characterized by selection criteria, roles and accountability, and priorities for leadership development for the new culture.
3. *Develop a coordinated plan to effect culture change.* First, managers should make a realistic assessment of the gap between the

current and desired culture, again along the nine elements. In the case of a merger, the gap would be defined for each company. Then initiatives should be identified for each of the key levers of culture change that will, in sum, close the gaps.

4. *Dedicate a cross-functional team.* Culture change is often delegated to the human resources (HR) function. As staff, HR cannot do this without the commitment and active involvement of senior managers and all managers down the line. The work involved is not that great in magnitude, but by definition it will not be "natural" to the organization and will, therefore, require a sustained focus. While HR might coordinate such a program, without the commitment and ongoing actions of line management HR will be a voice in the wilderness.
5. *Manage the change like a project.* Do not let your next acquisition be regarded by the organization as "another program" with speeches, workshops, newsletters, and the like, but no deliverables. Having a list of the key elements of the desired culture makes it possible to set goals for each. The specific actions to encourage and enable change can be scheduled and monitored. Actions will have far greater impact if they are coordinated and directed at established goals. In addition, the effect of the project on the nine elements can also be measured and communicated broadly to reinforce the goals of the change.

Developing and using a definitive process for management of cultural integrations can improve the entire M&A process, including the search and screen phase. While others might pass on an organization with an undesirable or ill-fitting corporate culture, skilled integrators will know if and how they can fix or align it.

PMI PROJECT MANAGEMENT

After a deal closes, what comes next? What should be the initial priorities?

A major merger marks the beginning of a large complex project. Integration leadership must define and lead key teams, integrate the deal logic into postdeal priorities and planning, and institute tracking of process and performance. Some key elements of postmerger productivity appear in Exhibit 10.2.

Note, however, that an overall process for postmerger integration is beyond the scope of this book.[13] The details of the process and team structures can fill binders. A few aspects important to the M&A strategy are emphasized here.

Everyone talks about the importance of speed. The emphasis here must be on doing the *right* things quickly. Again, this requires a focus on the deal logic and the needed changes in organization and culture, both consistent with the longer-term strategy of the enterprise.

The transition phase from announcement to a stable organization is critical. On the one hand, it is a time of low productivity when people are wondering about their job and the integration exercise is taking resources away from customers and the day-to-day business. On the other hand, the organization will never be as ready for change. So the company should move quickly on the organizational changes that will influence culture and on those aspects of the deal logic that can be implemented early.

This is in contrast to the common wisdom that culture takes years to change and integrate. The reason so many organizations experience slow cultural change and years of "we–they" references is because many PMI processes miss this window of opportunity of the disrupted organization and allow the organization to stabilize or "refreeze" in the wrong state.

Exhibit 10.2. Typical postmerger productivity.

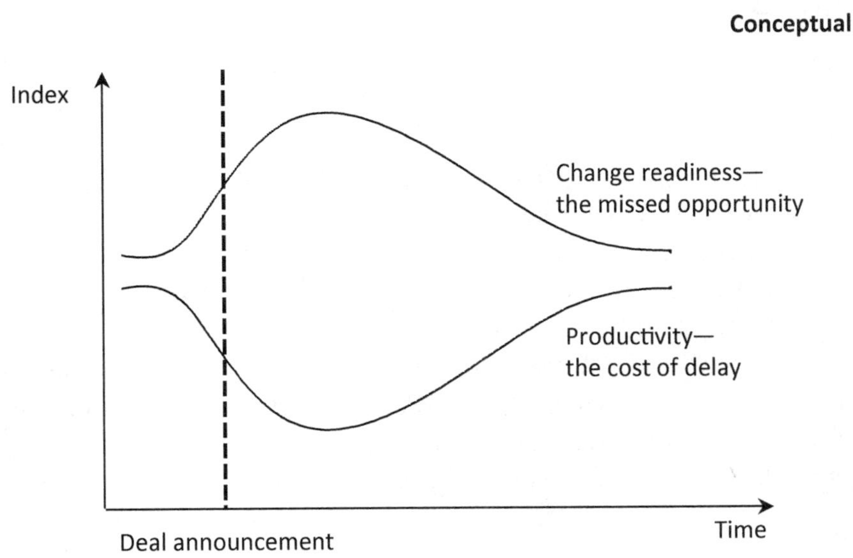

How do you ensure the rest of the deal logic is not forgotten?

Completing a transition, however, should not be viewed as completing implementation. Many aspects of the deal logic will require benchmarking, evaluation of alternatives, and significant effort over the next 6 to 12 months to ensure successful implementation. Pooled sourcing, technology integration, and joint business development programs, for example, may be worth hundred of millions in synergy benefits if implemented fully and effectively. It is important, therefore, that every element of the deal logic has a plan and an owner.

Initially, there is usually a hierarchy of teams engaged in a firmwide planning effort centered around the domain experts in each firm. However, after the transition phase most people have a line or staff responsibility in addition to their role on an integration team. This makes it difficult for them to maintain focus and momentum past the initial stages. The best way to maintain focus on the deal logic and to motivate the organization comes from metrics—tracking the ongoing progress and measuring performance impact. Software tools on the market are a good alternative to writing your own or becoming dependent on a consultant-supplied tracking program.

How can the management of the PMI affect the broader strategy?

Success in PMI and the speed of that success create value for the shareholder and build the confidence of the board and the markets for the next deal. In addition, if the PMI decisions are made in the context of the broader strategy, then each deal strengthens the company and improves its ability to derive value from the next deal.

Finally, in each deal there are new insights from things that worked and from things that didn't. A company that fails to learn from these lessons at the end of the deal will go on making the same mistakes at the beginning of the next one, when assessing synergies and selecting and pricing targets. The company that learns from every deal and from every achieved and frustrated aspect of the deal logic will have an advantage in the M&A market—the wisdom of experience.

Endnotes

1. Alexandra R. Lajoux, *The Art of M&A Integration: A Guide to Merging Resources, Processes, and Responsibilities*, 2nd ed. (New York: McGraw-Hill, 2006).
2. Financial engineering periodically backfires, giving its architects (generally Wall Street investment bankers) a bad name. Examples include the collapse of the high-yield "junk" bond market in the late 1980s caused in part by overvaluations, the catastrophic bankruptcy of Enron in late 2001 caused in part by the poor performance of funds that did not appear on the company's balance sheet, and the meltdown of the home mortgage business in 2008–2009 caused in part by nontransparent securitization of bad loans.
3. See Appendix to Part I for discussion of time periods for shareholder value assessment of major deals.
4. For guidance on how to combat the perils of short-termism, see Alfred Rappaport, *Saving Capitalism from Short-Termism: How to Build Long-Term Value and Take Back Our Financial Future* (New York: McGraw-Hill, 2011).
5. Michael Hammer and James Champy, *Reengineering the Corporation: A Manifesto for the Business Revolution* (New York: HarperBusiness, 1994).
6. TD Bank, N.A. "Company History," 2011, http://www.tdbank.com/aboutus/company_history.html.
7. Acquisitions of private companies perform significantly better for the acquirer in part because the seller is motivated to get rid of the asset. See the Appendix to Part I for the analysis and explanation.
8. For ongoing research into the underlying causes of failures, see the Appendix to Part I.
9. This list is based in part on the writings of John H. Bodley, *Cultural Anthropology: Tribes, States, and the Global System* (Lanham, MD: AltaMira Press, 1994), cited in Lajoux, *The Art of M&A Integration,* op. cit., note 1. Professor Bodley is the chair of the Department of Anthropology at Washington State University.
10. For guidance on how to build an innovative culture, see Suzanne Harrison and Patrick Sullivan, *Edison Returns to the Boardroom* (New York: John Wiley, 2011).
11. Michael Hammer and James Champy. op. cit., note 5.
12. See, for example, the techniques posted with the M&A Leadership Council at http://www.macouncil.org/services.php.
13. We refer the reader to Lajoux, *The Art of M&A Integration*; and to the Merger and Acquisition Leadership Council, http://www.macouncil.org/leadership.php, for details on process, tools, and support.

CHAPTER 11

Building a Sustainable M&A Program with the Help of Advisors

The lawyer that represents himself has a fool for a client.

—*Adage of the profession*

The pace of change in business is escalating. Globalization and technology are increasing the complexity of strategic planning and, in particular, changing the competitive landscape and the scope of opportunities for M&A strategy. Staying current and advancing the company in the right direction is at the same time more important and more difficult than ever.

The company's own leadership team and internal resources obviously play a vital role, and many companies have increased their capacity in key areas relating to the changing context and opportunities. However, many have also turned to external advisors for specific skills and for the capacity to achieve the needed pace in M&A strategy development and execution, and to get addition insights on these major decisions.

This chapter describes the roles that various advisors can play throughout the M&A process, from M&A strategy; to search and screen; to deal structuring and negotiation; to due diligence, closing, and post-merger integration.

Going outside of the company for help on any issue is not taken lightly in most companies. First, it means additional cost—the cost of the service plus the cost of the company's time or resources to work with an external party, explaining the business and the situation, discussing the service requirements, reviewing proposals, and finally managing the work. Second, it can result in frustration when the service provider exceeds the time or budget, delivers work that is subpar, or provides advice that is not aligned with your intentions. Such disappointments occur with internal work as well, but third-party work seems more outside of a company's direct control, and the costs are directly out of pocket.

However, most companies do go outside for help when the situation warrants it. Sometimes regulation requires an external resource, such as external auditors. Sometimes a particular skill is needed that few companies maintain in house, such as a litigator. Sometimes there is a peak in workload for which it would not be economic to hire permanent staff, such as a seasonal rush of work common in retail. Sometimes a situation calls for knowledge that you do not have in house, such as insight into an overseas market you are considering entering.

M&A—from the planning phase through the transactional phase, on through to postmerger integration—incorporates all these conditions and two more in addition. Major deals are *high stakes* and *high risk.* Given the value at stake and the failure rates of M&A, getting the right help in the right parts of the process makes good sense.

The purpose of this chapter is to outline which types of advisors can be helpful at each stage of the process, what value they bring, how to manage costs, and how to ensure independent and sound advice. The chapter is structured according to the stages of the M&A process from start to finish. Throughout, we will look at how help can be used in the individual transactions as well as how advisors can support a sustaining M&A program over time.

M&A STRATEGY ADVISORS

How common is it to use strategy consultants for M&A?

M&A and strategy go hand in hand. Although not every strategy includes an M&A plan, every strategy must at least consider M&A as an option, and every M&A plan must link back to strategy.

Therefore, as discussed in Chapter 5, M&A strategy should ideally be part of the overall strategy development process. Many companies get help with strategy from strategy consultants, either annually or occasionally, because they find that the independent perspective and the analytical research services most firms offer are a helpful addition to the internal capabilities.

The board is ultimately responsible for the strategic direction of the company. Management, in collaboration with the board and with or without the help of consultants, will develop the strategy—management needs to "own it" and be accountable for the results. The role of consultants, whether facilitating the process, augmenting the analysis, or offering recommendations, is to *support* management and the board.

How are strategy consultants used most effectively during the M&A strategy phase?

First of all, you may not need advisors at this stage at all. If your organization is effective at strategy development and has experience in M&A considerations, then this can probably be handled in house. Most of the portfolio companies, for example, would handle this stage internally. However, they may revert to outside help when considering an unfamiliar sector or geography, using a consultant to develop an analysis of the market and the key players.

If strategy consultants are already assisting with strategy development, there is great synergy in asking the same consultants to include M&A strategy in the scope of their engagement, if they are not doing so already. They will be starting with an understanding of the industry, the context, and the strategic intent.

If consultants are not involved in strategy development, new M&A considerations may warrant their addition. When strategy turns to M&A, as mentioned earlier, the stakes go up and so do the risks. Most executives have only limited experience in M&A strategy development, except those in portfolio companies or serial acquirers.

When consultants are engaged, expect them to think upstream and downstream from M&A strategy.

- *Upstream*: To be effective, strategy consultants need to know where a strategy came from. If you have a well thought-out strategic direction, they will need to understand it, at least, and they may challenge it.
- *Downstream*: Strategy consultants can also be helpful in seeing where an existing strategy may lead. The best strategy consultants can offer insights into the industry, as well as the business and operational challenges.

For a downstream example, understanding of industry dynamics and company operations can be helpful in considering the impact of a merger with a competitor. An advisor that did not know the courier business well would be hard-pressed to understand the benefits and postmerger integration challenges of a merger with a competitor. However, with an understanding of the industry, and drivers of profitability—pick up density, line-haul capacity utilization, hub capacity utilization, etc.—a consultant can help model how the companies would fit together and how a merger would affect them. Short of this, merger considerations in that industry are just guesswork.

Consultants with postmerger integration experience can be particularly valuable throughout the M&A process because they understand how the value will ultimately be created and how difficult it will be to achieve.

Are there any caveats when it comes to using the same strategy consultants for M&A integration?

The use of strategy consultants for postmerger integration does raise the issue of independence. If strategy consultants know that their fee will be higher if a transaction goes through (because the firm will win the postmerger integration work), they may have a bias toward deal completion. Therefore, the engagement should be quite separate, with no guarantee of the postmerger assignment. In fact, clients sometimes entice firms to offer a lower fee for the pre-deal work with the promise of the postmerger integration assignment. This should be avoided—pay the firm properly for the M&A strategy advice as a separate engagement, and insist on an objective perspective on the company's buy-versus-build options.

Are there alternatives to strategy consultants at the M&A strategy stage?

The most commonly used alternative to strategy consultants in the M&A strategy phase are investment bankers, and there are some advantages. First, the senior bankers have seen a lot of deals, and many have excellent instincts on what kind of deals are needed in an industry. Second, investment banks usually charge a work fee that is only cost recovery or less. The bulk of their fees is contingent on a deal closing.

However, therein also lie the disadvantages. First, the M&A department of an investment bank is much more about deal making than strategy. They will not have experience with organic growth strategies and will typically not be as skilled at weighing internal versus external strategy solutions. In other words, they know how to buy, but they do not know how to build. Their analytics are excellent on financial matters, but they lack operational understanding and experience in deep industry analysis. Finally, they have no experience in postmerger integration. In fact, many investment bankers refer clients to strategy consultants for postmerger integration. Lacking experience in postmerger integration, while most investment bankers have a good understanding of the potential to create value, they may have a somewhat superficial understanding of what it takes to realize that potential after the deal.

Second, the contingent fee structure is not consistent with the need for independent strategy advice. If the only way the advisor can profit from an assignment is to make a deal, they just might be inclined to recommend one, and the bigger, the better. Note that if a deal is consummated, the fees of the investment banker are typically far higher than the fees of a strategy consultant. Thus, while the consultant may have higher rates up front, their fees, and hopefully their advice, are independent of the deal.

Investment banks are valuable partners further downstream, as we will discuss, but they are an unlikely choice for strategy.

How do you choose the right advisory firm for M&A strategy?

Do not choose the firm; choose the partner. The experience and reputation of the senior professional that you may come to know and trust is the key choice. The most successful partners in any of the major professional services firms—whether or not they bill themselves as "strategy consultants"—can, in turn, assemble the best resources in their firm and scope and lead the work to meet their commitments to you.

The choice of professional services is personal in the end. In addition to skill, there must be mutual respect and trust, including trust that they will tell you what you may not want to hear.

In some cases, the right firm may not be a firm at all. For smaller assignments, there are many excellent independent consultants, some of whom are successful alumni of the major firms.

Strategy consultants are expensive—how can the costs be scaled to the situation?

Again, you may not need consultants at this stage at all. If you do, then strategy consultants will seem expensive because they are getting paid for the work, not a share of the deal.

The effort and cost of the assignment needs to be scaled to the stakes at hand. A smaller company does not need the $1 million M&A strategy study that one of the major firms would conduct for a multibillion-dollar client.

Some of the strategy firms and, more often, independent consultants will offer alternatives to the full-scale engagement. A lower-cost approach can involve the facilitation of an internal team through a defined process or the preparation and facilitation of a series of off-site executive meetings or retreats.

There can be advantages other than cost to the facilitator approach. If the facilitating consultant is working closely with internal resources and management, the process will usually result in better knowledge transfer and buy-in. Many a facilitated retreat has resulted in new directions and creative M&A strategies. There are also many expensive strategy consultant reports that never got implemented at all because the concepts and enthusiasm were not adequately transferred to the client. Thus, it is not always the most expensive approach that gets the best results.

SEARCH-AND-SCREEN ADVISOR

What kind of advisor is most helpful at the search-and-screen stage?

The most likely choice for outside help in the search-and-screen stage is an investment bank or other advisor working as a finder and/or broker, but strategy consultants and other advisors such as independent finders and brokers can also be used. An investment bank (or other broker or finder) will be the best choice when it is clear what type of firm you seek, whereas a strategy consultant can add more value if insight into the potential synergies will be needed throughout the search-and-screen process.

What exactly is an investment bank?

An investment bank is a financial institution that helps operating companies raise debt and equity capital in securities markets. Despite its name, it is not actually an investor or a bank in the traditional sense.[1] First, while an investment bank may take a position in equity offerings, it has restrictions on its role as an investor.[2] Second, although it may own a stock brokerage firm that manages client money, it does not offer traditional depository banking services. The main role of an investment bank is to act as an intermediary between saving and investing.

Investment banks often raise capital through underwriting—the purchase and resale of a new offering of equity securities. Investment banks also help market the new stock, distributing it to retail stockbrokers, often through a retail brokerage unit affiliated directly with the bank. These brokerage units in turn may have securities analysts who make recommendations to buy, sell, or hold particular issues (called *sell-side analysts* because in essence, they are promoting the sale of equity issues).

Also, some investment bankers get retained to locate entire businesses to buy, and so act as finders or brokers. They may also represent stockholder groups wanting to sell a company or one or more of its divisions, generally by a practice known as an "auction." However, it is nothing like the usual auction; it usually winds up in an extensive negotiation as to price and terms. As a result, they might get a series of fees—finder's, broker's, consulting, origination, and underwriting fees, and, if the securities are exchanged through their offices, a "security broker's fee." Finally, investments bankers may render a "fairness opinion" on a transaction, if they are not the ones getting a commission from it.

Together, all these fees are called "investment banking fees." In times of heavy merger activity, these fees bring in as much revenue as their retail stock brokerage and, some years, considerably more.

Investment banking firms typically have research departments that issue reports on equities. Prior to 2002, those firms would often include reports on client companies—including positive reports on companies whose stock the firm was bringing to market. Since passage of the Sarbanes-Oxley Act, such potential conflicts of interest have come under heavy regulation.[3]

What is the difference between the M&A services offered by an investment bank and those offered by a commercial bank?

In today's increasingly competitive market for financial services, the differences in M&A services offered by investment banks and at least some commercial banks have narrowed considerably. As commercial banks' lending margins have shrunk in recent years, they have sought other sources of income.

The commercial banks' capabilities include developing strategies for their clients with respect to acquisitions, recapitalizations, and leveraged buyouts, and acting as dealer-manager in tender offers, as well as rendering fairness opinions (as long as they are not the ones receiving a fee on a transaction). Investment banks, meanwhile, began to invade some of the commercial banks' traditional territories by offering to commit their capital in the form of "bridge loans" to their M&A clients to underwrite at least a portion of the cost of an acquisition, something that commercial banks may not do.

Commercial and investment banks often share clients. For example, a Wall Street investment banker might act as an adviser to a company doing an acquisition and take its deal to a commercial bank to obtain an acquisition bridge loan plus the long-term senior bank debt needed to refinance existing senior debt, later refinancing some or all of the bank debt with a private placement and/or an underwriting of senior or subordinated public debt.

When is the investment banker the best choice versus the strategy consultant in search and screen?

Investment banks have deep skills and efficiency in financial analysis and are experienced at approaching companies. Thus, with a clearly defined strategy and target criteria, they can be very effective at delivering a set of options that meet the criteria and are willing to talk.

However, if the criteria are less definable and/or relate to an understanding of operational synergies, strategy consultants can be more effective. A case in point is the search for a buyer of the downstream assets of the pulp and paper company referenced in Chapter 7. The strategy consultancy in that case was able to complete an accurate estimate of synergies from the outside in for a range of potential buyers for each of the businesses—this was possible because they understood the industry well and knew the specific integration opportunities and challenges. In this case, this advance strategy work supported the investment bankers who ultimately approached the companies and structured the deals.

By contrast, the investment banks on a loosely defined search can waste a lot of their time and yours with deals that do not fit. Given that their skills are more financially oriented than operational, they will tend to generate a lot of ideas that will quickly be seen by the client as nonstarters. You can expect only about half of these ideas to be worthwhile and only 1 in 20 to reach close.[4] This works for their business model but may not work for you.

Investment banks can also act as brokers, whereas the strategy consultant is qualified as a finder but cannot act as a broker. In addition to investment banks and strategy consultants, there are other consultancies that can serve as finders and/or brokers—e.g., licensed business brokers.

What is the difference between a broker and a finder?

A *broker* is an agent and a legal fiduciary with all the responsibilities and restrictions that those terms imply in law.[5] Brokers may represent only one side in a transaction. The rules governing their behavior have been established for nearly six centuries by the common law. Many M&A matchmakers have lost their fees because they were ignorant of these rules. Generally, brokers represent sellers and as fiduciaries must try to get a top price for a company. There can be civil or even criminal lawsuits if the broker favors the other side or is found not to be independent of the other side.

Finders, as opposed to brokers, are not agents of or for anyone. They are not fiduciaries. Unlike brokers, they represent the deal rather than one of the parties. Finders can be paid by both parties or by either party, even without the knowledge of the other. Finders, however, must be careful not to negotiate, for it is the act of negotiation that takes them out of the finder class, creates an act of agency, and places them squarely in the broker category, creating fiduciary responsibilities and putting them under regulatory supervision. Depending on the location, a "business opportunity" or "business chance" broker's license may be required. Payments to a finder, if he or she is deemed an unlicensed broker, can cause an entire transaction to violate securities laws, giving investors a right to undo the deal.[6]

What is an intermediary?

This is a straddling category that can be risky. Intermediaries are supposed to negotiate, and a *negotiating intermediary* is an agent of one party or the other in a contemplated transaction unless both sides have agreed—usually in writing—that the negotiation is in their common interest. People who are foggy about the distinction between brokers and finders, or want to play both sides, try to solve their dilemma by calling themselves intermediaries. Clients of brokers who turn into "intermediaries" should be cautious; the intermediary, depending on the language of the agreement, may be relieved of his or her fiduciary duties as a broker.

How do you decide whether to use a simple finder versus a broker versus a major investment bank?

The size of the planned acquisition will help determine your choice. If you know what kind of company (or companies) you are looking for, and it is (or they are) relatively small, it is perfectly adequate to use an independent finder or broker for your purposes. Larger transactions may need the clout of a major financial institution, such as an investment bank. Whether using a boutique finder or broker or a major investment bank, you will need to choose carefully.

How do you choose the right investment bank or other broker or finder?

As when selecting a strategy consultant, it is important to choose the right senior banker —one with a track record and one you trust. However, there is a difference in culture between the firms, with some being more transaction driven and some more client driven. This shows in the value created for their clients over time, with the client-driven firms creating more value over time.

In a recent study, editors of *Global Finance*, with input from industry experts, used a series of criteria to name Morgan Stanley as the top M&A investment bank for 2011 overall. (Additional banks won this distinction for their work in particular industries or countries.) The editors considered market share, number and size of deals, service and advice, structuring capabilities, distribution network, efforts to address market conditions, innovation, pricing, after-market performance of underwritings, and market reputation.[7] Publisher Joseph D. Giarraputo noted, "The best institutions are those that have a business model focused on customer needs."[8]

One of the greatest customer needs, and arguably the most valid one, is postmerger financial performance. In this respect, a 2010 study by

SECOR Consulting of 10 years of U.S. deals found that deals advised by some firms created an average of 10 to 18 percent shareholder value over industry during the three years following announcement, while deals of other firms resulted in performance 25 to 39 percent below industry. (See Exhibit 11.1.)

These two studies differed from the usual "league tables," ranking firms by the amount of money they receive from transactions.[11] Public companies and their advisors routinely disclose investment banking fees, so it is understandable to focus on them. However, league tables emphasize fees received, not value created. In choosing an investment banker, ask them about the latter. If they do not track postmerger value, that suggests they are more transaction oriented than client oriented.

Given the norms of contingency fees and/or postmerger consulting opportunities, can you get independent advice?

Contingency fees are problematic in that even when the advice is good, the clients are sometimes suspicious of the motivations. Given the above data, some skepticism may be warranted. Some options to avoid or mitigate the risk are:

Exhibit 11.1. Deal performance[9] by advisor for major U.S. acquisitions.

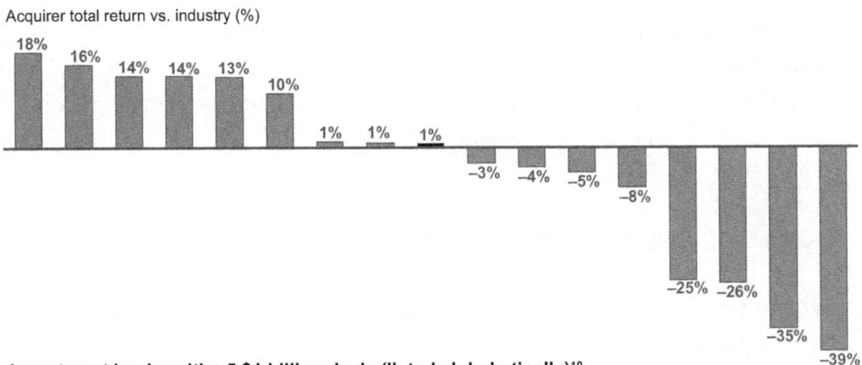

Investment banks with >5 $1 billion deals (listed alphabetically)[10]

Bank of America	Deutshe Bank	JPMorgan	UBS
Chase Manhattan	Donaldson Lufkin*	Lazard	Wachovia***
CIBC	Dresdner Kleinwort**	Merrill Lynch	
Citi	Evercore Partner	Morgan Stanley	
Credit Suisse	Goldman Sachs	Thomas Weisel	

*Acquired by Credit Suisse in 2000, but still uses the Donaldson brand name.
**Rebranded under Commerzbank in September 2009.
***Absorbed by Wells Fargo during recent recession.

Source: Bloomberg, *SECOR Analysis*

- Use a strategy consultant for the search-and-screen phase, alone or in conjunction with an investment bank. Pay going rates, and make it clear that the firm cannot count on post-merger work (lest they think of the strategy work as a loss leader into follow-on work and lose their independence).
- Ask the investment bank to play a finder role in the search and screen—full fees for time and materials; again, no obligation to use the given firm in the event of a negotiation.
- Hire a separate strategy firm to complete a due diligence on the synergy potential.

The third option has the added benefit of advancing the postmerger integration assessment and planning, which should ideally be completed at some level before negotiation in any case.

Once an acquirer has identified a company of interest, who should approach the company?

There is a hierarchy of value in approaching a company—from the low-level "mass mailing" that verges on spam; to the use of commissioned salespeople, retained advisors, or company officers to make calls on the phone or in person; to the "high touch" of a CEO calling or visiting a CEO.[12]

Many an acquisition door has been opened through the services of a veteran salesperson that has a gift of drawing people out. Of course, nothing is more credible than having a senior officer make the call. However, these leaders have a business to run. Thus, it is best to use others for initial screening; by the time an officer of the company is engaged, the target list should be small.

VALUATION AND NEGOTIATION

What guidance do you have on the use of advisors for valuation?

The choice of an advisor will depend in part on the valuation philosophy of the acquirer. There are many different approaches to company valuation, and different advisors are more expert in different approaches. The best professional services firms can offer a team of experts with a variety of professional backgrounds.

Here is a list of the some possible valuation approaches, followed by the type of advisor most experienced in the particular approach. Note that knowledge of the company's strategy is key to all of these approaches.

- *Valuation based on assets*: Professional appraisers are most qualified to give an opinion on the value of any asset, including an interest in an operating company viewed as an asset. The Uniform Standards of Professional Appraisal includes standards on business appraisal development and reporting of value.[13] One standard, for example, emphasizes the importance of "future prospects" when analyzing the value of a company or its securities.[14]
- *Valuation based on earnings*: Accountants are most qualified to give an opinion on the quality of earnings of an enterprise. The training it takes to become a certified public accountant includes mastery of accounting principles, especially generally accepted accounting principles (GAAP) in the United States but also their convergence with International Financial Reporting Standards globally. Accounting numbers including earnings must meet the four main recognition criteria of GAAP (definitions, measurability, relevance, and reliability) and must conform to the fundamental concepts of accounting (accounting period and principles including accrual, conservatism, consistency, cost, going concern, matching, and money measurement).[15]
- *Valuation based on discounted future cash flow, anticipated future stock price, or hybrid approaches such as economic value added, cash flow return on investment, and the like:* Here we are moving beyond the domain of company assets and financial reports and are considering a more complex array of phenomena. The appraiser or accountant may or may not be versed in such matters; a financial professional will be needed. The most expert outside valuation opinions will come from investment bankers or from major commercial bankers who have experience with peer companies. Any of these advisors may seek the services of credit rating agencies such as DBRS, Fitch, Moody's, or Standard & Poor's. During the most recent financial crisis, when the U.S. government purchased company securities, it used an investment bank for its analysis.[16]

Bear in mind that valuation of a company in an M&A setting is highly relative to the buyer and so is inextricably related to *negotiation*, which also requires advisors—generally lawyers. The price paid is interrelated with other deal factors such as the acquirer's plans for the senior management, the employees, and various other stakeholders (often referred to generally as *social issues*). Numerous issues must be negotiated in connection with an acquisition agreement—both business and legal.

What is a fairness opinion and who generally gives it?

A fairness opinion, as its name suggests, is an opinion about the fairness of a transaction. It is provided by an independent third party (an auditor, investment bank, or valuation firm) on the financial terms of a merger or other transaction. Such letters are used especially when a transaction can create a conflict of interest between the parties to this transaction—for example, a management buyout that by definition pits the interests of the insider managers who are buying against the shareholders of the company that is selling. Submitted in the form of a letter, the fairness opinion is most frequently based on detailed valuation work. The purpose of rendering the opinion is to provide the directors and/or shareholders who will have to make the M&A decision with deeper insight into its value from an independent source.[17]

Any qualified professional with no stake in the transaction, including an independent appraiser, accountant, investment banker, or commercial banker, may render a fairness opinion.

There is a protocol of what needs to go into a fairness option. Traditionally, the scope of fairness opinions was considered under state law, but in recent years, for securities brokers regulated by the Financial Industry Regulatory Authority (FINRA), a federal standard has emerged: FINRA 2290. The rule requires all FINRA member firms that issue fairness opinions to disclose whether they have material relationships with any party to the transaction. They are also required to disclose whether their fee is contingent on the success of the transaction. Procedurally, FINRA member firms are required to have written procedures outlining processes and to disclose whether a fairness committee was involved in approving opinions issued. They must also disclose whether they have relied on independently verified information in coming to a conclusion on fairness and whether they expressed any opinion on the fairness of compensation to be received by insiders as a result of the transaction relative to shareholders.[18]

DUE DILIGENCE

What exactly is M&A due diligence, and what kinds of advisors perform it?

M&A due diligence refers to a study of a company to identify material risks that it could pose in a transaction. It is similar to the due diligence conducted on a company prior to an equity offering, where the term *due diligence* is also used. Typically, due diligence means looking at the company's management and operations, financial statements, and legal compliance, as well as conducting a thorough study of the transaction's own documents and process.

To conduct due diligence, the acquirer typically supplements in-house sources of expertise with retained consultants and advisors. While inside managers may assess the target company's management and operations, outsiders are often used for the other aspects of due diligence. At a minimum, the due diligence team will include accounting personnel for the financial statement review and legal personnel for the liability exposure and transactional review—right up to closing.

The accountants and the lawyers engaged have separate and distinct responsibilities, although they may communicate with each other. The acquirer may also bring in management consultants, financial advisors, engineers, environmental experts, or other professional talent as needed. Typically, the acquirer's outside counsel directs the review, with help from a variety of other agents of the acquirer. These agents might include senior management (especially the chief financial officer), internal legal and accounting staff, external accountants, and investment bankers. The party directing the review should be free from any conflicts of interest.

What is bringdown due diligence, and how can advisors help?

"Bringdown" due diligence is the performance of due diligence right up until the closing date.[19] Dealmakers speak of "bringing down" the due diligence through additional meetings and conference calls to update seller warrantees and representations. This can protect a buyer against a claim that it should have uncovered or some eleventh-hour development that was not included in representations and warranties. Advisors can help make sure that all the material information about the seller—including those impacting strategy for the future combined company—gets disclosed.

Qualified legal counsel will help ensure that the acquisition agreement includes a section explaining conditions to closing, which in turn will include a "bringdown provision." This will state that the deal may not close if the seller has breached any of the deal's covenants, or if any of the representations and warranties were not true when made or are no longer true as of the closing date. The burden will be on the seller to update the information in the agreement (generally through reference attachments), but advisors on both the seller and the buyer side can encourage thoroughness.

POSTMERGER INTEGRATION

What are the benefits of using outsiders in planning integration?

Consultants can provide experience, expertise, and objectivity.[20] Managers should consider using the services of outsiders to compensate for their deficiencies in one or more of these regards or if the postmerger integration work simply requires more resources. Experienced acquirers tend to achieve better postmerger returns because they are more likely than inexperienced companies to have a clear plan and to implement it effectively and quickly. If an inexperienced acquirer wants to achieve these things, it may hire one or more outside parties who can help it form, implement, and accelerate a postmerger strategy.

Also, when merging with a competitor, using an outside consultant is a way to do planning before the deal closes without violating antitrust laws. When a merger may cause market concentration, it requires approval from antitrust authorities. Until that approval is obtained, the companies are not allowed to begin integration. They may, however, have an independent third party begin the planning work at "arm's length."

What are the drawbacks of using outsiders to help in M&A integration planning?

Once at the postmerger integration stage, independence issues raised earlier are usually less of a concern. However, some consultants will propose fees contingent on postmerger savings. This can be tempting but undermines the independence of the consultants and risks that costs are cut and resources lost that should not have been.

The biggest risk in depending on consultants at this stage is that the company may not learn from the process. With or without consultants, management should be sufficiently engaged to ensure that:

1. The deal logic is implemented to the full extent possible and that the resulting organization and culture are as intended.
2. Any lessons from the implementation regarding the practicality and true value of synergies can be applied to the assessment of subsequent deals.
3. Over time, each postmerger experience deepens the skills of the company in postmerger management toward development of competitive core competence in all aspects of M&A.

Endnotes

1. Updated from *The Art of M&A Financing: Sources and Instruments for Growth* (New York: McGraw-Hill, 1999), p. 224.
2. A provision of the Dodd-Frank Act of 2010 known as the Volcker Rule prohibits banks from trading for their own profit in securities, derivatives, and certain other financial instruments. See "Prohibitions and Restrictions on Proprietary Trading and Certain Interests in, and Relationships With, Hedge Funds and Private Equity Funds, Securities Exchange Act" Release No. 65545 (Oct. 12, 2011), available at http://www.sec.gov/rules/proposed/2011/34-65545.pdf.
3. In May 2002, SEC approved conflict of interest rules proposed by National Association of Securities Dealers and New York Stock Exchange, as requested by Sarbanes-Oxley Act, Section 501. See www.sec.gov/rules/final/33-8193.htm.
4. The source for this estimate is a series of interviews by Ken Smith, conducted with investment bankers and their clients, as background for the other research cited in this book.
5. This section on finders and brokers is based in part on Stanley Foster Reed Alexandra Reed Lajoux, and H. Peter Nesvold, *The Art of M&A: A Merger/Acquisition/Buyout Guide*, 4th ed. (New York: McGraw-Hill, 2007), Chapter 2.
6. See Wendy Fried, "The Secret World of Finders," *Inc.* March 2005.

7. Read more at www.gfmag.com/tools/best-banks/11097-worlds-best-investment-banks-2011.html#ixzz1TcOuNVmA.
8. "World's Best Investment Banks 2011, *Global Finance*. www.gfmag.com/tools/best-banks/11097-worlds-best-investment-banks-2011.html#ixzz1Tc1NZzjz.
9. SECOR Consulting; see Appendix to Part I for explanation of metric.
10. SECOR Consulting has the rank ordering, but the authors are not including it here, since such rankings are subject to many factors and change over time.
11. See for example "Investment Banking Scorecard" July 21, 2011 from Thomson Reuters, dmi.thomsonreuters.com/DealsIntelligence.
12. A combination approach can be effective in a roll-up, in which an acquirer buys many independent companies to create a large scale company. There may be too many potential targets to call directly, so a skilled consultant may be retained to screen them first for direct calls from the vice president of development or CEO.
13. Uniform Standards of Professional Appraisal Practice, 2010–2011; www.uspap.org/USPAP/frwrd/uspap_toc.htm. Standard 9 (and five related rules) focuses on business appraisal development, and Standard 10 (and four related rules) focuses on business appraisal reporting. These standards, as well as certification of appraisers, are overseen by an Appraisal Standards Board, which is appointed by the board of trustees of the Appraisal Foundation.
14. Uniform Standards of Professional Appraisal Practice, 2010–2011, www.uspap.org/USPAP/frwrd/uspap_toc.htm, Rule 9-4 b iv.
15. For more about the use of accounting concepts in valuation, see Robert A. G. Monks and Alexandra R. Lajoux, *Corporate Valuation for Portfolio Investment: Analyzing Earnings, Cash Flow, Stock Price, Governance, and Special Situations* (Hoboken, N.J.: John Wiley & Sons, 2011).
16. See Valuing Treasury's Acquisitions, Congressional Oversight Panel, February 6, 2009, featuring valuation material from Duff & Phelps, an investment banking firm (not affiliated with the rating agency by the same name that merged into Fitch). cybercemetery.unt.edu/archive/cop/20110402010539, cop.senate.gov/documents/cop-020609-report.pdf. For the final report on the TARP program, see cybercemetery.unt.edu/archive/cop/20110401223133/, cop.senate.gov/reports/library/report-031611-cop.cfm.
17. This answer is based in part on a succinct discussion by BNP Paribas, a diversified financial institution offering both commercial and investment banking services. See carteachat.bnpparibas.com/fairness-opinions.
18. See "Maximize the Utility of Fairness Opinions," Chris Ruggeri, reprinted from *Directorship* 2008, www.deloitte.com/view/en_US/us/Services/Financial-Advisory-Services/765a8ed08aff d110VgnVCM100000ba42f00aRCRD.htm.
19. For more on bringdown due diligence, see Alexandra R. Lajoux and Charles M. Elson, *The Art of M&A Due Diligence: Navigating Critical Steps and Uncovering Crucial Data*, 2nd ed. (New York: McGraw-Hill, 2011).
20. For more on the use of consultants in postmerger integration, see Alexandra R. Lajoux, *The Art of M&A Integration: A Guide to Merging Resources, Processes, and Responsibilities* (New York: McGraw-Hill, 2006).

CHAPTER 12

M&A as a Core Competence

The more I practice the luckier I get.

—*Arnold Palmer*

Mergers and acquisitions, once a realm dominated by conglomerates and corporate raiders, are now relevant for most corporations. As a result of fundamental changes in technology, deregulation, and globalization, most industries are restructuring and, therefore, most companies will be either buyers or sellers, or both. In fact, while historically major deals were a once-in-a-lifetime experience for most companies, today, most companies and executives will experience many deals.

In Part I of this book, we outlined how, in this context of restructuring industries, M&A can create value in different types of portfolio companies, in consolidation plays, in revenue growth, and in the creation of real options. In Part II, we applied this to strategy development, noting in the opening chapter that a company had better know how it would create value in M&A because the skills and the competitors for each type of M&A strategy are different.

Moreover, when M&A becomes central to the strategy, the company enters a new arena of competition. While a company may have had competitive skills relating to its underlying business or businesses, such as product development, sourcing, manufacturing, marketing, or sales, these skills are not enough to ensure competitiveness in the market for corporate control.

C. K. Prahalad and Gary Hamel, in their landmark article, "The Core Competence of the Corporation,"[1] characterize core competence as advantage derived, not from physical assets, but from "collective learnings . . . across organization boundaries . . . which are enhanced as they are applied and shared." Given the need to acquire and merge in today's restructuring industries, and given the persistently high failure rates from mergers, the message is clear: superior skills in M&A not only are valuable to individual deal success, but they also provide a powerful basis of competitive advantage. In other words, by Prahalad and Hamel's definition, those with superior M&A skills hold a core competence for today's business.

This chapter examines the steps in M&A strategy development and execution to identify the skills or collective learnings from which advantage can be derived: strategy development, defining the role of M&A in the strategy, candidate search, screening, negotiation and pricing, due diligence, and postmerger integration (PMI). Note that the point is not to define all the skills required, but rather, to identify those skills that can serve to differentiate a company in the M&A arena, and therefore can create competitive advantage based on core competence.

PRE-DEAL COMPETENCIES

How can strategy development capabilities provide competitive advantage in M&A?

While good strategic planning may have been a competitive differentiator 20 years ago, most companies are now quite capable of the basics. There are many well-documented processes,[2] trained and sometimes dedicated internal staff, and many well-qualified consultants if needed.

What is seldom done well and is vital to winning in restructuring industries is the development of *a truly insightful strategic vision*. Many regard the vision as merely a statement of a long-term goal or, worse, an aspirational statement designed to motivate. However, as defined in Chapter 5, a strategic vision should be based on the following:

1. An insightful view on the *future* industry context
2. Considered *choices* as to where the company will compete
3. Determination of the *competencies* or the basis of competitive advantage that will be required.

On each of these three, the winners succeed where others fail. Consider some of the examples discussed in this book. Thomson saw the sustainable advantage in gathering information with long-term value to professionals (versus the ephemeral news aimed at general readers), and they chose to develop and compete in this space by acquiring the businesses and competencies required to succeed. Time Inc. chose to remain in the (advertising-funded) news business but went on to develop the competencies needed in a multimedia digital world. As the Internet grew, the eventual impact it would have on print media was well understood. However, most media companies planned to a short time horizon. Most believed, correctly, that there was "plenty of juice" left in the old business, and it was the old business that they knew best. They "stuck to their knitting." This was not necessarily wrong for these companies in the context of their respective industries.

However, in the context of the industry restructuring that was to occur, those that took a long view to reposition (like Thomson) or build skills (like Time Inc.) had competitive advantage. Those that arrive late to a new or changing industry usually find the most attractive assets gone and/or are playing catch-up on skill development.

Similarly, the companies that foresaw the potential restructuring of their industry (e.g., BHP Billiton in mining, Interbrew in beverages, and Manulife in financial services) acquired some of the best assets (e.g., Alcan, Anheuser-Busch, and John Hancock, respectively) and had years of practice before others mustered up the courage.

Courage, while not a competency, is also a requirement for strategic M&A. In the early 1990s, as the global brewing consolidation was warming up, Molson surprised the market by investing further in diversification and selling down its brewing position to Miller.[3] Molson has more recently ventured in[4] but late to the party, with many of the best assets gone. No one today can say they have not been warned about the impact that globalization will have on the structure of most industries, yet most in the United States are choosing not to act and are quickly losing ground, as outlined in Chapter 9.

In defining the role of M&A in strategy, what competencies set the best acquirers—the winners—apart?

There are two imperatives for the role that M&A will play: first, there needs to be *alignment between the M&A strategy and the skills to perform it*; second, the skills need to be *competitive*.

The first requirement is mostly a matter of discipline, assuming the strategy is sound. For example, Berkshire Hathaway has to resist the temptation to take on a turnaround, even if it seems a bargain, because as a controller, they have not built the skills and capacity to manage turnarounds. A portfolio company that adds value through industry knowledge needs to stay within the sectors it knows best.

The same is true for operating companies. For example, companies that have focused on consolidation may have become expert at rapidly and fully integrating acquisitions. That approach taken to a product-market play, such as IBM's acquisition of Lotus, would have failed. IBM, Cisco, and others have learned that revenue growth requires limited integration, and too much integration can ruin the entrepreneurial cultures of acquired firms.

Alternatively, if the company needs to deploy M&A for a purpose beyond its experience and skills, then it needs to recognize the situation and get help if necessary. Note that a mismatch of strategy and skills can create exposures throughout the process. For example, a company that does not have experience with consolidation in an in-market consolidation (e.g., two banks) will typically overestimate the cost synergies, underestimate the time to achieve them, and count on positive revenue synergies when they will be negative instead. All this can result in errors in partner selection and pricing, the wrong focus in pre-deal planning and due diligence, and a PMI calamity. Many of the failed bank consolidation deals were in fact with companies that had been successful in cross-product or cross-market deals previously.

The second requirement is that the skills associated with the chosen role or roles for M&A need to be competitive with others that could be competing for the same assets. Note that the competitors for an asset could be unlike each other, interested in the asset in the context of quite different M&A strategies—interested buyers may include in-market competitors, adjacent market players seeking to expand, or financial buyers. The point is that it may not be good enough to be the best consolidator in your industry, for example. You may have to be better than that to win against a range of players that see value in different places.

Ideally, skills will be diverse. Every deal has some elements of financial engineering (even if only the deal structure), elements of cost synergies through consolidation (even if just headquarters), some elements of revenue development (even if only limiting the customer defections), and some elements of real options (even if only the new opportunities created through new scale or scope). Therefore, a skilled acquirer will have competencies in all these areas and will ideally be best in class in one of them.

The core competencies that are distinct for each M&A role will be noted as we move through the subsequent steps of the M&A process.

What particular competencies differentiate the winners in the search-and-screen stages?

This list can be derived from revisiting some of the key points of Chapter 6. First, the leading acquirers are all proactive, not limited to the deals that walk in the door or even by the companies that may be interested and looking for a partner. This suggests two differentiating competencies: a corporate development function that can manage a wider scope of search and corporate leadership skilled at nurturing relationships.

The first is simply a matter of recruiting the right team of analytically competent people and providing them with the right strategic direction. In a small company, this can be too expensive so, alternatively, one can use a consultant or broker to maintain the screening matrices (see Chapters 6 and 11) and revisit them from time to time. However, if the company uses a third party, then it is not a strong differentiator. Also, to the extent that a company's competitors have this same competence (often the case), it will not be a differentiator.

The ability to nurture relationships is less common and more difficult, and it is more often a differentiator of the winners. For example, Reuters was not looking for a deal and was proudly independent before Thomson approached. There were many months of confidential discussions exploring the common interests and values of Thomson and Reuters, discussions that included Ken Thomson himself.[5] Similarly, the developments of Southam Newspapers in Canada and Gannett in the United States were characterized by patient discussions over many years with the founders of the big-city dailies. The founders needed to know that the new owner would respect the principles behind these proud properties and that it was time to let go. The companies that sell to Berkshire Hathaway do not have to sell, and it is critical to Berkshire Hathaway that the management is competent and stays on.

In all these cases, the buyer is "selling" in that they are convincing an owner or management team of the virtues of the deal, a deal for which they were not looking and which they do not need. This is a *differentiator* because it is uncommon due to its difficulty. It is also a true *competence* because it can be applied and further developed over many deals. Through such differentiation, some companies develop a reputation in the market as an attractive buyer, that is, a company that one would prefer to be acquired by versus others.

A reputation as an attractive buyer can be very valuable in a restructuring industry. For example, in the technology sector Cisco became known for offering growth to the companies it acquired and leaving them relatively autonomous. As a result, many early-stage companies approached Cisco when it was time for the next stage of growth.

Is being an attractive buyer essential to every deal?

Not necessarily. As noted earlier, hostile transactions have very good success rates. However, a hostile transaction is not possible when there is a controlling shareholder. Also, hostile deals cannot be dependent on the good graces of the founder or the incumbent management. They are executed under the assumption that key positions will be filled from the outside and are closely managed by the acquirer. Thus, while the relationship skills may not be required, the hostile buyer must compensate with hands-on management of the acquired assets.

DEAL-MAKING COMPETENCIES

Are there differentiating competencies for the pricing and negotiation stage?

In a competitive M&A environment, the market essentially determines the price. The differentiating competency is knowing what you can afford to pay.

Particularly in restructuring industries, the most attractive targets are attractive to others as well. As a result, the competitive market will force higher premiums—premiums commensurate with the higher potential to create value. For example, many acquirers seek targets that have demonstrated superior growth. Research shows that the acquisitions of companies with high growth rates before the deal do not outperform acquisitions of low- or declining-growth companies. Higher-growth companies are rightly assigned higher multiples, but sometimes too high for the average acquirer's own good—they cannot sustain growth at the same level after the deal. Thus, it is difficult for the purchaser to earn back the acquisition premiums and provide a net positive return to shareholders.

Essentially, you get what you pay for. The market will force higher prices for strategic industry restructurings and for the most attractive targets. The net effect is that *price is the great equalizer*. In other words, the market for major deals is reasonably efficient. Price premium is not a good indicator of deal success because the premium one has to pay above stock trading prices will generally be in line with the potential value inherent in the deal. There are as many high-price deals that succeed as there are bargains that fail.

This hardly means that price does not matter. The price paid in an individual deal determines how much value needs to be created from the deal in order to break even or better.

The differentiator is knowing enough about the future for the company and the industry, the value you can create, and your alternatives to the acquisition to know how far you can go. This works in two ways. First, knowing the value you can create can prevent you from paying more than you can recover from the deal. Many companies get engaged in a competitive bidding process and stretch their own analysis of synergies in order to justify staying in the game. They might win the battle but then lose the war because they wind up paying a price that they cannot recover from the synergies.

Second, knowing the value potential with confidence may allow you to pay more than others. This includes consideration of the make-versus-buy analysis for an acquisition that is being considered as an option for an essential strategic investment. (As discussed in Chapter 5, such acquisitions cannot be valued in isolation but need to be weighed against the alternatives of "make" or "do nothing.") If you are truly the buyer that can derive the most value, then you can pay more. In the heat of the bidding, some disclosure of the potential benefits can also be cause for pause for the other bidders, whose boards might start asking questions.

In addition, when the buyer's stock is used as currency in the transaction, a clear and compelling explanation of the value creation potential will need to be part of the pitch. As noted in Chapter 7, the sellers in a stock-based transaction need to ensure the deal is win-win.

Knowing what you can afford to pay and still create value also applies to the bargain hunter or opportunist that seeks to buy undervalued assets. It is dangerous to assume that an asset is simply undervalued by the market. Acquisition of an apparently undervalued asset needs to be based on a clear understanding of how the asset will perform in the buyer's hands to result in a higher future value. Even in the case of companies that are able to acquire in down markets, such as Berkshire Hathaway, as discussed in Chapter 6, they are not so much betting that the market's valuation is inaccurate as they are betting on the future performance of the company and its sector.

What are the differentiating competencies in deal structuring and due diligence?

A recommended practice in this stage of the process is the integration of detailed postdeal planning into the deal structuring and due diligence. This is not a common practice yet, so it differentiates winning acquirers from others.

In every deal, the value is created after the deal is done, so the best acquirers develop a postdeal plan in conjunction with the deal structure to ensure that the structure supports the actions required. For example, every acquisition agreement includes a list of "representations, warranties, and covenants" that the seller and buyer make to each other. Representations are statements assumed to be true. Warranties are guarantees about those statements. Covenants are promises about the future. Ideally, all of these will be consistent with the acquirer's plans and projects for postdeal actions and results.

The consideration of postdeal plans in due diligence is also a recommended practice, which, if followed, can differentiate an acquirer. The traditional due diligence exercise is a confirmation that what you are buying is what you thought it was. It is essentially an audit of the company. If the postdeal plans are incorporated in the due diligence, then the potential synergies can also be audited. This inclusion forces earlier planning, a benefit in and of itself, and usually results in better plans with clear financial metrics and milestones.

POSTDEAL COMPETENCIES

What are the differentiating competencies in integration itself?

Effective postmerger integration builds on the pre-deal and deal-making competencies described earlier—for example, the choices and skills defined in the strategic vision, the alignment of the M&A role with the skills to execute, the ability to know what to pay based on superior insight into how value will be created postdeal, and the structure and due diligence with the postdeal action plan in mind. In addition, however, some competencies focus on the actual integration itself.

In Chapter 10, we mentioned the virtuous circle completed by effective postdeal execution—companies that implement well have better insight into how they can *really* create value in the next deal, which can affect target selection and negotiation and can support paying the price required to win because of the confidence in implementation ability and performance outcomes. Effective and timely postdeal execution also supports the stock price, which in turn puts the company back in the market ahead of others.

Superior postmerger management skill is therefore a potentially powerful advantage in restructuring industries—all the greater advantage because it is a difficult skill to acquire.

Why is it difficult to develop PMI skills?

Most executives would agree that the most common cause of acquisition failure is poor PMI. Yet most acquirers boast skills in integration—and resources offering help and insights abound. So why are the failure rates still 40 to 50 percent?

Developing PMI skill is in fact very difficult to do. It is a multidimensional challenge that is getting increasingly difficult as deal success increasingly relies on hard-to-get strategic synergies and the integration of large, complex international organizations and cultures.

There are three main stumbling blocks to postmerger management: *difficulty of retaining focus on deal logic*, the *challenge of culture integration*, and the *size and scope of the postmerger integration project.*

Why is it difficult to retain focus on the deal logic?

Although most deals have a stated logic, many fail to implement it. Postdeal audits conducted by one of the authors typically found that in failed transactions, only 30 percent of planned postdeal actions were implemented successfully. (See Exhibit 12.1.)

What happened to the rest? About 15 percent of the planned postdeal actions were either tried and failed or reconsidered after the deal. This is not unreasonable—after the deal, when all the facts are on the table, it should be expected that some of the ideas prove to be impractical.

The shocking statistic is that the remaining 55 percent of planned actions were essentially *forgotten or ignored.* In other words, more than half of the deal logic was not even tried.

Exhibit 12.1. Typical postacquisition implementation results (% of proposed value).

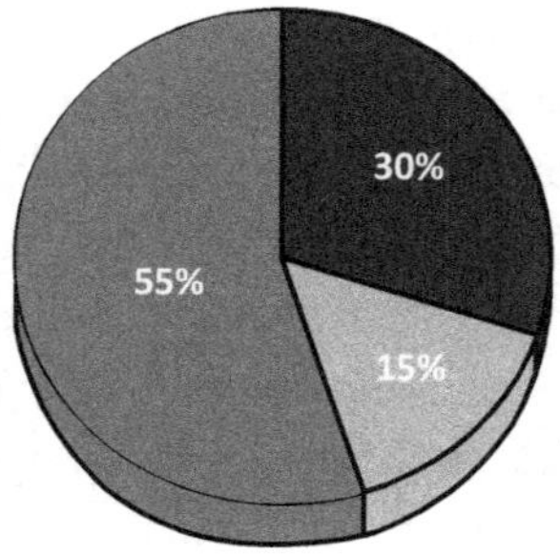

There are several reasons for this seemingly irrational corporate behavior. First, usually, only a very small number of executives and advisors know the details of the sources of deal synergies before the deal is announced—sometimes by necessity. Second, the planning and communications challenge is always underestimated, and the great ideas of the few who get to lead are never sufficiently understood and/or accepted by the many who have to implement. In fact, many deals are handed off to an implementation team with little more than a speech. Third, the postdeal environment is, at best, confusing and sometimes hostile. Urgent issues such as job assignments, outplacement, and customer retention consume everyone's attention. Without a strong focus on the high-value postdeal actions, the urgent will continue to squeeze out the important.

How can cultural issues impede merger progress?

While all agree on its importance, few know how to properly assess or integrate corporate cultures.

Cultural problems can begin even before the deal is signed. Some potentially attractive deals for shareholders are never even considered because of cultural rivalry: "They are our competitors; they have stolen our people and customers; they are the enemy." Similarly, a deal may be considered out of the question due to some perceived cultural weakness: "Those people are too bureaucratic." Sometimes merger discussions are abandoned because of perceived differences or clashes of corporate cultures that become evident during negotiations.

But often, the greatest failures happen after closing. Of the deals that close and fail, executives often cite failure in culture integration as a key reason. Part of the reason is the gap between lip service and action.

Executives often promise to respect cultures going into a deal, yet culture remains a mismanaged aspect of merger integration.

Most of the work goes into issues of structure—putting names in boxes—and the critical issues of culture integration are left to chance. The challenge is even greater with international deals involving not only intercompany differences but also intercountry contrasts.

How do the size and scope of the postmerger integration project affect success rates?

The project management challenge associated with a large merger is frequently underestimated. Allocation of resources tells the story. While companies may commit their best and brightest to high-level strategic planning on paper before the deal actually occurs, and then make heavy investments in outside help to negotiate and close, that is often when the attention ends. The leaders who were focusing on the transaction before it happened are now off on another vision, and the advisors are long gone. The detailed planning and implementation are left to the hastily assembled integration task forces, which often work on integration issues on a part-time basis while maintaining some or all of their usual responsibilities.

This lack of attention to deal implementation is odd given the enormous stakes involved. Not surprisingly, the deals that gloss over integration can bring misery in their wake.

The merger between Western Pacific Airlines and Frontier Airlines in 1997 closed in spite of the unresolved integration issues. The merger held the promise of more planes, more passengers, more destinations, more recognition, and more revenues. However, the two airlines were unable to come to a consensus on the process of merging pilot seniority lists. In addition, the schedule integration was incomplete and untested. On the first weekend of joint operations, flights were overbooked because of code foul-ups, and Western Pacific had new staff dealing with frustrated customers. In the fall of 1997, the deal was called off. Western Pacific later filed for bankruptcy, and in February 1998, the company shut down.

As we go to press, the warnings are sounding about cultural issues between Caribbean Airlines and Air Jamaica.[6] Time will tell on that deal, but often, the lessons of past failures are not leveraged, and history repeats itself. Many a distressed company can trace the cause of its economic decline to "that deal" and the poor integration that followed.

The effects of poor integration can impact an entire industry or worse. The effective moratorium on railway mergers mentioned in Chapter 6 can be traced to the poorly planned integration of Union Pacific and Southern Pacific in the merger of 1996. As a result of integrated rail schedules that just did not work, difficulties in negotiating workforce integrations, and a new computerized integrated control system behind schedule, there were acute and widespread service delays that affected economic output.[7] In our own day, the campaign by some to reinstate the Glass-Steagall wall between commercial and investment banking can be traced in part to acquisition-built empires that did not properly integrate, in this case appropriately separate, their diversified financial offerings. The U.S. government's report on the causes of the 2008-2009 financial crisis includes multiple references to mergers.[8]

What are the core competencies associated with postdeal implementation?

Chapter 10 provides an outline of the aspects of PMI most relevant to M&A strategy for the serial acquirer. We will use that outline as a framework, focusing on associated skills that are applicable across multiple deals and that are differentiators in the market. These are the core competencies associated with PMI for the serial acquirer.

What are the core PMI competencies associated with the focus on the deal logic?

Again, the components of value in the deal logic can be categorized into four areas: financial engineering, cost synergies, revenue synergies, and strategic options, corresponding roughly to the four ways M&A can create value outlined in Part I of this book. The first two are usually well executed. The latter two are more difficult and therefore represent greater potential for competitive advantage.

How important are financial engineering skills in the market for corporate control?

The mechanics of financial engineering are important to an acquisitive company, but most companies need not develop a core competence in this area. These skills are required only in the finance department and only apply to a specific and narrow set of integration benefits. While the associated benefits can be of substantial value, (e.g., unused tax losses, pension fund surplus, capital restructuring), the actions require involvement of very few people, and much of the technical detail can even be outsourced to investment advisors, tax accountants, and lawyers. Only a company in the business of M&A, such as the portfolio companies, need to build this skill as a core competence.

However, we outlined in Chapter 10 the importance of the promoting transactions to the market so that the stock price reflects the value as early as possible. This is a subtle task. It would hurt the company in the long run if the focus on the short-term market reaction prevented the company from undertaking deals with longer-term payoff in revenue growth and strategic options. Yet ignoring the valuation of the market in the short term hurts the value of the currency and makes it more difficult and costly to raise new capital. Therefore, the company must stay on course with longer-term potential and at the same time gain the support of the market without the benefit of short-term evidence from the deal in question.

This ability to earn the market's confidence and gain early positive valuation on the potential of a deal is, therefore, a difficult and differentiating skill. It is difficult because just the marketing of the deal and stock will not work unless it is accompanied by a track record of success in creating value in prior deals. It is differentiating because few companies have a sustained record of success in acquisitions.

What about cost synergies? How can an acquirer stand out from others in developing these skills?

Cost reduction is an important skill in most companies, but it is especially important for mergers, which often require changes in personnel and operations to reduce costs and achieve economies of scale. However, after two decades of reengineering and consolidation, most companies have now developed these skills. The postmerger cost-cutting exercise is often an extension of programs already underway. To the extent that competitors also have these skills, the acquirer's added value may have been negotiated away in the deal, leaving little opportunity for competitive advantage.

The key to success here lies in finding undiscovered sources of cost-savings or in getting faster or more effective at achieving the savings.

The most likely sources of undiscovered cost-savings are in the supply chain—vendors and customers. While the overlap between two merging companies' operations and organizations is usually clear, the opportunities to outsource, resource, or restructure the supply chain are often less obvious and less fully implemented. Thus, these competencies are more likely to be the source of some competitive advantage. They are not specifically M&A-related skills, but in a restructuring industry, the accumulated knowledge of the players and opportunities in the supply chain can be a source of advantage from one deal to the next.

In addition, the speed of cost-cutting can be an advantage. Experience, accumulated benchmarks, and codified processes can provide an ability to realize cost-savings faster or more effectively. This is not rocket science. Such experience, knowledge, and processes can save months of unproductive and even counterproductive effort, debate, and uncertainty, and in larger deals can be worth millions simply in the time value of money.

What is the best way to gain competitive advantage as an acquirer through revenue synergies?

Some of the more difficult and rare skills related to revenue synergies are in segmentation, pricing, and the maintenance of entrepreneurial cultures.

Everybody understands the importance of segmentation, but few do it well, and fewer still segment the market with a view to application in the M&A strategy. Especially in consumer-oriented industries, segmentations are often theoretical characterizations that are interesting but not actionable. There is little use in the definition of a statistical cluster of "socially concerned politically active idealists," for example, if you cannot identify them when they walk in the door or sign onto your website.

A segmentation of value in a restructuring industry is one that defines and distinguishes recognizable customers, customers that you can choose to have more or less of, and for whom you can take practical steps to treat differently. For example, a courier company can measure the average parcel weight and pieces per shipment of customers and price differently on these bases, and furthermore can use such a measure to assess the value to the company of the customers that could be acquired in an acquisition.

Product and service pricing in and of itself is an uncommon skill. Only in the travel industry, especially airlines and hotels, is there evidence of any real science. Those companies that sell what they regard as commodities simply accept their prices from the market. For most of the rest, there is a heavy reliance on cost plus margin as the benchmark for price, contrary to the market opportunity in many cases.

A superior competence in product/service pricing is of high value in a merger. Even in commodities for wholesale, such as petroleum and forest products, pricing can make a difference in postmerger performance. For example, the acquisition of Texaco's Canadian assets by Imperial Oil Limited (Exxon's Canadian affiliate) resulted in immediate price improvements through the implementation of Imperial's rack pricing system, including strict management of discounts. (Other aspects of this PMI were less effective.)

Thus, the core competence for PMI in pricing is twofold. First, the companies that are good at pricing already have an advantage against competitors in most industries. Second, the ability to use the opportunity of a merger to selectively improve pricing (rather than reverting to the lowest common denominator for each product-market segment) requires confidence in the pricing model that most companies do not have.

In the acquisitions of high-growth companies, acquirers frequently "kill the goose that laid the golden eggs"; that is, the entrepreneurial culture. As noted in Chapter 10, culture assessment, alignment, and integration are difficult and rare skills. In particular, the loss of the founder's drive and the entrepreneurial culture of a company may eliminate much of the value of a high-growth company.

If the acquisition of high-growth companies is a component of the industry's restructuring, then a systematic approach to integration that retains the growth cultures of the acquired firms can be a competitive advantage. Cisco's approach to acquire and only minimally integrate is an example of a repeatable approach that maintained the growth rates of acquired companies and was a core competence for Cisco's M&A strategy during the restructuring of its industry at the turn of the century.

How can the pursuit of strategic (real) options set an acquirer apart?

Real options are a relatively new science for management, except perhaps in the mining sector and some utilities. The skills are therefore uncommon. In addition, almost every deal has some real options embedded, so these skills can be developed and then leveraged going forward. Hence, this is a core competency in M&A and can be a competitive advantage, especially in industries where real options are not commonly identified and managed.

In the context of PMI, what matters most is not *identifying* the real options (which presumably has already occurred) but actually *managing* them. This means analyzing how changes in the company or its context may have increased or decreased their value and acting accordingly. Much like the management of protected intellectual property, which must be catalogued and managed to ensure currency,[9] so it is with real options.

PMI must include the ongoing management of real options well into the future (not just the first 100 days or so typical of intensive PMI management), as their timeframe is typically longer than the postdeal implementation project.

In particular, it is in the extended implementation period when some options may be exercised. It could be the sale of an asset (divestiture option), the investment to complete a product under development (growth option), or a change in strategy or asset use (flexibility option). Many companies would have long forgotten about such options acquired years previously. The competency to manage and exercise options at the right time is therefore a differentiator in PMI.

What are the core PMI competencies associated with the integration of corporate cultures?

Developing core competence in organization and culture integration requires that the company first refuse to accept the common view that corporate culture is some mysterious organization factor that takes years to influence.

As outlined in Chapter 10, *most* of what determines corporate culture is associated with concrete, manageable organizational elements. By describing corporate culture in terms of the composite of values, work rituals, and leadership, we identified nine concrete elements that can be designed and managed. Collective values are largely determined by the people who make up an organization, by what is understood about corporate values, and by what is reinforced or motivated. Work rituals are determined by business processes, decision processes, and a combination of informal and formal norms and standards. Leadership influence on the organization is determined by the selection of leaders, their positions and accountability, and their development.

Many companies define values, but few know how to manage towards values consistent with a desirable strategic outcome. While the skills to manage the work rituals are more common today thanks to process reengineering, reengineering is seldom done with clear goals for the desired culture. Managers today understand the importance of leadership selection, but few companies are undertaking leadership development to extend, deepen, and accelerate change. All three are important, but given the rarity of values management and leadership development components of culture, these are key differentiators in culture integration for competitive advantage in M&A programs. More than ever, it is important for an acquirer to have a deliberate approach to developing culture and values, in particular, and the right leadership development program can be instrumental.

It is a mistake to let cultural integration occur on its own without management. Indeed, the winning acquirer will select and manage key aspects of the culture needed in the new organization to implement the deal logic and ultimately the strategic vision. It need not be one organization's culture or the other's. It is almost certainly not the averaging of the two cultures that is most often achieved by simply pushing people together. We illustrated this in Chapter 10 with three representative cases: A. Newco takes on the culture of one of the merging companies; B. Cultures remain independent of one another; C. A new culture is formed that is different from both previous cultures.

Many companies define values, but few know how to manage towards values consistent with a desirable strategic outcome. The skills to manage the work rituals are more common today with all the experience in process reengineering, especially. The importance of leadership selection is well understood, but the potential for leadership development to extend, deepen, and accelerate change is not.

Thus, the key differentiators in culture integration for competitive advantage in M&A programs are having a deliberate approach to developing culture and values, in particular, and having the leadership development model to influence the behavior of a large organization.

IBM, as described in Chapter 3, following the earlier failures in culture integration would be a positive example, in particular keeping some aspects of culture separate while continuing to build a single company with common values. IBM made significant investments in leadership development to have a common understanding and approach across the many divisions and geographies of the company.

General Electric, with a very different approach, is another example. General Electric's focus has been on a performance culture, and the company has leveraged business processes, such as Six Sigma, and leadership development in the institute in Crotonville, New York, to make change happen across highly diversified holdings.

Are there core competencies associated with the management of the PMI project?

Integration leadership must define and lead key teams, integrate the deal logic into postdeal priorities and planning, and institute tracking of process and performance. The steps and processes are now well documented, and help is readily available.

However, many managers will be doing this for the first time and will benefit from training, support, and coaching. It will be a competence when the leadership skill is developed, the key tools and processes are codified, and the company can manage PMI more effectively and efficiently than competitors in the M&A market.

GE Capital, Cisco, and the best of the U.S. bank consolidators all have speed and effectiveness superior to their competitors. The planning process starts as part of synergy assessment. By the time of announcement, they can outline the plan to employees. The transition phase can be complete not long after close. Finally, the work on the more significant projects can then start earlier than anywhere else and start delivering value before less capable companies have their teams fully underway.

The GE Capital process is described in their "Wheel of Fortune"[10] model with four action stages: preacquisition, foundation building, rapid integration, and assimilation. Cultural assessment is the first step in the first stage. Processes and "nonnegotiables" are standardized. Plans are jointly developed with learning loops built in. An integration audit is completed at the conclusion of the process. Finally, the tools and practices are sharpened and taken into the next deal cycle.

Can a buyer be attractive to would-be merger partners and to the financial markets at the same time?

This is difficult but not impossible—and it is imperative for those who wish to succeed in the long term as acquirers. For many, mergers and acquisitions represent a nasty side of business. The phrase "we're being acquired" conjures up images of hostility, dislocation, and layoffs. Yet, in restructuring industries, being a buyer or a seller may be preferable to the alternatives, which often include retrenchment or eventual failure and bankruptcy.

Companies that manage the M&A process, especially the PMI process, with professionalism and respect will be noticed and potentially welcomed by other companies that determine they need an external solution. As it takes time and experience to develop such a reputation, this too is a core competency that can distinguish a company in a competitive market for corporate control.

There are three requirements to develop a reputation as an attractive acquirer without sacrificing the attraction on Wall Street: integrity, professionalism, and compassion.

1. *Integrity*

Playing fairly does not mean there will be no injuries and, in the end, no losers. In fact, it is this very process that will lead to competitiveness and value creation.

However, cheating and carelessness fail on both social and financial grounds. For example, hindsight analysis shows that on average, the share price of most target stocks increases significantly in the weeks before a transaction is announced. The inescapable conclusion is that this characteristic run-up is at least partly the result of leaks and insider trading.

That is not fair. It is also not good capitalism. The share price swings translate into billions of dollars stolen from the market to line the pockets of some unethical traders and investors. It is not easy to maintain confidentiality, but many executives have demonstrated that leaks can be controlled even in very large transactions.

2. *Professionalism*

Historically, most major acquisitions have failed to create value for shareholders. Our research shows that most of these deals had the potential to create value, even at the prices paid. These deals failed the shareholder in the execution—in the actions taken *or not taken* after the deal. That is when leadership, investment of time and resources, and outstanding project management become the make-or-break issues. Deals succeed when there is competence and professional execution. As outlined earlier, this requires zealous attention to three postdeal issues, which again align social and financial goals:

- *Deal logic*. Organizations that fail to act on the potential of the deal will not live to do many others. Major acquisitions come at a high price, and a failure to implement will ultimately erode capital, retard growth or worse, and thus fail both shareholders and employees.
- *Organization and culture*. The presence of competing or conflicting policies, procedures, traditions, and practices can paralyze an organization, and make some employees feel vanquished and others supreme. Careful attention to matters of culture integration is good for employees and is a key success factor for deal success and value creation.
- *Transition speed*. As the process drags on, the ideas that made the deal so promising do not get implemented. At the same time, the anxiety of the staff and the unproductive behavior can destroy a culture and waste human energy. Again, moving quickly benefits employees and helps ensure value capture.

3. Compassion

Mergers represent a crisis, even in the best-managed instances. At a minimum, employees and their families must deal with uncertainty and often loss. Job loss is one of the most stressful events in life, according to psychology studies.

There are mergers in which people have been fired by voice mail. This was not the intention of senior management (and hopefully never would be) but rather was the result of a postmerger process out of control. The shareholders as well as employees pay a price for poor project management.

Speed is a factor here as well, for employees that will stay and those that will go. A caring railway CEO confided: "I decided to implement gradually to minimize the pain to employees. It had the opposite effect. I should have acted more decisively."

Companies need to continue to develop acquisition and postmerger management skills—particularly to succeed in restructuring industries.

Acting with integrity, professionalism, and compassion will pay off in a reputation as an attractive buyer, making it easier to negotiate and implement deals in the future. At the same time, the shareholders will reap rewards from more effective implementation of mergers and from the capital markets that make them possible.

Endnotes

1. C. K. Prahalad and Gary Hamel, "The Core Competence of the Corporation," *Harvard Business Review*, May-June 1990.
2. See Selected Readings in Strategy and Strategic Planning Methodologies in the Appendix to Part II.
3. See Andrea Mandel-Campbell, *Why Mexicans Don't Drink Molson* (Douglas & McIntyre, 2007); also see www.fundinguniverse.com/company-histories/The-Molson-Companies-Limited-Company-History.html.
4. In 2002, Molson Coors bought Brazil's second largest brewery, Kaiser. In 2006, the Mexican FEMSA Cerveza acquired 68 percent of Kaiser Brewery from Molson Coors. Molson Coors still holds 15 percent of Kaiser brewery shares, and Heineken holds the remaining 17 percent. Source: Annual reports.
5. Speech by Geoff Beattie, President, Woodbridge Corporation, (family holding company of Thomson Corporation), Seminar of the Institute of Corporate Directors, Toronto, November 2008.
6. Peter Berkeley, "CAL/Air Jamaic: Odds Stacked Against Successful Post-Merger Integration," July 25, 2011, caricomnewsnetwork.com.
7. Denis A. Breen, *The Union Pacific/Southern Pacific Rail Merger: A Retrospective on Merger Benefits,* March 11, 2004, Sourced from www.ftc.gov/be/work papers/wp269.pdf; see also Russell Pittman, *Train Wreck: A Lesson in Megamergers,* manuscript, June 1, 1998.
8. For a detailed description of what went wrong in financial markets during the 2008–2009 financial crisis, see The Financial Crisis Inquiry Report: Final Report of the National Commission on the Causes of the Financial and Economic Crisis in the United States (Washington, D.C.: January 2011). "John Reed, former co-CEO of Citigroup, attributed the firm's failures in part to a culture change that occurred when the bank took on Salomon Brothers as part of the Travelers merger. He said that Salomon executives 'were used to taking big risks' and 'had a history . . . [of] making a lot of money . . . but then getting into trouble'" (p. 265) http://www.gpo.gov/fdsys/pkg/GPO-FCIC/pdf/GPO-FCIC.pdf.
9. See Suzanne Harrison and Patrick Sullivan, *Edison Returns to the Boardroom* (Hoboken, NJ: Wiley, 2011).
10. Ronald N. Ashkenas, Lawrence J. DeMonaco, and Suzanne C. Francis, "Making the Deal Real: How GE Capital Integrates Acquisitions," *Harvard Business Review*, January-February 1998.

CONCLUSION

The business environment has been changing and will continue to change in significant ways over the next few decades. While some of this change will be impossible to predict—the "black swans" strategists rightly fear—some trend lines are evident. As consumer markets in the United States and Europe emerge from the financial crisis, they will continue to grow more conservative about leverage, more concerned about the environment, and more globally aware. The middle classes in the developing economies will continue to expand and will soon dominate consumer spending. Inexpensive and pervasive media and communications technology will continue to homogenize markets and mindsets internationally. At the same time, freer trade and greater ease of ethnic migration will create cultural mosaics in every open economy.

Such market forces are causing an ongoing transformation in the requirements for business success. Consumers will continue to expect more responsible corporate behavior locally and globally. For most industries, markets are becoming or will become multicultural, multinational, or both. Many companies will require global scale and scope to compete. International supply chains are replacing domestic vertical integration. International wage gaps are narrowing. Moreover, the size and shape of most industries will change and, with them, so will the bases of competitive advantage.

As companies expand internationally, they will have to adapt to not only new regulatory regimes but also new cultures. Operating internationally is not simply a matter of knowing the regulations. Companies are increasingly recognizing the importance of the underlying cultural differences, e.g., the tax rates and restrictive labor laws in parts of Europe as a function of more socialist values, the bases in religion and tradition of Muslim lending rules and gender gaps, the nationalist pride in the centrally managed economies of Asia, the competitive character of the new capitalists in emerging economies, and the many and varied forms of greed and corruption in both old and new economies.

As companies reshape themselves to compete in these changing industry environments, M&A will play an increasing role in business strategy. First, acquisitions and divestitures can accelerate needed change. The reshaping of the company, the entry into a new market, or the development of critical new skills that could take a decade or two to complete organically can take a deal or two instead. Second, the cultural, market, and local policy understanding is very difficult to develop from the outside. An acquisition, merger, or joint venture can incorporate the needed insider knowledge and cultural sensitivity instantly.

Finally and most importantly, whether in the domestic or international market, M&A can accelerate growth and strategy execution. M&A programs that advance the company's strategy, position the company as a leader in the new industry context, and are well executed can multiply shareholder value. However, throughout this book, in addition to the examples of successful acquirers, we have provided examples and statistics of the failures. Still close to half of major deals fail to create shareholder value. M&A is high stakes and high risk.

Certainly, it could be tempting to walk away from the challenge, but in most industries, there is no choice. With the degree of change in customer markets, policy environments, technology, and the scale and scope of competitive businesses, those that are not buyers will eventually be sellers. Thus, an M&A strategy is needed, even if that strategy is to sell well, eventually.

With this context in mind, we have sought to provide in this book some ideas and guidance for strategists, leaders, and future leaders on the development and execution of M&A strategies that create value.

- Part I outlined how M&A can create value in strategy in each of a range of corporate strategy situations. The M&A strategies of multibusiness enterprises were characterized according to the typical roles and skills of their corporate centers. The motivation for consolidation and the particular challenges in creating value through cost consolidation were outlined. We then demonstrated the higher potential for value creation in acquisitions that facilitate new revenue growth and in acquisitions that create options in a changing industry environment.

- Part II provided guidance on the development and execution of M&A strategy. Beginning with strategy and the make-versus-buy decision, we then outlined how to search and screen for the right business combinations. However, in addition to make-versus-buy, every company must also consider buy-versus-sell. This led into the discussion of the board's role—the "sell" option may be presented unexpectedly to the board in the form of a takeover offer. Thrust into the front line, directors need to know and consider the true value of the alternatives. This underscored the importance for the company to develop and follow a suitably ambitious long-term growth plan.
- In Part III, we threw down a global gauntlet. Most industries are restructuring on a global basis, and M&A strategies will meet multifaceted challenges. Companies need to get better at M&A—and international M&A especially. Postmerger integration is fundamental to value creation, so PMI will be integral to M&A strategy for those who will acquire often. Help is available throughout the M&A cycle, and smart companies get the right help for the right tasks. However, people cannot expect third parties that are available to everyone to make up their competitive advantage in M&A. Thus, we concluded by summarizing the core competencies required throughout the M&A process. The company that accumulates experience and leverages these distinct skills will have a competitive advantage in the market for corporate control.

We hope that this book will inspire a greater confidence and ambition to acquire—and acquire *well*—to develop competitive corporations for the twenty-first century. The reshaping of our industries is an undeniable trend. The winners in industry restructuring, in most cases, will need to employ M&A in their strategies. This requires a set of skills well beyond those needed in the underlying core business, whatever that business may be. While many of the key skills are uncommon, they can be developed readily if a company recognizes the opportunity for growth through M&A and commits to developing excellence.

APPENDIX I.1

On the Success and Failure of Major Deals

"Shareholder value" appears throughout this book, and especially in Part I, as a way to measure deal success and failure. This appendix defines this metric, outlines the basis for it, and summarizes some of the key findings from the analysis of major deals.

THEORY AND LIMITATIONS

In theory, an acquisition is an investment like any other. An investment can be defined as "successful" if the net present value (NPV) of the all the relevant cash flows relating to the invested capital, the expenses, and the returns exceeds zero. Ideally, such calculations use free cash flow (FCF) so that noncash accounting numbers such as depreciation are ignored and the effects on taxes are taken into account. The discount rate is generally the weighted average cost of capital (WACC) of the company, although in theory this may vary for some types of investments.

There are difficulties in applying this metric to acquisitions, even for an insider and especially from the outside in. First, there is a problem isolating the FCF related to the acquisition. If the acquisition is kept entirely separate there is no measurement problem, but then there would be no synergies either. Usually there is integration of some functions at least; and some revenue or expense benefit of the acquired company to the buyer and/or some revenue or expense benefit of the buyer to the acquired company. So what is the incremental FCF that represents the returns on such a transaction? In addition to the fact the numbers being difficult to isolate, there are other things affecting the numbers, such as changes in market conditions and strategic initiatives unrelated to the deal.

Second, if stock is used as a currency, how should it be valued for the NPV calculation? If it is valued based on its trading value at the time of the deal, the market has already assumed some level of success or failure for the transaction, so the price of the stock includes some of the impact of the deal on the FCF. While this may provide a basis for an NPV calculation, it ignores the value gained or lost by shareholders leading up to the deal, typically a volatile period for the stock.

From the outside in, it is of course even more difficult. FCF can be approximated using required disclosures of public companies, but it will be even more difficult to isolate the FCF effect of the acquisition. In addition, if the insider can isolate the FCF impact of the deal, the insider may also be able to project the impact into the future—typically a significant component of the NPV. This will be much more difficult from the outside in.

Finally, the strategic value of the deal, that is, the value of the deal to the positioning of the company and the options created (growth options, flexibility options, divestiture options) is not accounted for in the FCF calculations.

BENEFITS OF AN EXTERNAL APPROXIMATION

In the long run, the market's valuation of any freely traded stock will approximate an FCF valuation.[1] While there are many inaccuracies in the stock market's assessment of a deal, there are some benefits of a stock-based metric as well, in addition to the fact that it is easier to find the data.

First, the impact of the deal can be measured from before it is announced and before the market begins to judge it. Measurement must start well before announcement—that is, before pre-announcement leaks and insider trading affect the stock price. Our analysis has shown that major deals begin to affect stock prices as early as three months prior to public announcement of a deal. So if the impact on shareholders of the acquiring company is to be measured, the base price must be set about three months prior to the announcement of the deal.

Second, there are industry indexes available so that changes in market conditions affecting all players can be factored out. Of course, any comparison must account for dividend policies. So if the total return to shareholders (stock appreciation plus dividends) is compared to the relevant index of total returns for the industry, then the differential performance for shareholders can be isolated.

Third, the market provides a perspective on current performance as well as future performance, incorporating projections of ongoing performance and the value of options. It is, after all, the market that we turn to for valuation of stock options, which are in turn used in the valuation of real options.[2] So if the market is given adequate time to consider the postdeal actions of the company and the resulting returns, it will account for the impact of postdeal actions as well as the continued progress. The market must be given time to see the impact, of course. For large deals that take time to close and implement, it would be at least two to three years before real impact could be evident.

Finally, our analysis indicates that for major deals, the postdeal impact of the deal overwhelms the performance impact of other activities of the company. In fact, postdeal stock performance is virtually independent of predeal performance,[3] suggesting that a major deal is a company-defining moment and as many previously well-performing companies fail as others.

THE METRIC: RELATIVE VALUE CREATED

We measure the total return to shareholders, relative to the industry. Starting three months before the announcement and measuring for two years (sometimes three for complex deals; it should be long enough for the market to see the real impact, but not so long that other factors confound the measure).

$$\text{Relative value created} = \frac{1 + (\text{two-year total return of acquirer})}{1 + (\text{two-year total return of industry index})}$$

where total return is share price appreciation plus dividends expressed as a percentage of stock value three months prior to announcement.

To illustrate, if the acquirer's total return was a 15 percent improvement over the base, and the industry's total return was 10 percent over the same time period, then the relative value created is (1 + .15)/(1 + .10) = ~1.045. So the deal has outperformed for shareholders by 4.5 percent. Put another way, $1 invested in the acquirer's stock got a 4.5 percent better return than if it had been invested in the index.

Similarly, if the acquirer's total return was only a 5 percent improvement in the same circumstances, then the relative value created is (1 + .05)/(1 + .10) = ~.955. So in this case the deal has underperformed for shareholders by 4.5 percent.

Using this metric, a deal is a success if the relative value created is >1 and a failure if <1. For major deals, this makes sense from a shareholder's perspective. If the company has made a large investment, and through astute postdeal management the company outperforms the industry index, then the shareholder is better off for having held stock in the company that did the deal. On the other hand, if all the capital was committed, and despite implementation of postdeal actions the company underperformed the industry, then the shareholder lost by betting on this company that did the deal.

For illustration, a sample of the U.S. deals of the 1990s is shown in Exhibit AI.1. This is a histogram of all the US$1 billion deals of the 1990s in Bloomberg. The bars show the number of deals with the relative value created indicated on the horizontal axis; for example, there were three deals with a relative return between 0.70 and 0.75, and 18 deals between 1 and 1.05.

The mean of 0.99 means that on average these acquirers performed 1 percent below their respective industry indexes during the measurement period, in this case the three years from the point three months before announcement. The standard deviation, or sigma, of 0.30 means that the

Exhibit AI.1. Illustrative sample, success of U.S. deals in the 1990s.

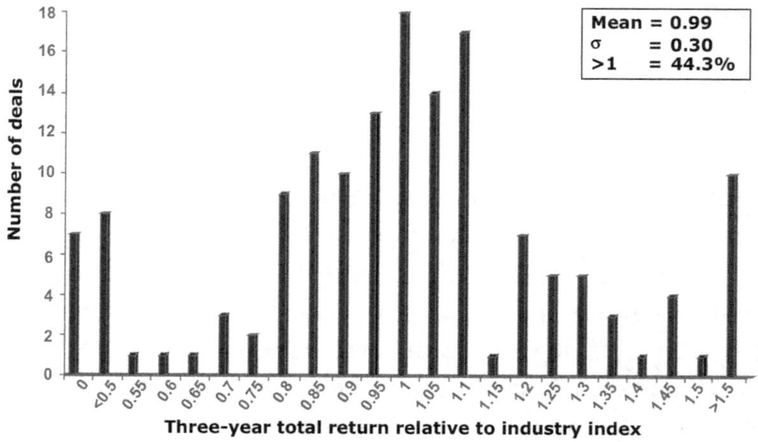

Source: Bloomberg, SDC, FP Datagroup.

performance range is relatively wide. The fact that 44.3 percent of the deals have relative value created >1 means that only 44.3 percent of the deals were successful by this measure and 55.7 percent failed to create value in excess of the industry.

Uses, misuses, and variations

This metric is more meaningful for an individual deal if the deal is large relative to the size of the company. A deal of 20 percent or more of the market value of the acquirer will typically be a significant commitment of capital or effort and will typically be material to the relative value created.

A given transaction may have extenuating circumstances. One cannot assume that a failure to achieve relative value created >1 is the fault of the deal or its implementation. However, from the shareholder's perspective it doesn't matter: the shareholder that held the stock from the point prior to the announcement of the deal for the two years to close the deal and implement has been worse off for holding that stock.

The start time of three months prior to announcement and the time period of two or sometimes three years may seem somewhat arbitrary. Regarding the start time, failure to account for preannouncement market action will distort the measure. Deals that are perceived to be bad ideas depress the acquirer's stock. Measuring from that depressed level would overvalue performance of the deal. Conversely, measuring from a point at which a deal perceived to be a good idea has been accounted for in the stock will result in undervaluing the deal impact.

Regarding the time period, less than two years is seldom enough time for the deal to close, actions to be taken, and performance impacts to be read by the market. For some complex deals a longer period may be needed. However, we have found a strong correlation between two-, three-, and four-year performance, suggesting that two years is adequate in most cases.

In contrast, there is a weak correlation between one- and two-year performance. This is consistent with the observation that large deals can seldom be closed and implemented in much less than two years from preannouncement.

The foregoing observations have been validated by analyzing the actual circumstances of some of the individual deals included in the statistical correlation analyses.

THE DATABASE AND THE STUDIES

This approach was first developed by one of the authors, and the results of the initial analysis were published in *BusinessWeek* in 1995.[4] There have been periodic updates of the database and analysis of a variety of sectors and M&A issues, including significant updates in 2003, 2007, and 2010.[5]

The most recent databases have included all deals tracked by Bloomberg >$1 billion in value, including domestic and international deals. For example, the 2010 database includes approximately 2,500 deals for which there are two years of performance data. (Some analyses of Canadian deals have included deals >$100 million in order to increase the number of deals for analytical purposes.)

In all analyses, the total population of deals in Bloomberg has been used above a specified size—that is, not a random sample. Bloomberg tracks all significant deals for which there are public disclosures.[6] Therefore, there is no notion of margin of error or statistical significance that applies. Rather, all analyses are based on all deals for which the relevant data are available.

SELECTED FINDINGS

Much analysis has been completed on this database and many of the findings have been published elsewhere. We have selected here a few of the most important findings, some of which underlay the themes of this book.

Price premium is not a key determinant of deal success

There is little correlation of price premium and relative value created in major deals. Exhibit AI.2 shows relative value created plotted against price premium. If price were a strong determinant of deal success, one would expect a pattern of higher premiums corresponding to lower value created. There is no such pattern. In fact the R^2 value (the statistical indicator of correlation) is very low at .0017 for Canada and .00000011 for the United States in this analysis.

This is not to say that price is unimportant—price determines the investment level and therefore the return that must be earned in order to break even or better on the investment. Rather, this finding indicates that

Exhibit AI.2. Price premium versus acquiring firms' three-year performance.

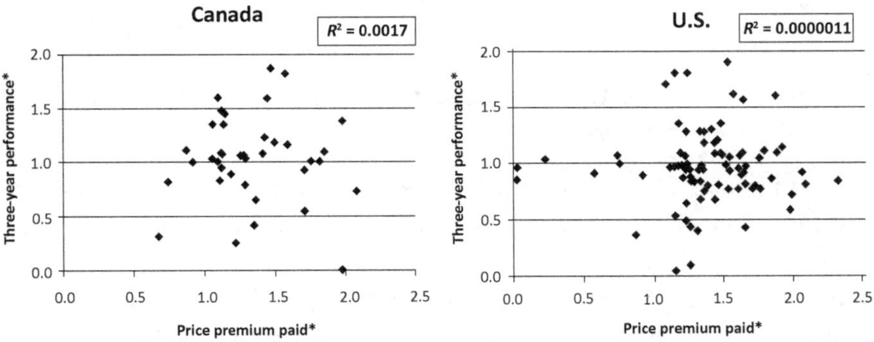

*Price Premium Paid per share versus stock trading price three months prior to announcement.
Source: Bloomberg, SDC, FP Datagroup.

companies are not succeeding or failing on the basis of the price paid, but based on other factors such as deal logic or postdeal execution. The market for major deals is determining the price that must be paid, and the buyers are succeeding or failing based on what they are able to do with the acquired company.[7]

In-market consolidation deals usually fail

Consolidation deals in which direct competitors merge perform worse than do related diversification deals. The performance gap is about 10 percent, with most related diversification deals successful and most consolidation deals failing. This is a surprising finding given that the overlap and cost synergies would clearly be higher in consolidation deals.

Investigation of selected transactions reveals three reasons for the relatively poor performance of in-market consolidation deals. First, as an industry consolidates, the benefits become well understood and the synergies easy to estimate. Second, each target is typically of interest to more than one consolidator, so the would-be buyers will negotiate away much of the synergy value. Finally, the cost synergies are typically more difficult and take longer to achieve than planned. As a result, most consolidation deals fail to create value for the buyers.

However, this does not mean that value is not created. While most of these deals fail, some succeed, and the most effective consolidators are able to implement well and beat the odds. In addition, there is value transferred to the shareholders of the sellers as a result of the bidding up of sale prices by competing buyers.

With the exception of U.S. acquirers, international deals perform well

International deals are typically based on growth—that is, revenue synergies more than cost synergies. In general, revenue synergies are harder to achieve but less likely to be negotiated away than in consolidation plays. The biggest challenge in international deals is to achieve success across borders and cultures. Most European companies have extensive experience working across languages and cultures, including many international acquisitions as industries reformed from domestic to EU industries.

By contrast, most U.S. companies have focused on the domestic market—understandable for companies based in what has been the largest market in the world for most industries. As a result, many U.S. companies have lacked international experience and have not been sensitized to the range of national and corporate cultures abroad. Many U.S. deals abroad have met surprises and have failed to meet objectives or worse.

U.S. companies are vulnerable in light of international M&A trends

The sources used for the M&A database are increasingly international in scope and the number and value of international deals have been increasing. So what is the "balance of trade" in M&A? To track this, we calculate for major deals a net value of international acquisitions as the value of acquisitions abroad less the value sales to foreign enterprises.

The findings, in short, are that the United States, the United Kingdom, and Canada are significant net sellers. The United States is the world's largest net seller in absolute terms. Canada is the largest net seller relative to the size of its economy; that is, it has the highest depletion rate of corporate control. Chapter 9 of this book provides a full discussion of these trends and implications.

It must be noted here in the context of deal success rates that the poor U.S. track record in international deal performance noted earlier, combined with the largest deficit in the global market for corporate control, presents a double challenge. If U.S. companies are to be competitive in global industry restructuring, they must be more aggressive internationally and achieve significantly better deal returns for shareholders.

Larger deals have higher failure rates

Deals valued at higher than 30 percent of the buyer's market capitalization fail more often than deals valued at 15 to 30 percent. (Relative value created is not a meaningful metric for deals valued at less than 15 percent, as smaller deals may not be material to the acquirer's total return).

This is not a surprise to anyone in the industry. However, the difference in performance levels is over 15 percent, with deals in the larger category failing ~60 percent of the time in the United States and Europe. Deals in the range of 15 percent to 30 percent of the acquirer's market capitalization usually correspond to superior shareholder returns over competitors.

Acquisitions of private companies perform better than acquisitions of public companies

In the United States, in particular, there is a performance spread of ~15 percent between public and private deals. Study of selected transactions suggests a number of reasons for the better performance of private transactions.

First, there is a motivated seller. Typically, these assets are wholly owned subsidiaries of corporations that have decided to exit a particular product line, market, or industry. While they seek a fair price for the asset, they have already decided to sell.

Second, the selection of the buyer is often conducted quietly. Often there are synergies with other divisions that the selling company wants to retain in some form, so it narrows the consideration to a group or an individual company with whom it wants to do business. Sometimes, the seller simply wants to keep the plan out of the press to prevent loss of key people or loss of customers from the unit, or to avoid some risk to its own stock price. Whatever the motivation, a negotiation with one or a few friendly buyers can result in more favorable pricing for the buyer.

Third, there is weak accountability to the seller's shareholders. The selling shareholders have to agree to the sale of a public company, but the sale of an individual asset of a company typically does not require shareholder approval. Directors should take note—the interests of the company are often compromised when management is motivated to "dump" an asset. There is a lack of accountability for the pricing of exit decisions. This is bad news for the selling shareholders, but their loss is the buying shareholders' gain.

Finally, because these transactions are often confidential and friendly, there is adequate time and access to data to properly plan integration.

Results vary by sector

Performance varies widely by sector, with the U.S. banking sector historically posting the worst results and telecommunications the best. Detailed analysis by sector has been completed from time to time, but such analysis is beyond the scope of this book.

Endnotes

1. Tom Copeland, Tim Koller, and Jack Murrin, *Valuation: Measuring and Managing the Value of Companies* (New York: John Wiley & Sons, 1990). Note: This book is now in its fifth edition, with the McKinsey firm as its main author.
2. See Alexander J. Triantis and Kenneth W. Smith in Lenos Trigeorgis, ed., *Real Options in Capital Investment* (Westport, CT: Praeger, 1995).
3. Early work included an analysis of the correlation of corporate performance in the three years prior to deal announcement versus the three years following deal announcement. The correlation coefficient, or R^2, was 0.027 on a database of all large deals of the 1990s. An R^2 this low suggests that pre-deal performance is in general a poor predictor of postdeal performance. This is a strong indicator that postdeal performance is significantly affected by the market's assessment of the deal and its implementation.
4. Phillip L. Zweig, "The Case Against Mergers," *BusinessWeek*, October 30, 1995, http://www.businessweek.com/archives/1995/b3448107.arc.htm. See also Chapter 4 in this book, "Real Option in M&A."
5. These data files and analyses were developed by SECOR Consulting under the leadership of Ken Smith, one of the coauthors of this book.
6. Bloomberg Financial tracks M&A activity (as do other financial information services, such as Thomson Reuters). Securities regulations require certain disclosures regarding significant acquisitions or sales of public companies so data are readily available for public companies. Bloomberg and others have had comprehensive data for U.S. deals since the early 1990s at least and have been increasingly inclusive of international data. The deal performance metrics used here are based on the buyers' total returns, so to measure performance we only require that the buyer is a public company and that the date of the transaction is

known. The total return of the acquirer and that of the acquirer's index are also based on publicly available data that are tracked by Bloomberg and others. Certain correlations of deal performance with other company factors of the buyer or seller (e.g., seller's previous growth rate) rely on public disclosures. Any deals for which the required data for an analysis are not disclosed are omitted from that analysis.

7. Note that the deal premium for the preceding analysis is determined from the trading price three months prior to announcement. As already noted, later values have expectation of the deal built in and are therefore less accurate estimates of the true premium being paid over market.

APPENDIX II.1

Suggested Readings in Strategy and Strategic Planning Methodologies

1. *The Art of War*, Sun Tzu, 500 BC. Translated by Lionel Giles in 1940 and reissued in 2011. (See also *The Art of War 3: The Cannons of Commerce,* David I. Goldenberg, Authorhouse, 2002)
2. *Strategic Management*, H. Igor Ansoff, Classic Edition reissued from 1979, Palgrave Macmillan, 2007
3. "How to Improve Strategic Planning," Renee Dye and Sibony Olivier, *McKinsey Quarterly*, August 2007
4. *Blue Ocean Strategy*, W. Chan Kim, Renee Mauborgne, Harvard Business School Press, 2005
5. *The Modern Firm*, John Roberts, Oxford University Press, 2004
6. *Strategy Maps: Converting Intangible Assets Into Tangible Outcomes*, Robert S. Kaplan and David P. Norton, Harvard Business School Press, 2004
7. "Scenarios for the 21st Century", Ged Davis, Probing the Future Conference, Strathclyde University, July 12, 2002
8. *Process-Based Strategic Planning*, Rudolf Grunig and Richard Kuhn, Springer-Verlag, 2001
9. *Good to Great: Why Some Companies Make the Leap . . . and Others Don't,* Jim Collins, HarperBusiness, 2001
10. *Real Options*, Martha Amram, Nalin Kulatilaka, Harvard Business School Press, 1999
11. "Strategy as a Portfolio of Real Options," Timothy Leuhrman, *Harvard Business Review*, September-October 1998
12. *Perspectives on Strategy*, Carl W. Stern and George Stalk, John Wiley & Sons, 1998
13. *Strategy Safari*, Henry Mintzberg, Bruce Ahlstrand, and Joseph Lampel, Free Press, 1998

14. *Competing by Design: The Power of Organizational Architecture*, David Nadler, Mark Nadler, and Michael L. Tushman, Oxford University Press, 1997
15. *The Art of the Long View: Paths to Strategic Insight for Yourself and Your Company*, Peter Schwartz, Doubleday Currency, 1996
16. *The Balanced Scorecard*, Robert S. Kaplan and David P. Norton, The President and Fellows of Harvard College, 1996
17. "What Is Strategy?" Michael Porter, *Harvard Business Review*, November-December 1996
18. *Value Migration*, Adrian J. Slywotsky, Harvard Business School Press, 1996
19. *Real Options in Capital Investment*, Lenos Trigeorgis, Praeger, 1995
20. *Grow to Be Great*, Dwight L. Gertz and Joao P. A. Baptista, Free Press, 1995
21. *The Rise and Fall of Strategic Planning*, Henry Mintzberg, Free Press, 1994
22. *Applied Strategic Planning: How to Develop a Plan That Really Works*, Leonard Goodstein, Timothy Nolan, and J. Pfeiffer, McGraw-Hill, 1993
23. *Competing Against Time: How Time-based Competition is Reshaping Global Markets*, George Stalk and Thomas M. Hout, Free Press, 1990
24. *The Mind of the Strategist*, Kenichi Ohmae, Penguin Books, 1982
25. *Competitive Strategy*, Michael E. Porter, Free Press, 1980

APPENDIX II.2

Wheel of Opportunity/ Fit Chart with Illustrative Delphi Scoring

From Stanley Foster Reed, Alexandra Reed Lajoux, and H. Peter Nesvold. *The Art of M&A: A Merger Acquisition Buyout Guide*, 4th ed. (New York: McGraw-Hill, 2007).

Exhibit 5.2. Wheel of opportunity/fit chart (with illustrative example).

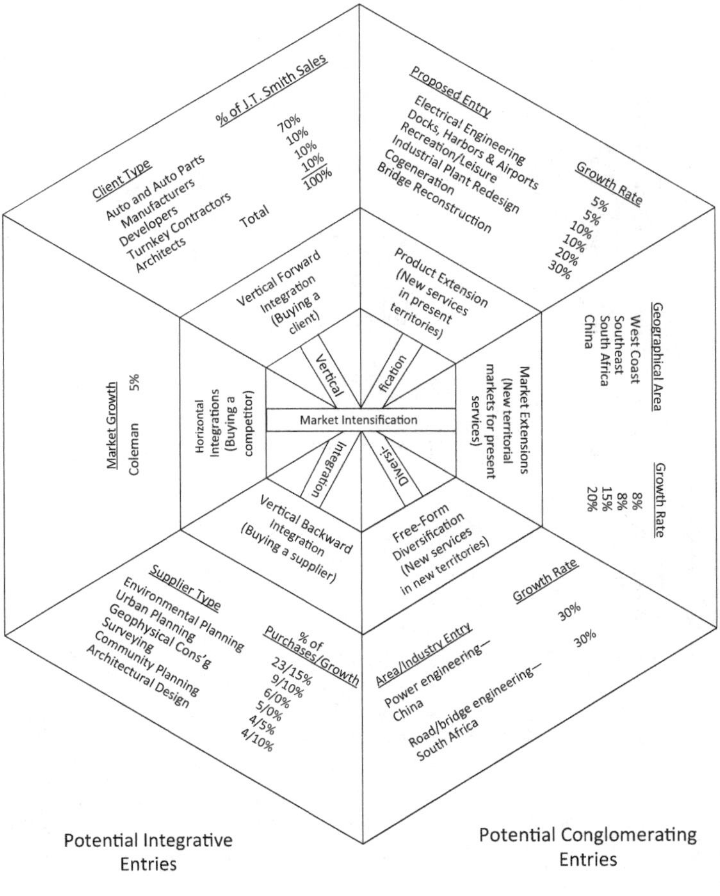

Instant Delphi Tally Sheet for Fit Chart

	Complements									Supplements									
	Cycle Res.	Billings Growth	Profit Improve-ment	Min. Mkt. Share	Fulfil-ling Pot'l	Customer Clout	Reduce Over-head	Reduce Down-time	Sub-total	Top Mg't Fit	Mid. Mg't Fit	Staff Skills Fit	Marketing Fit	Client Fit	EDP Fit	Synergy	Sub-total	Efficiency	Rank Order
ROUND 1:																			
J.T. Smith, CHRM & CEO	0	0	100	0	300	0	0	100	500	0	0	100	0	200	0	200	500	100	-
Tom Jones, Pres. & COO	200	200	100	0	0	0	100	100	700	100	0	0	0	100	100	0	300	1000	-
H. Miller, Ex. VP	150	150	100	0	0	0	0	0	400	200	100	100	0	50	50	0	600	1000	-
H. Teets, VP Marketing	100	100	100	200	200	0	0	0	700	0	0	110	90	0	0	100	300	1000	-
W. Clarke, VP Finance	0	100	100	0	0	0	100	100	400	0	100	180	0	200	0	120	600	1000	-
J. Walsh, VP Eng'g	0	50	100	0	0	50	80	70	350	300	150	100	50	0	50	0	650	1000	-
Carole Henry, Comptroller	100	100	100	0	200	90	0	0	590	100	0	110	0	150	50	0	410	1000	-
Total	550	700	700	200	700	140	280	370	3640	700	350	700	140	700	350	420	3360	7000	-
Average	79	100	100	100	100	29	40	53	520	100	50	100	20	100	50	60	480	1000	-
ROUND 2:																			
Bill Smith, CHRM & CEO	0	70	30	0	300	0	0	100	500	0	0	100	x	200	0	200	500	1000	-
Tom Jones, Pres. & CEO	200	200	0	0	0	0	100	100	600	300	100	0	x	0	0	0	400	1000	-
H. Miller, Ex. VP	150	150	0	0	100	0	0	0	400	200	150	100	x	100	50	0	600	1000	-
H. Teets, VP Marketing	100	100	0	200	300	0	0	0	700	0	0	0	x	300	0	0	300	1000	-
W. Clarke, VP Finance	0	100	110	10	0	0	100	80	400	0	0	110	x	40	300	150	600	1000	-
J. Walsh, VP Eng'g	10	50	0	0	0	0	140	150	350	300	200	0	x	100	50	0	650	1000	-
Carole Henry, Comptroller	100	100	0	0	70	70	80	60	480	40	250	40	x	100	90	0	520	1000	-
Total	560	770	140	210	770	70	420	490	3430	840	700	350	x	840	490	350	3570	7000	-
Average	80	110	20	30	110	10	60	70	490	120	100	50	x	120	70	50	510	1000	-

ROUND 3:																			
Bill Smith, CHRM & CEO	80	100	x	x	300	x	0	0	480	100	0	0	x	200	20	200	520	1000	-
Tom Jones, Pres. & COO	200	240	x	x	100	x	100	0	640	300	60	0	x	0	0	0	360	1000	-
H. Miller, Ex. VP	150	200	x	x	100	x	100	0	550	200	200	40	x	10	0	0	450	1000	-
H. Teets, VP Marketing	100	100	x	x	300	x	0	0	550	0	200	0	x	300	0	0	500	1000	-
W. Clarke, VP Finance	0	200	x	x	40	x	200	100	540	10	0	0	x	0	300	150	460	1000	-
J. Walsh, VP Eng'g	0	0	x	x	0	x	90	200	290	200	10	100	x	300	100	0	710	1000	-
Carole Henry, Comptroller	100	0	x	x	0	x	0	190	290	100	360	0	x	100	140	10	710	1000	-
Total	630	840	x	x	840	x	490	490	3290	910	830	140	x	910	560	360	3710	7000	-
Average	90	120	x	x	120	x	70	70	470	130	1190	20	x	130	80	51	530	1000	-
ROUND 4:																			
Bill Smith, CHRM & CEO	100	200	x	x	300	x	0	0	600	300	30	x	x	70	0	x	400	1000	-
Tom Jones, Pres. & COO	200	200	x	x	100	x	0	0	500	300	200	x	x	0	0	x	500	1000	-
H. Miller, Ex. VP	150	200	x	x	100	x	10	40	500	200	210	x	x	0	90	x	500	1000	-
H. Teets, VP Marketing	100	40	x	x	300	x	0	0	440	0	200	x	x	300	60	x	560	1000	-
W. Clarke, VP Finance	50	200	x	x	0	x	200	100	550	20	0	x	x	130	300	x	450	1000	-
J. Walsh, VP Eng'g	0	0	x	x	10	x	0	300	310	200	40	x	x	300	150	x	690	1000	-
Carole Henry, Comptroller	100	0	x	x	100	x	0	50	250	100	300	x	x	250	100	x	750	1000	-
Total	700	840	x	x	910	x	210	490	3150	1120	980	x	x	1050	700	x	3850	7000	-
Average	100	120	x	x	130	x	30	70	450	10	140	x	x	150	100	x	550	1000	-

Fit Chart: J.T. Smith Consultants

	Complements									Supplements									
[Growth rates in Brakets]	Cycle Res.	Billings Growth	Profit Improve-ment	Min. Mkt. Share	Fulfil-ling Pot'l	Customer Clout	Reduce Over-head	Reduce Down-time	Sub-total	Top Mg't Fit	Mid. Mg't Fit	Staff Skills Fit	Marketing Fit	Client Fit	EDP Fit	Synergy	Sub-total	Efficiency	Rank Order
COLUMN NUMBER	**1**	**2**	**4**	**5**	**6**	**7**	**8**	**9**		**10**	**11**	**12**	**13**	**14**	**15**	**16**	**17**	**18**	**19**
1st approximation	79	100	100	29	100	20	40	53	520	100	50	100	20	100	50	60	480	1000	-
2nd approximation	80	110	20	30	110	10	60	70	490	120	100	50	0	120	70	50	510	1000	-
3rd approximation	90	120	x	x	120	x	70	70	470	130	119	20	x	130	80	51	530	1000	-
Final (4th approximation)	100	120	x	x	130	x	30	70	450	160	140	x	x	150	100	x	550	1000	-
HORIZONTAL INTEGRATION																			
Coleman, Detroit	60	120	x	x	40	x	30	70	320	160	140	x	x	150	100	x	550	870	1
MARKET EXTENSION																			
West Coast [8%]	0	40	x	x	30	x	10	30	110	160	70	x	x	0	50	x	280	390	-
Southeast [8%]	80	80	x	x	30	x	10	30	230	100	70	x	x	0	50	x	220	450	-
South Africa [85]	80	120	x	x	0	x	0	0	200	40	0	x	x	0	50	x	90	290	-
China [20%]	100	120	x	x	0	x	0	0	220	40	0	x	x	0	50	x	90	310	-
SUBTOTAL MARKET INTENSIFICATION MODE																	Average:	480	

VERTICAL BACKWARD INTEGRATION																			
Environmental planning [15%]	40	40	x	x	0	x	10	10	100	40	35	x	x	50	50	x	175	275	
Urban planning [10%]	40	40	x	x	0	x	10	10	100	40	35	x	x	50	50	x	175	275	
Geophysical consulting [0%]	0	0	x	x	0	x	0	0	0	0	0	x	x	0	50	x	50	50	
Surveying	0	0	x	x	30	x	20	0	50	80	35	x	x	100	50	x	256	315	
Community planning [5%]	40	40	x	x	0	x	10	20	110	40	35	x	x	50	50	x	175	285	
Architectural design [10%]	0	0	x	x	130	x	30	70	230	120	70	x	x	100	100	x	390	620	3
VERTICAL FORWARD INTEGRATION																			
Auto and auto parts mfg. [5%]	0	0	x	x	0	x	0	0	0	0	0	x	x	0	0	x	0	0	
Architectural design svcs [8%]	0	0	x	x	130	x	30	70	230	120	35	x	x	100	100	x	355	585	4
Turnkey contractors [5%]	0	0	x	x	0	x	0	0	0	100	70	x	x	50	100	x	320	320	
Developers [0%]	0	0	x	x	0	x	0	0	0	100	35	x	x	50	100	x	285	285	
SUBTOTAL VERTICAL INTEGRATION MODE																	Average:	334	

Fit Chart: J.T. Smith Consultants (*continued*)

[Growth rates in Brakets]	Complements									Supplements									
	Cycle Res.	Billings Growth	Profit Improve-ment	Min. Mkt. Share	Fulfil-ling Pot'l	Customer Clout	Reduce Over-head	Reduce Down-time	Sub-total	Top Mg't Fit	Mid. Mg't Fit	Staff Skills Fit	Marketing Fit	Client Fit	EDP Fit	Synergy	Sub-total	Efficiency	Rank Order
COLUMN NUMBER	**1**	**2**	**4**	**5**	**6**	**7**	**8**	**9**		**10**	**11**	**12**	**13**	**14**	**15**	**16**	**17**	**18**	**19**
PRODUCT OR SERVICE EXTENSION																			
Electrical engineering [5%]	0	0	x	x	130	x	30	70	230	100	70	x	x	150	100	x	420	650	2
Docks, harbors, and airports [5%]	60	0	x	x	60	x	20	60	200	150	70	x	x	25	100	x	345	545	
Recreation/leisure [10%]	40	40	x	x	0	x	20	40	140	100	70	x	x	50	100	x	320	460	
Industrial plant redesign [15%]	40	30	x	x	60	x	30	70	230	50	105	x	x	50	100	x	305	535	
Power engineering [20%]	40	60	x	x	130	x	10	50	350	50	70	x	x	0	100	x	220	570	5
Bridge/Reconstruction [30%]	100	120	x	x	60	x	20	40	300	50	70	x	x	0	100	x	220	520	
FREE FROM EXTENSION																			
Power engineering—China	50	120	x	x	60	x	0	0	230	80	70	x	x	0	100	x	250	530	
Road/bridge engineering—South Africa	100	120	x	x	60	x	0	0	280	80	70	x	x	0	50	x	200	480	
SUBTOTAL DIVERSIFICATION MODE																			

APPENDIX II.3

Information Sources and Tips for Target Screening

Updated from Stanley Foster Reed, Alexandra Reed Lajoux, and H. Peter Nesvold. *The Art of M&A: A Merger Acquisition Buyout Guide*, 4th ed. (New York: McGraw-Hill, 2007).

How should list of industry players be developed and then researched?

It takes a combination of sources, in person, in print, on the telephone, and, of course, online. Here are just a few of the steps to consider:

- Join the target industry's trade association(s) and obtain the membership directories. Network with association members and the staff of the association.
- Attend industry trade shows. You can physically see the target products/services and talk directly with potential acquisition candidates in some cases. Also, most trade shows attract industry gurus. They seem to know before management when something is going to be sold off. If you're interested in expansion by serial consolidation, trade shows are the place to start. Many a management buyout, leveraged or not, has been started right on the exhibit floor.
- Create your own lists. Develop contact lists to conduct one-on-one telephone interviews with the leading players, including corporate development functions. If the relevant universe is large, consider initial surveying by email or with questionnaires.
- Review required disclosures. Take advantage of the free information available because of securities disclosure rules affecting public companies. Look to annual reports, SEC filings (10Ks, 10Qs, prospectuses, and proxy statements at http://www. sec.gov), press releases, product literature, catalogs, company case studies, and executive speeches. The

U.S. Treasury also has good data based on tax filings (www.irs.gov/taxstats/index).

- Gather research reports. If you are considering publicly held targets, don't overlook the reports of securities research firms. There are hundreds of such firms worldwide; many affiliated with major brokerage houses. They are listed annually in *Nelson's Directory of Investment Research.*
- Other sources for public companies include the *Value Line Investment Survey* (http://www.valueline.com), Standard & Poor's publications (http://www2.standardandpoors.com), *Directory of Corporate Affiliations—Who Owns Whom* (www.lexisnexis.com/dca), and various Moody's publications (http://www.moodys.com) will also serve.
- Use reference books such as *Thomas Register* (http://www.thomasnet.com) and trade periodical buyer's guides. These reference books normally group companies by the product or service sold. For example, the researcher looking for companies that manufacture fluid-bed dryers should start by referencing fluid-bed dryers in the *Thomas Register.*
- Study special industry research reports by independent research firms. Prospectuses for these studies are listed and indexed by subject in *Findex* and are also on Lockheed's Dialog database (http://library.dialog.com/bluesheets/html/bl0196.html). These prospectuses contain the study's table of contents, which usually discloses the names of key industry players. Another good source of specialized industry information is Frost & Sullivan (http://www.frost.com). Also, both trade association and industry/company reports are invaluable information centers for industry data. These normally cover an entire industry's structure or a particular product/market segment's structure. They can be expensive—sometimes in the $25,000 range. But the publisher will send you a précis that in itself can be very valuable in helping you decide if you want to study making an entry.

How can a buyer find information on private companies?

A good starting place is Dun & Bradstreet's *Million Dollar Directory*, which lists both public and private companies. Dun & Bradstreet also has online services at http://www.dnb.com/us/.

If D&B does not have financial information on a particular private company, it is extremely difficult to obtain the information without getting it directly from the company itself. However, many states, especially those with extractive activity, require both public and private businesses, whether incorporated or not, to file annually various types of information, including year of establishment, names of principal owners, key personnel, number of employees, annual sales, principal lines of business, plant size, and import/export activity. Sometimes asset, liability, and profit information must also be submitted.

Some states compile the information through their chambers of commerce or their economic development programs and publish it via private companies such as Harris InfoSource (http://www.harrisinfo.com), formerly Harris Publishing Company, of Twinsburg, Ohio. Harris has state, regional, national, and industry editions. Private companies rarely give out financial information such as balance sheet and profit and loss numbers. Even when they have done it for credit purposes, many do not keep it up to date. Even smaller public companies fail to update. Gross sales information is often four to five years old. Normally D&B will give some numbers, such as the number of employees. Thus, to get a ballpark figure for a potential target's annual sales volume, the buyer can generate a sales-per-employee number and apply. Service company information is harder to come by than manufacturers' as their trade organizations, if they exist, often do not collect hard numbers.

Also scan the academic literature. Both public and private companies may be the subject of academic research for which the company has volunteered information or interviews. Private companies sometimes agree to be the subject of a study case as well, so the search should include cases being used in business schools.

How does the researcher develop a contact list of industry gurus?

The World Wide Web—and in particular, search engines such as google.com—have revolutionized research. By typing in the name of a particular industry, one is immediately led to seminars, publications, and other sources of information about it. One can pick up the names of experts/gurus from the speaker lists at trade shows and meetings of technical societies. Most such gurus publish articles about their specialties in technical journals and the trade press. For books, the largest collection is of course at the Amazon website (www.Amazon.com), which lists some five million titles accessible by subject. For articles, the best place to start is with the *Business Periodicals Index*, which lists tens of thousands of technical and nontechnical articles arranged by industry. LexisNexis also offers an in-depth service for searching articles by subject matter—actually counting the number of times a given word or phrase (e.g., "iron and coal") appears.

In many cases, a trade association maintains a list of consultants who specialize in their industry. Also, list brokers, such as National Business Lists, may have special contact lists for your industry.

As with research on industry players, don't stop at the printed word. Developing a contact list requires a great deal of telephone work, such as conducting target industry surveys.

When conducting target industry surveys, what is the best approach?

Superior results come from talking to "users" over the telephone and going over a questionnaire with them. A user is someone who makes decisions to buy, or use, a product or a service. Talking to these users is especially helpful. Many a good lead has been developed this way, as a major user might help you target a company and might even be interested in helping you finance the deal! Such conversations are easily started: "Who there buys high-capacity filter presses?" You should talk to both the end user and the purchasing person.

One caveat: the direct approach works well *once you know the industry.* If you don't know what a filter press looks like, do some research. When you place that call you may have more up-to-date information than the industry player. You can trade information in a telephone call. Key personnel generally open up and talk about their own company if they have learned something new about the industry from you.

A word of warning: it may take many hours and even days before one gains a sense of the industry, so never start with the target company, even if you have one in mind. Learn the industry on the peripherals. Always talk to customers first and discover what they are looking for.

What information should be accumulated in a target's file?

After completing basic research, the potential acquirer needs to decide whether moving into this industry is desirable. If that decision is positive, the buyer puts together a target profile on each of the acquisition candidates. This may entail a technology and manufacturing audit to make sure the target's process will survive in the future. A marketing audit may be highly revealing and may support a premium price for the company. These audits are the very beginning of the buyer's due diligence.

Other information that goes into the target company's file includes annual reports, 10Ks, D&B credit reports, company fact books and product catalogs, press releases, print advertisements, published articles and executive speeches, and director and officer profiles. *Forbes*, *Fortune*, the *Wall Street Journal*, and many other publications do summary articles on industries—especially emerging high-tech industries. Researchers can obtain much of this information and more using Internet search engines such as Google.

At this time the potential buyer must rank-order targets. What is the best way to do this?

If the buyer's team is using the fit chart or a similar approach, it should now run specific targets through the fit chart and rate them against the buyer's specific weaknesses and strengths (as complements and supplements). The first company evaluated may have a strong marketing force and weak technology, whereas the fifth in line may have the opposite. That might lead a strong marketer to the decision to buy number five, believing that it can be integrated into its own strong marketing and distribution channels.

Who should be contacted at the target company?

Callers should start at the top. The principals contacted may include the CEO, the CFO, or the COO. In a wide-ranging search, the target's directors, outside counsel, accountants, and bankers—both commercial and investment—can also be contacted. Contacting a target's outside counsel is usually unproductive. First, attorneys, because of attorney–client confidentiality, are not supposed to give out any information, and second, they have their own agendas. They may want to initiate the deal so that they will continue to be retained, and they will try to discourage you. The same thing, to a lesser extent, applies to the target's accounting firm.

Try to structure any conversation with a principal officer or owner so as to avoid a direct turndown. One technique that has been honed to a fine art by executive headhunters is to call target executives and ask if they know of an executive who might be available. They might then offer themselves. It works the same way in an acquisition search. Tell a prospective target that you are considering making an entry in the industry either by a de novo entry (a start-up) or an acquisition and ask if they know anyone for sale. That is sure to get their attention; their response might just be, "Well, if the price were right, *we* might be for sale."

If the acquisition proposal involves a relatively small subsidiary of any relatively large company, the contact person should be the senior vice president of corporate planning or corporate development—but don't call the division head unless it is public knowledge that the unit is on the block. And even then it is best to deal with planning at either the corporate, sector, or business unit level rather than with the executives who might be intimately affected by a sale and may, in fact, be trying to buy the operation themselves.

What should the caller say–and not say?

The target company's nonowner management will be impressed with any expertise demonstrated by the caller. The target profile will give the buyer more "information leverage" because the target will often know very little about the buyer. To set the management more at ease, the buyer or its agent should provide some useful information about itself or the target's management.

The ultimate goal of the initial conversation is to set up a meeting to discuss "working together" or "teaming up" through a possible "business combination." The business combination could be a merger, acquisition, or joint venture. The more broadly you define it, the better. No mention of price should be made at this stage of the process.

Where should buyer and target representatives meet at this early stage?

The parties have to agree on a mutually satisfactory meeting place. Visiting the target may start the rumor mill, and that can hurt a deal. On the other hand, the buyer can get a better feel for the target's operations and personnel if they are at least eyeballed. But the usual practice of a large group of "suits" visiting a target should be discouraged.

An alternative would be a meeting at the offices of an investment banker or law firm, or in neutral territory, such as a conference room at a hotel. Try not to meet in airline clubs, hotel lobbies, restaurants, or other public places—it starts the rumor mill going and can create competition for the target.

A good cover for meetings is the prospect of a joint venture or a supplier or customer relationship. This plays very well where a company is not on the block. But be careful of any out-and-out misrepresentation.

Having agreed on a meeting place and prior to the meeting, the buyer should obtain the target's financials. (We assume you already have all of the sales literature, D&B reports, and, if it's a public company, the 10Ks.) The target may ask you to sign a confidentiality agreement at this point. By all means do so, but make sure you are protected.

With such information in hand, an agenda for the meeting can be easily set. It is important to have a written agenda, at least for your side, so that all of the important subjects will be covered.

It is also important to recast the target's historical financials into a more easily read form such as common-size, trended, and industry comparisons. When these are done, it is easy to compile a list of questions identifying the financial and operating anomalies for discussion.

What are common-size, trended, and industry comparisons?

These are invaluable techniques for identifying problems and isolating areas for potential profit improvement. As such they can be an important tool in the negotiation process and can influence price.

Instead of looking at absolute numbers, common-size and trended analyses uncover hard-to-detect anomalies that may exist in a company's balance sheet or income statement. Common-size financial statements utilize a common denominator such as net worth for balance sheets; all the components are entered as percentages and are easily compared year to year. The operating statements use net sales as a base and the cost components as percentages of that base. Trended analyses use an appropriately selected base year or period that represents 100 for all items of the balance sheet and income statement. All dollar amounts for each item on the balance sheet and income statement in years subsequent to the base year are expressed as a percentage of the base year amounts. The anomalies become immediately apparent as areas for further investigation and become part of the negotiating process because they must be explained.

For example, if accounts receivable and inventory combined accounted for 50 percent of total assets during the first year and increased to 62 percent the second year while sales only increased a meager 2 percent, the company may be boosting sales by serving customers who have poorer credit. As a result, the buyer will want to double-check the collection period for accounts receivable by interviewing customers and suppliers. Although, this is a point of stress for sellers—especially the customer interviews—and generally can take place only at advanced stages in the negotiation; the buyer should let the seller know that it is expected.

What else can be accomplished at the first meeting with a target?

The meeting should give the buyer a sense of the company and its operations, whether there are any skeletons in the seller's closets that may preclude a deal, and whether the chemistry is right if there are to be any continuing management relationships. The meeting should give the target management a sense of the buyer and its management and the benefits to target managers if they are to stay and to owners if they are to continue to own.

There must be *reasons* for combining companies corporately and operationally. In most cases these are discussed in the early meetings, unless the buyer wants to keep plans confidential. However, if the target is a public company, this is a sensitive area; whether and how a company discloses or conceals future plans can trigger legal exposure.

For public companies, it is good to have copies of any financial analysis performed by investment bankers—even if issued by a regional house. Also ask the sellers if they ever had a management consultant in to run a survey. If they did, ask to see the report, no matter how old it may be. And ask to see the outside auditors' management letters or reports. Find out if the company has changed auditors within the past five years, and if so, get permission to talk to the earlier auditors.

In this meeting, it is important for the seller to avoid making exaggerated claims. When sellers make representations that later prove untrue, buyers can sue, citing fraudulent conveyance, also called fraudulent transfer. The Uniform Fraudulent Transfer Act, like the other "uniform" acts in the United States, was drafted by the National Conference of Commissions of Uniform State Laws (Uniform Law Commissioners), a group of law professors, former judges, and lawyers who have volunteered to set these standards. The Uniform Law Commissioners propose uniform laws to the states for ratification. To date 41 states have ratified this act.

APPENDIX 11.4

NACD Guidance on the Board's Role in M&A and Strategy

Topic: The Board's Role in M&A

Summary: This memo provides guidance to board members with respect to M&A (buying, selling, or merging with another company).

GOVERNANCE PRINCIPLES

Principle IV: Board Accountability and Objectivity: Governance structures and practices should be designed to ensure the accountability of the board to shareholders and the objectivity of board decisions.

Principle VII: Attention to Information, Agenda and Strategy: Governance structures and practices should be designed to support the board in determining its own priorities, resultant agenda, and information needs and to assist the board in focusing on strategy (and associated risks).

Source: *Key Agreed Principles to Strengthen Corporate Governance for U.S. Publicly Traded Companies.* Download a complimentary copy at www.NACDonline.org/LeadingtheWay.

Key Findings

OVERVIEW OF THE ROLE OF THE BOARD IN M&A

Corporate directors have duties of care and loyalty under state law, and these duties apply to the merger context. (The overarching duty of good faith need not be discussed here.) The duty of care requires that directors be informed and exercise appropriate diligence and good faith as they make business decisions and otherwise fulfill their general oversight responsibilities. The duty of loyalty requires that a director act in the best interests of the corporation.

When reviewing plans to buy another company, sell a company unit, or merge with another company, the board needs to exercise proper oversight of management (duty of care) especially apply in issues of strategy, pricing, and compliance with various legal obligations such as disclosure obligations.

The board also needs to exercise independence (duty of loyalty). It can do this by appointing a standing committee of the board composed entirely of independent directors to review a particular transaction.

Source:

- *Report of the NACD Blue Ribbon Commission on the Role of the Board in Strategy*
- *Art of M&A* Series, McGraw-Hill

THE ROLE OF THE BOARD IN STRATEGY

- Boards should be constructively engaged with management to ensure the appropriate development, execution, and modification of the company's strategy.
- The nature and extent of the board's involvement in strategy will depend on the particular circumstances of the company and the industry in which it is operating.
- While the board can—and in some cases should—use a committee of the board or an advisory board to analyze specific aspects of a proposed strategy, the full board should be engaged in the evolution of the strategy.
- Strategy development should be a cooperative process. Management and the board should jointly establish the process the company will use to develop its strategy, including an understanding of the respective roles of management and the board.
- Management and the board should agree on specific steps for strategy development.
- To participate effectively in the strategic thinking process, boards should be prepared to ask incisive questions—anticipating, rather than reacting to, issues of major concern.

Source: *Report of the NACD Blue Ribbon Commission on the Role of the Board in Strategy*

THE ROLE OF THE BOARD IN BUYING ANOTHER COMPANY

By being actively engaged in formulation of strategy, boards will typically already have some involvement in considering possible acquisitions, since all acquisitions should be consistent with a company's strategy.

The extent of the board's involvement in a proposed transaction (e.g., questions of disclosure, financing, pricing, structuring, and due diligence) will vary depending on the size of the acquisition and the risks that it may pose. If a very large company regularly buys small companies in its industry, and has already developed a process for finding, acquiring, and integrating these small transactions, boards need not focus on the details of any particular transaction. They can and should, however, periodically review the entire merger process, from strategy to integration, in the context of strategy opportunities, attendant risks, and operational implications, to make sure that the process is working.

M&A transactions need not trigger micromanaging on the part of the board. Directors can help management achieve greater effectiveness. Individual board members may have expertise in various phases along the M&A route and can help improve the process. Management would be wise to take full advantage of this expertise on an as-needed basis. Major transactions merit formation of an independent committee of the board to analyze the value of the transaction with the help of an independent third party, who can render a fairness opinion.

Source: *Art of M&A* Series, McGraw-Hill

THE ROLE OF THE BOARD IN SELLING THE COMPANY

The negotiation of a public transaction involves fiduciary and disclosure considerations. The board of directors of a public company being acquired via a tender offer must be mindful of its fiduciary responsibilities under state corporate law. Traditionally under state law, as represented by Delaware law and the Model Business Corporation Act, the directors' fiduciary duty is to shareholders. In the landmark case of *Revlon Inc. vs. MacAndrews & Forbes holdings* (1986), the court described the role of the board of directors as that of a price-oriented "neutral auctioneer" once a decision has been made to sell the company.

Source: *Art of M&A* Series, McGraw-Hill

INFORMATION FLOW TO THE BOARD REGARDING M&A

One of the key ingredients for empowerment of any board is knowledge. Information flow, therefore, is a key prerequisite for directors to fulfill their oversight and decision-making functions. Of course, the specific type, quantity, format, timing, and source of the information that fuels board knowledge will vary from board to board and over time for a particular board. It will even vary among board members, who have different levels of experience and expertise with different topics.

Information flow is critical for directors with respect to capital allocation decisions, and in particular mergers and acquisitions. This area requires special attention to the long-term interests of the corporation and the ways in which management interests may affect transactions. The board and management should continually discuss the opportunities for and threats to the company, even in the absence of any planned or foreseen transactions, so that directors have an understanding of the business context in which these issues may arise.

Depending on the size and business context of the company, directors should periodically receive information related to, and discuss with management, the following:

- Comparative studies and analysis concerning whether the company would be more viable by merging with, or entering into alliances with, another candidate, or standing alone
- Possible acquisition candidates. When discussing the fulfillment of certain of the company's business strategies, such as entering into new lines of business, directors should receive information on possible alternatives, such as an acquisition or strategic alliance, to achieve the same objectives.
- The merger activity of competitors, including the impact of recent activities on the company's market share. Competitive analysis as to other suitors for the same potential acquisition candidates might also be warranted.

Maintaining an up-to-date understanding of these issues will help directors to remain prepared for the time when management actually proposes a transaction. Since some deals are time sensitive and decisions must be made quickly but on an informed basis, laying some groundwork for such decisions will be useful to both management and directors.

In evaluating a particular transaction, directors should seek specific information about the price, timing, and certainty of the transaction, and should be proactive in overseeing negotiations. Directors should understand how the transaction will be financed and the projected financial impact on the company under reasonably likely scenarios. Where the sale of the transaction warrants it, directors should seek independent financial advice from outside experts to consider together with management's financial assessment.

Directors should also obtain a high-level analysis of the merger documentation, including an understanding of the most important representations, covenants, and indemnities contained therein and their application to the company and the transaction. In addition, directors should receive input from market and investor relations experts about the best manner in which to position the transaction and the likely reception from investors and creditors. As with any other matter before them, directors should crucially evaluate all the information they have obtained and arrive at an independent assessment instead of relying exclusively on management's views.

Directors should also be alert to the ways that the interests of management may differ from those of stockholders in negotiating a particular transaction—for example, who will continue to work for the merged company and with what responsibilities—while stockholders generally are not significantly concerned about such issues.

In addition, directors of public companies should understand the company's plans and legal options for responding to unsolicited takeover offers.
Source: *Report of the NACD Blue Ribbon Commission on Director Liability*

Citations summary

- *Key Agreed Principles to Strengthen Corporate Governance for U.S. Publicly Traded Companies*
- *Report of the NACD Blue Ribbon Commission on the Role of the Board in Strategy*
- *Art of M&A* Series, McGraw-Hill
- *Report of the NACD Blue Ribbon Commission on Director Liability*

Additional resources

- NACD White Papers Series I: "Risk Oversight, Transparency, Strategy, Executive Compensation"

For additional updates or insights on this NACD ExpresSource™ memo, visit www.nacdonline.org and use the search function for your topic.

About NACD

Founded in 1977, the National Association of Corporate Directors (NACD) is a nonprofit membership organization based in Washington, DC. Although primarily national in focus, NACD collaborates with similar organizations around the world by sharing best practices in governance. With over 11,000 members, NACD advances exemplary board leadership by empowering members through education, forums for peers to share ideas, and an extensive knowledge base of information and publications. NACD fosters collaboration among directors and governance stakeholders to shape the future of corporate governance.

APPENDIX III.1

Public Policy and Corporate Growth: Selected SECOR Consulting Case Studies Regarding the Role of Public Policy in International M&A[1]

This appendix provides case studies in the telecommunications, mining, manufacturing, and financial services industries which illustrate contributing factors in the development of global leaders, in particular highlighting relevant public policy.

We offer no economic theory here, much less prescriptions for industrial policy. Rather, our aim is to reveal the competitive reality faced by companies in the global economy. The cases demonstrate how a wide range of government policies can impact corporate competitiveness in the market for corporate control. Indeed, each company profiled here owes its leadership position in some measure to supportive public policy on control issues. In each case, the success of the company internationally has resulted in significant benefits at home, for its domestic consumers, industry clusters, economies, and/or capital markets.

BHP BILLITON: AUSTRALIA'S DEFENSE OF A STRATEGIC INDUSTRY

The Australian government has made significant investments in exploration in order to develop its mining industry. Geological and geophysical surveys throughout the country improved the public understanding of Australia's geology, a key factor in the surge of mineral discoveries that began in the late 1940s. This knowledge was expanded further by the establishment of the Bureau of Mineral Resources in 1946. Explorers were then better able to search for deposits. Combined with political stability, this infrastructure led to an influx of foreign mining companies in the 1960s.

Beyond exploration jobs and expenditure, these companies brought with them new ideas and expertise. In the late 1950s the government undertook measures to encourage further mineral exploration, including a subsidy scheme enticing overseas and local companies to explore both onshore and offshore in Australia. As a result, most of the existing Australian crude oil reserves were discovered under this scheme. Companies like BHP and Billiton benefited greatly from continued support for their investments in exploration between 1957 and 1974. It allowed them to grow their productivity and to become increasingly competitive internationally.

The rest of Australia's mining industry is also a pertinent example of how building adjacent industry groups fosters the development of strong industry clusters. Australia emerged as one of the world's leaders in the development and provision of mining technology services (MTSs) due to its position as a leading mining nation. In 2000, CSIRO Australia stunned the industry by demonstrating mine modeling with Internet-based virtual reality capabilities. This advancement allowed for increased productivity and reduced risk with regard to investment and safety. In line with such capabilities, the Australian Bureau of Agriculture and Resource Economics estimates that Australia's MTS exports in 2004–2005 were approximately $1.2 billion.

Many believe that Australia currently has the world's most advanced geoscientific map coverage in terms of level of detail and physical reach. This strength is a result of the National Geosciences Mapping Accord, a joint program between the federal government and the Northern Territory. Launched in 1999, the accord provided a new realm of geoscientific maps and databases of important resource areas. The Australian government has also started a new $59 million program over five years that will acquire new seismic reflection survey data and other specialized geophysical data. These advancements in industry groups that support the mining sector contribute to the strength and productivity of the mining cluster overall as well as the strength of Australia's mining corporations in the market for corporate control.

The merger of BHP Ltd. and Billiton Plc.

The merger of BHP Ltd. (from Australia) and Billiton Plc. (from the United Kingdom) is an example of a successful government-driven defensive strategy in an M&A context. The new entity, BHP Billiton, started operating under a dual listed companies (DLC) structure in 2001. In this case, the Australian government used its power to ensure that foreign investment would not be contrary to the "national interest." It regulated the terms of the merger in some detail and allowed time for the development of an Australian solution.

Under the Foreign Acquisitions and Takeover Act of 1975 (FATA), the Australian government has the power to block foreign acquisitions determined to be contrary to the national interest. The FATA applies to the acquisition of interest greater than AU$100 million in an Australian company. In 2004, the U.S. Free Trade Agreement increased this threshold to AU$871 million for U.S. investments in nonsensitive sectors, but the threshold remained at AU$100 million for sensitive sectors such as banking and media.

In the case of BHP Billiton, the proposed merger was not blocked. Instead, the Australian Foreign Investment Review Board (FIRB) influenced the deal from a corporate control point of view. The FIRB's conditions for merger approval prescribed the following:

- BHP Billiton should continue to be an Australian company, managed in Australia and listed on the Australian Stock Exchange.
- The global headquarters of BHP Billiton should be in Australia.
- The global headquarters of BHP Billiton should be publicly acknowledged as being in Australia in significant public announcements and in all public documents.
- Both the company's CEO and CFO should have their principal place of residence, offices, and key supporting functions in Australia.
- The majority of all regularly scheduled board meetings and executive committee meetings in any calendar year should occur in Australia.

These requirements are specific enough to ensure that the Australian office will be a true executive office, keeping executive jobs, industry expertise, and supporting professional services and capital markets that might have been lost should the global headquarters have moved from the country. Perhaps more importantly, Australia ensured that decisions regarding the future of the newly formed entity would be made in Australia, maintaining Australia as a global platform for the mining industry, not only from a production point of view but also from a decision-making point of view.

The considerable economic and social significance of the mining industry in Australia might explain the high level of scrutiny applied by the Australian government in the review and negotiation of the deal. The Australian government might also have acted based on its learning from the merger of Rio Tinto–Consolidated Zinc Corporation (RTZ), from the United Kingdom, and Consolidated Zinc Corporation (CRA), from Australia.

A DLC structure united RTZ and CRA at the end of 1995. The new company, soon to be named Rio Tinto, had two headquarters (Melbourne and London) and a single board. In this case, the Australian treasurer imposed weaker demands, including the following:

- At least one-third of the board of the DLC should be Australians, in order to protect Australia's national interest.
- CRA should be allocated responsibility for the two companies' Latin American assets (5 percent of the group's assets at that time).
- Rio Tinto's headquarters could be in London, but the CEO should be Australian.

In the course of the integration, much of the power was transferred to London. Indeed, the International Coal Report[2] stated the following after the completion of the deal:

> What was promoted as a friendly merger between two giant mining companies, RTZ and CRA, is now more looking like a take-over. . . . The reorganisation will see a halving of the management team at the CRA's Melbourne office and London becoming the headquarters of the combined operation. In the future, Rio Tinto will have six divisions based on products rather than geographical location. The Melbourne office will be a support organisation for the aluminium, energy and iron ore business units headquartered in Australia.

Government intervention in all major deals is not an approach that would foster investor confidence in a country's openness to foreign direct investment. However, the BHP Billiton example highlights that government intervention can be desirable and, in some cases, the only solution for smaller economies to keep control of leading firms that may play a strategic role in an industry cluster. It is important to note that such government intervention does not necessarily require explicitly restrictive rules: overall, Australian rules encourage foreign investment, but the existence of the "national interest" test means that the government retains the right to say no and can therefore influence a deal when it deems necessary.

BOEING: BUILDING A GLOBAL LEADER TO PROTECT STRATEGIC INTERESTS

The Boeing Company is an American business involved in the design, development, manufacturing, sale, and support of commercial and military aircraft, equipment, and services. Boeing's growth toward leadership in the aerospace industry is unique. However, we might learn from the U.S. government's approach to enabling the development of such a global leader.

The U.S. government and its agencies provided Boeing with privileged access to the domestic market through large orders in the military and nonmilitary areas. The links between Boeing and the U.S. government date back to as early as WWI when the Navy ordered 50 model C training seaplanes, the first "all-Boeing" design and the company's first financial success. This relationship lasts to this day:

- In 1999, the Department of Defense selected Boeing as the lead integrator for the National Missile Defense, a three-year contract worth more than $1.5 billion.
- In 2000, the Navy granted Boeing a multiyear contract worth $8.9 billion for the production of more than 200 Super Hornet strike fighters.
- Finally, NASA and Boeing officials signed, in 1995, a $5.6 billion contract to design and develop the International Space Station. The company then topped the NASA's list of contractors by contract value awarded in both 1996 and 1997 and still ranked in the top four in 2005 and 2006.

Beyond its role as a prime customer, many suspect that the U.S. government also supported Boeing by allowing its consolidation with Douglas Aircraft Company, McDonnell Aircraft Corporation, North American Aviation, and Hughes Aircraft. Indeed, in its majority ruling allowing the merger of Boeing with McDonnell Douglas in 1997, the Federal Trade

Commission noted that it posed "serious antitrust concerns." However, the commissioners specifically stated that "the national champion argument does not explain [their] decision."

Overall, Boeing would likely not have the significant scale that it has today without the support of the U.S. government. That support continues for reasons of both national security and benefits to adjacent industries.

The case of Boeing illustrates how government subsidies for R&D have helped a company improve its productivity. In the aerospace industry, both Boeing and its European competitor Airbus benefit from significant government subsidies. Between 1992 and 2005, under pressure from European innovations like the Concorde plane and the A-380 aircraft, Boeing received more than $29 billion in direct and indirect support.

In an epic face-off at the World Trade Organization, the European Union accused Boeing of receiving important subsidies to finance its R&D and be more competitive through innovation. In addition to direct financing, the U.S. government allegedly helped the firm through R&D tax breaks and loans under preferential conditions. Boeing also received support in the context of its relationship with NASA, in the form of resource transfer at terms more favorable than market conditions as well as exclusive access to data, test results, trade secrets, and patents. Finally, the company benefited from access to privileged data and results through its participation in research programs for the Department of Defense.

The support of the various levels of U.S. government and agencies does not only impact Boeing's productivity. Overall, the U.S. aerospace industry includes about 1,500 companies with combined annual revenue of $125 billion. Players such as Goodrich and Honeywell also benefit from U.S. government expenditures in the defense sector because of tight links between institutional spending and growth in civil segments.

Research and other projects that are funded by military budgets are also later used at the civil level. For example, government programs like Vision for Space Exploration have been pushed forward in part to ensure that the United States will continue as a space-faring global leader and take advantage of the scientific, national security, and economic benefits borne of innovative space programs.

CEMEX: ALLOWING SCALE TO IMPROVE PRODUCTIVITY AND EXPAND ABROAD

Cementos Mexicanos (CEMEX) is the leading cement manufacturer in Mexico. CEMEX has been a part of Mexico's modernization in both real estate and infrastructure ever since its creation as a result of the merger of Cementos Hidalgo and Cementos Portland Monterrey in 1931.

Favorable domestic conditions

An emerging economy, Mexico continues to be a dynamic market for concrete and aggregates. With a GDP of US$840 billion at current prices, the country is now one of the world's 15 largest markets. Its economy has been growing at an average pace of 3.6 percent over the last decade.

The lack of infrastructure that characterized Mexico and the developing nature of the Mexican economy made the Mexican cement market attractive. In addition, the country's abundant mineral resources and the high cost of concrete and aggregate transportation, due to its weight and volume, gave an advantage to local operators.

Government support

The government of Mexico contributed to the growth of the cement industry through its support of cement-intensive development projects. It also supported the emergence of CEMEX most specifically through its tolerance with regard to consolidation in the industry and limits on foreign participation.

In the lower income segment only, CEMEX benefited from major development projects, including Piso Firme (1995, 200,000 self-built houses); Patrimonio Hoy (2000, expected to benefit 2 million families by 2010); Construmex (2001, provides financing for Mexicans living in the United States who want to build or remodel a house in Mexico).

To penetrate the vast and fragmented domestic cement market, CEMEX had to increase its capacity in many Mexican regions. It did so through the acquisition of several companies, to the point of capturing approximately 55 percent of the domestic market in 2006.

The government of Mexico tolerated such a high concentration. Indeed, CEMEX's lower cost of production allows for better prices on large-scale development projects despite the drawbacks of market dominance (the "efficiency defense"). High transportation costs also imply that the market would remain concentrated regionally even if it was not nationally. In other words, structural regional oligopolies are natural in this industry.

International expansion

After becoming the largest Mexican producer in 1976, CEMEX started to expand its activities globally with acquisitions in Europe, South America, and Asia during the 1980s. Following the signature of NAFTA in 1994, CEMEX leveraged its proximity and privileged access to the U.S. market by acquiring plants there. The company pursued its U.S. expansion to the point that most of its revenues now come from the United States.

In March 2005, CEMEX doubled its revenues and ready-mix capacity by acquiring RMC Group Plc. of the United Kingdom. The company then offered over US$14 billion for the purchase of the Australian Rinker Group Ltd. The board's approval of the transaction in April 2007 promises to increase the company's annual sales by 32 percent. CEMEX is now the world's largest producer of ready-mix, with activities spanning the Americas, Europe, Africa, the Middle East, and Asia.

It is only after CEMEX could strengthen its position on international markets and in the United States that restrictions on foreign direct investment in the cement industry were relaxed domestically in Mexico. Until then, foreign participation was limited to less than 50 percent, which explains the late entry of the two leading international players, Holcim and Lafarge, in the 1990s.

In summary, it appears that the government supported a three-step approach for CEMEX's growth: building a dominant position in a protected domestic market, leveraging this position to expand abroad through strategic M&A deals, and, finally, allowing competition domestically once the company had built a solid position in Mexico and abroad.

DEUTSCHE TELEKOM: USING THE DOMESTIC MARKET AS A SPRINGBOARD FOR INTERNATIONAL GROWTH

Until the late 1980s, the domestic telecommunications markets in Europe were dominated by state-owned monopolies of the likes of Deutsche

Telekom, France Telecom, and Telefonica. After 1987, the EU policy was adjusted to promote low prices, quality, and choice through greater competition and harmonization across EU countries. European telecom markets were thus gradually liberalized until 1998. However, each country's regulatory body continued to act based on a domestic agenda in order to ensure "fair" competition.

Since market liberalization, European incumbents (often formerly state owned) continued to grow and managed to outperform the telecommunications industry globally in terms of revenues. A group of eight reference European telecom incumbents recorded a compound annual growth rate (CAGR) of 7.3 percent between 1996 and 2006, whereas the global telecom industry's CAGR averaged 6.7 percent.

In order to better understand how some formerly state-owned monopolies became global telecommunications powerhouses, we will look at the case of Deutsche Telekom.

Aggressive M&A strategy

After 1996, the growth of European telecom incumbents was fueled mostly by foreign acquisitions. Deutsche Telekom is not an exception, as it followed an aggressive international M&A strategy after market liberalization. Between 1999 and 2001, the company made more than US$40 billion worth of cross-border acquisitions, focusing on gaining critical mass and differentiation in the UK and U.S. mobile markets, respectively. The company was driven to gain scale internationally and did so at the expense of reduced margins and large debt financing, raising its long-term liabilities to nearly US$60 billion in 2001 and its debt-to-equity ratio to 2.

Maintained domestic leadership

Simultaneously, Deutsche Telekom maintained a leading market share in both fixed-line and mobile telephony on its domestic market. On the fixed-line segment, its former monopoly share only eroded to 83 percent between 1997 and 2006. In the mobile segment, its share only dropped from 45 percent to 36 percent over the same period.

Deutsche Telekom's dominant position allowed it to use its domestic market as a springboard to cross-subsidize its aggressive international M&A policy.

With a population of more than 80 million people, the German market is the largest market in Europe for telecommunications. It is home to 40 million fixed-network subscribers, 91 million mobile subscribers, and 20 million broadband lines.

Government support

As Deutsche Telekom was under development, the company benefited from regulatory tolerance in the German domestic market:

- *Broadband services pricing*: Competitors accused Deutsche Telekom of dumping, but the company continued to operate almost as a monopoly while the regulator RegTP conducted a multiyear investigation.
- *Access to the local loop*: Deutsche Telekom undercut competitor prices by charging 12 percent less than the price set by RegTP for voice services.
- *Carrier selection*: Germany offered the service only in late 2003, more than three years after it should have been available according to EU regulations, thus maintaining heightened entry barriers as long as possible.

Furthermore, some RegTP decisions have been appealed by Deutsche Telekom, such as the application of wholesale flat-rate Internet access, and were suspended by the German court of appeals before implementation.

Laterally, the German market has fully opened up to foreign competition, but not before Deutsche Telekom developed into a global industry leader.

Repeated pattern and local impact

Another formerly state-owned monopoly, France Telecom, benefited from similar tolerance by regulatory authorities. The government's support helped France Telecom maintain high market shares in the fixed and mobile domestic market segments. This strong position at home allowed the company to roll out an aggressive US$40 billion-plus acquisition strategy in mobile, cable, and Internet services across Europe.

It is noteworthy that consumers in Germany and France enjoy competitive service penetration and prices despite the presence of a dominant player in their respective markets. We analyzed competition across 11 OECD countries in the telecommunications industry, and found that competition is not hindered by the presence of a strong incumbent in the public telephony market.

Residential and small-business fixed telephony is slightly cheaper for countries where the incumbent is less dominant but prices for large businesses are unaffected. We also found that prices for broadband and mobile services are not correlated to the relative market share of the incumbent player. Furthermore, a strong incumbent did not slow market penetration in the broadband segment and even favored it in the mobile segment.

BANCO SANTANDER: DOMESTIC MERGERS TO BUILD EUROPEAN STATUS

Banco Santander SA was founded in 1857. At first, it operated only in some regional markets of the fragmented financial industry in Spain. The group's small scale made competition difficult in foreign markets. The two primary drivers of growth in the financial industry being market-size growth and favorable macroeconomic conditions, the strong performance of the Spanish economy facilitated the expansion of its domestic banks, including Santander.

Government support

During the process of financial liberalization required by the European Union in the late 1990s, Spain loosened its regulations, allowing Spanish banks to merge. The government supported a series of mergers within the banking industry, hoping that emerging champions could compete effectively against European rivals.

These efforts led to large-scale mergers:

- A testament to its proactive stance, the Spanish government brought together all the state-owned banking institutions to form Corporación Bancaria de España (Argentaria). Starting in 1993, the government gradually privatized it completely, eventually leaving the banking sector entirely in private hands.
- Banco de Vizcaya and Banco de Bilbao merged to form Banco Bilbao Vizcaya (BBV).

- Banco Central and Banco Hispanoamericano merged to form Banco Central Hispanoamercano (BCH).
- Finally, Banco Santander first acquired Bank Banesto in 1998. It then merged with BCH to create the third-largest European bank by market capitalization at the time.

International expansion

The fragmentation and small size of the Spanish economy forced domestic banks to venture rapidly abroad. As a result, Banco Santander was the first bank to challenge Europe's reluctance to allow large cross-border bank mergers and the bank eventually won its case against EU regulatory authorities.

Banco Santander's aggressive expansion strategy, enabled by domestic consolidation, led to ventures into Portugal, Latin America, and England, all regions that offered strong growth potential and often stronger cultural fit. The bank has now become a source of pride for Spaniards, having grown at an accelerated pace to become one of the world's 10 largest institutions by assets.

ING followed a similar growth path. The company built scale in its domestic market with a merger in 1991 when the legal restrictions on mergers between financial institutions were lifted in the Netherlands. From that base, ING evolved from a Dutch company that had some international business to a true multinational firm. Significant acquisitions have been made both in the Benelux region (e.g., Belgian Bank Brussels Lambert) and in other parts of the world (e.g., in the United States: Equitable of Iowa, ReliaStar, Aetna Financial Services, and merchant bank Furman Selz). Today, ING is the 13th largest bank by market value with a capitalization of €68 billion.

CONCLUSION

The case studies on Boeing, CEMEX, Deutsche Telekom, and Banco Santander provide examples of successful government support to domestic firms as *national champions*, allowing them to achieve competitive scale and productivity. This support relied on privileged access to the domestic market and tolerance of domestic consolidation. It is important to note, however, that such government support has been temporary. It has aimed at facilitating the development of ambitious and successful firms to face strong international competition. The case of Boeing, which continues to enjoy governmental support, would be an exception, perhaps because it plays in a highly sensitive industry related to U.S. national security.

Three types of government levers emerge from our analysis of cases in the telecommunications, mining, manufacturing, and financial services industries:

- Emergency tools
- Transition tools
- Long-term strategies.

Emergency tools are defensive, reactive decisions to regulate against deals that threaten the national interest. They are a last recourse that may, however, be a small country's only way to retain decision-making centers when facing acquisitions by players from major economies. The decision of the Australian government to adopt a strong stance regarding the BHP-Billiton deal shows that the country's leaders considered it their only recourse after their moderate approach in the Rio Tinto case, which was ineffective. In some particular cases, government intervention may be desirable and the only solution for smaller economies to keep control of leading firms.

Transition tools are temporary measures that allow domestic companies to strengthen and gain scale before having to face the global leaders in their industry. This approach appears to be widely used by governments that demonstrate tolerance regarding the dominance of targeted firms or protect the domestic market from international competition. Contrary to popular belief, government tolerance toward dominant incumbent players does not necessarily result in an uncompetitive market detrimental to consumers, as illustrated by examples from telecommunications incumbents. A similar approach was adopted in Canada when life insurers were demutualized: the government required that Sun Life and Manulife be widely owned in order to prevent their likely acquisition by foreign investors.

Finally, long-term strategies correspond to attempts by governments to develop national competitive advantages. They may be some of the most constructive attitudes that governments can adopt, not only to favor specific firms but mostly to trigger productivity spillover in adjacent industries and across the economy.

A drawback of open and explicit government support is the risk of conflict with the terms of international trade agreements and foreign commercial retaliation. This is well illustrated by the high-profile dispute between the European Union and the Clinton administration over the government support given to Boeing at the time of its acquisition of McDonnell Douglas. The American firm finally had to make concessions by giving up exclusivity clauses with three carriers to avoid an all out commercial war. However, government support has been the source of positive externalities for industries, the development of clusters, and the broader economy in the cases reviewed here.

However, the support of national champions is a competitive reality. While competing jurisdictions will complain, they are all supporting their own national champions and actively developing competitive advantage, as is evident in the foregoing case examples and many others. By choosing not to allow and facilitate the development of national champions and by choosing not to aggressively support international growth, a nation risks putting its firms at a disadvantage relative to others.

Endnotes

1. The cases are condensed from *The Global Market for Corporate Control,* Submission to the Federal Panel on Competitiveness, 2007; with permission from SECOR Consulting. Ken Smith, the lead author of this book, led this work while at the firm. For the full report, see http://www.secorgroup.com/files/pdf/SECOR_final_report_on_Canada_s_MA_competitiveness.pdf.
2. *International Coal Report*, 1995. For archives, visit http://www.platts.com/IM.Platts.Content/ProductsServices/Products/intlcoalreport.pdf.

INDEX

B

ABOUT THE AUTHORS

Ken Smith has practiced as a strategy consultant for over 25 years, initially with McKinsey & Company and most recently with SECOR Consulting, where he was also a managing partner and chair. He is an associate professor at the University of Guelph and associate dean of executive programs in the university's College of Management and Economics. Smith lives in Toronto, Canada.

Alexandra Reed Lajoux, chief knowledge officer at the National Association of Corporate Directors (NACD), has three decades of experience in business information and has served as editor for *Directors & Boards, Mergers & Acquisitions*, and *Export Today*. She is the author or coauthor of all books to date in McGraw-Hill's acclaimed Art of M&A series. She lives in Fairfax, VA.

CPSIA information can be obtained
at www.ICGtesting.com
Printed in the USA
BVHW04*1341240918
527887BV00007B/146/P

9 780071 756211